REMEDIES FOR DISREPAIR

AUSTRALIA
LBC Information Services
Sydney

CANADA and USA
Carswell
Toronto

NEW ZEALAND
Brooker's
Auckland

SINGAPORE and MALAYSIA
Thomson Information (S.E.Asia)
Singapore

REMEDIES FOR DISREPAIR
AND OTHER BUILDING DEFECTS

by

STEPHEN KNAFLER

LONDON
SWEET & MAXWELL
1996

Published in 1996 by
Sweet and Maxwell Limited of
100 Avenue Road, London NW3
Computerset by Interactive Sciences Ltd, Gloucester
Printed and bound in Great Britain by
Hartnolls Ltd, Bodmin

No natural forests were destroyed to make this product;
only farmed timber was used and replanted

**A CIP catalogue record for this book is
available from the British Library**

ISBN 0 421 58230 8

FOREWORD

I am indebted to many lawyers, including the long-suffering county court judges of London, who have over the years generously and patiently shown me the error of my legal ways. Particular thanks go to Linda Pearce, Sarah Pearce, James Bowen and Terry Gallivan, who read and amended the draft of this book. I have tried to state the law as at January 1997.

CONTENTS

PART ONE
GENERAL PRINCIPLES AND EXPRESS TERMS

PART TWO
REPAIR

PART THREE
OTHER TYPES OF OBLIGATION TO CARRY OUT WORK

7. Other Types of Obligation to Carry Out Work

PART FOUR
IMPLIED TERMS OF THE CONTRACT

8. Terms Implied by Common Law or by the Express Terms of the Contract Itself

Terms generally implied into certain types of tenancy

PART FIVE
OTHER RELEVANT OBLIGATIONS OWED BY LANDLORDS TO TENANTS

12. Nuisance

13. Breach of the Covenant of Quiet Enjoyment and Derogation from Grant

PART SIX
WHAT THE LANDLORD OR TENANT HAS AGREED
TO CARRY OUT WORK TO

16. Obligations Relating to the Whole of the Premises

17. Obligations Relating to the Structure of the Premises

PART SEVEN
DAMAGES

PART EIGHT
OTHER REMEDIES

27. Specific Performance Interlocutory Injunctions and the
    Special Rights of Secure Tenants

28. Other Remedies

PART NINE
MISCELLANEOUS

29 The Limitation Acts

TABLE OF CASES

TABLE OF STATUTES

PART ONE

GENERAL PRINCIPLES AND EXPRESS TERMS

CHAPTER ONE

General Principles of Liability

Basic ingredients of liability

The relationship between landlord and tenant is essentially con-   **1–01**
tractual. Liability to repair or improve first and foremost depends
upon what the parties have agreed. Statute and common law
extend, restrict and create repairing obligations: but questions of
both liability and quantum are basically resolved by reference to
the contractual intentions of the parties.

   The advisor who wishes to ascertain the extent of a landlord's or
a tenant's liability to carry out works to land must consider:

(1) The express and implied terms of the contract;
(2) Relevant statute law: the Landlord and Tenant Act 1927,
     the Occupiers Liability Act 1957, the Defective Premises
     Act 1972, the Landlord and Tenant Act 1985 and the
     Environmental Protection Act 1990;
(3) Common law extensions and restrictions on liability and the
     common law context generally, which may impose liability
     for nuisance or (exceptionally) negligence.

Analytical tools: the 5-stage and 2-stage tests

   Reported cases on disrepair extend back over 200 years. In those   **1–02**
cases, judges state or develop the law in a variety of factual
contexts. It is not surprising that cases are not always easy to
reconcile with each other, or to apply to a particular tenancy
agreement in a particular set of circumstances.

   One solution is to extract a principled approach from the cases.
In *Dilapidations: The Modern Law and Practice* (1995) by Nicholas

3

Dowding and Kirk Reynolds Q.C., the authors advocate an approach based on five key questions:

"The following questions must be asked and answered in the following order:

(1) *What is the physical subject matter of the covenant?*

This part of the approach is directed to the inquiry that logically must come first, namely, the identification of the physical premises which the party giving the covenant has bound himself to repair.

(2) *Is the subject matter in a damaged or deteriorated condition?*

Before any question of repair arises it must first be asked whether the premises are in disrepair. This involves asking whether there has been a deterioration from some previous physical state. If the answer is no, then there has been no breach of covenant notwithstanding the fact that the premises may be unsuitable for occupation or use for some other reason.

(3) *Is the nature of the damage or deterioration such as to bring the subject matter below the standard contemplated by the covenant?*

Not every occasion of physical damage or deterioration will give rise to a liability under the covenant. It must be asked whether such damage or deterioration results in the premises not being in the state and condition that the parties contemplated they should be in. This involves identifying the standard imposed by the covenant and comparing it with the actual state of the premises. Again, if the answer is no, then there has been no breach.

(4) *What work is necessary in order to put the subject matter of the covenant into the contemplated condition?*

Once it has been ascertained that the state of the premises falls below that required by the covenant, the next stage is to identify what work is required to put them into the required state.

(5) *Is that work nonetheless of such a nature that the parties did not contemplate that it would be the liability of the covenanting party?*

The nature of the work identified as necessary may be such that it goes outside what the parties intended the covenantor to have to carry out. This 'fact and degree' test is variously formulated in the authorities . . .

It should be noted that the five stages will not necessarily be entirely self-contained in every case. Depending on the facts, similar consideration may apply at more than one stage. In particular, the second, third, fourth and fifth stages may overlap each other in practice."

Dowding and Reynold's 5-stage approach is the best around, but is not perfect. It focuses attention on obligations to repair and distracts attention from the other activities which landlords and tenants these days are increasingly bound to perform: decorating, keeping in good condition, building and improving. Secondly, it focuses attention on the law of disrepair as a distinct entity and distracts attention from the law of disrepair as an element in the package of obligations owed by landlords and tenants to each other, subject essentially to principles of construction and enforcement common to all contracts. Thirdly, while these five clearly articulated questions clarify many problems, five separate questions applied to one problem can create distinctions which confuse rather than clarify.

The material in this work can easily be adapted to formulate **1–03** answers to Dowding and Reynold's 5 questions. It is, however, set out so as to reflect a simpler 2-stage approach, as follows:

(1) *What activity is the landlord or tenant obliged to perform?*

The activity might be to repair, to build, to alter, to maintain in a certain condition, to decorate or to improve. The responsibility might arise out of the express or out of the implied terms of the tenancy agreement, or it might be imposed by statute or the common law. The activity may be specified in more or less detail in the relevant tenancy agreement.

(2) *On which parts of the rented premises is the landlord or tenant obliged to perform this activity?*

In other words, one has to ask: what is the landlord (or tenant) obliged to do; and to what is the landlord (or tenant) obliged to do it?

The disadvantage of this 2-stage approach is that it risks sending the advisor back to grapple in the raw with perplexities from which a 5-stage approach might have freed him or her. It assumes that issues of breach and remedy can be resolved simply by reference to the nature of the duty fully explained, which is often not the case.

CHAPTER TWO

Ascertaining the Express Terms of the Agreement

The relevance of express terms

2–01   The activities for which landlord or tenants are responsible are defined primarily by the express terms of the tenancy agreement or lease, to which reference should be made in the first instance. Only after considering the express terms of the agreement is it necessary to consider whether any implied terms arise, or the extent to which the landlord's or tenant's responsibilities are extended, reduced or created by the common law or by statute.

Identifying the written agreement

2–02   If there is a written agreement the first task is to obtain a copy of it and ascertain what express obligations it contains. It may be that the original written document has been varied, orally or in writing, in which case further instructions or documentary material will be required: see below at paras. 2–05, 2–06.

It frequently occurs that those who act for tenants of short or periodic tenancies, particularly secure tenants, do not take sufficient trouble to obtain a copy of the written agreement, but rely instead on the repairing terms implied in the case of such tenancies by section 11 of the Landlord and Tenant Act 1985.

Such an approach is acceptable only when all the defects complained of clearly fall within the terms of section 11 of the Landlord and Tenant Act 1985. Otherwise, it is misconceived. The express terms of the agreement (or implied terms arising therefrom) often impose obligations on landlords which are more

6

extensive than those implied by section 11 of the Landlord and Tenant Act 1985. Reliance on such terms will result in orders of specific performance which are more extensive and awards of damage which are higher than they otherwise would have been.

A graphic example of additional liability arising as a result of the express terms of a periodic secure tenancy can be found in the case of *Johnson v. Sheffield City Council*.[1] The tenancy agreement expressly provided that the landlord would keep the house "fit to live in". The landlord was accordingly liable for severe condensation and mould growth caused by the inherently defective construction of the house. The landlord would not in this case have been held liable had the tenant relied only on section 11 of the Landlord and Tenant Act 1985.

Oral and implied agreements

Before considering the nature of repairing obligations in oral or implied agreements, it is desirable to briefly explain the nature of such agreements.   **2–03**

The basic rule is that a deed is required to create out of the contract a legal (as opposed to an equitable) estate in the land.[2] Repairing obligations in equitable tenancies can be enforced for most practicable purposes under the doctrine in *Walsh v. Lonsdale*[3]: but may not be enforced in certain circumstances, most commonly if specific performance of the underlying agreement would for some reason no longer be granted: *IRC v. Derby (Earl)*.[4] It can therefore be of importance that the contract between the parties creates a legal rather than an equitable interest in the land.

A legal (as opposed to equitable) tenancy can be created orally or in writing rather than by deed providing the tenancy takes effect in possession for a term not exceeding three years at the best rent which can reasonably be obtained without taking a premium.[5]

Periodic tenancies can be created orally and become legal estates in the land, even though they are capable of continuing for over three years: *Kushner v. Law Society*.[6]

Periodic tenancies may be created by conduct rather than words. The most common example is when the owner of land accepts payments from the occupier of the land. Unless those payments are

[1] *Legal Action*, August 1994, p. 16.
[2] s.52 Law of Property Act 1925; *City of London Corporation v. Fell* [1994] 1 A.C. 458.
[3] (1882) 21 Ch.D. 9.
[4] [1914] 3 K.B. 1186.
[5] s.54(2) Law of Property Act 1925, preserving the common law rule permitting the creation of such tenancies orally, recognised in *Ryley v. Hicks* (1713) 1 Str. 651.
[6] [1952] 1 K.B. 264.

referable to some non-landlord and tenant legal relationship, unless the occupier does not have exclusive possession or unless there was no intention to enter into a legal relationship, it will be inferred that a tenancy has been created: *Street v. Mountford*.[7]

Repairing obligations can be agreed orally just as other terms, for example as to rent, can be agreed orally. If the tenancy is a legal tenancy, such terms become part of the legal estate and can bind the landlord as well as the tenant in case of assignment (which must be by deed even in the case of a legal tenancy created in writing or orally[8]). It is a question of ascertaining what the parties agreed, expressly or by their conduct. Careful and detailed instructions are required.

Agreements partly oral and partly written

2–04   There may be a written tenancy agreement, or a lease made by deed, containing repairing obligations. The parties may, however, have orally agreed additional or varied terms.

When there is a written agreement, the parol evidence rule excludes evidence of oral agreements which is inconsistent with the written agreement. The parol evidence rule does not, however, apply where the plaintiff is able to establish collateral contract, estoppel, misrepresentation, mutual mistake, entitlement to rectification or that the contract as written down was not intended to contain the entire agreement: *Hutton v. Watling*.[9]

In *Brikom Investments Limited v. Carr*[10] the landlord agreed orally with the sitting tenants that if they entered into the proposed long leases by deed the landlord would not enforce the tenants' obligation to repair the roof but would repair the roof itself at its own expense. The Court of Appeal held that the oral agreement created a collateral contract.

In *Mann v. Nunn*[11] the court required the landlord to perform an oral promise to carry out repairs not included in the lease subsequently drawn up. The decision was again on the basis that there had been a collateral contract.[12]

---

[7] [1985] A.C. 809; *Antoniades v. Villiers and Bridges* (1989, unreported); *A–G Securities v. Vaughan* [1990] 1 A.C. 417.

[8] s.53(1)(a) Law of Property Act 1925; *Crago v. Julian* [1992] 1 W.L.R. 372.

[9] [1948] Ch. 398.

[10] [1979] Q.B. 467.

[11] (1874) 30 L.T. 526.

[12] See also *Angell v. Duke* (1875) 32 L.T.R. 320 (no collateral contract to repair or furnish as inconsistent with express terms in the written agreement); *Kennard v. Ashman* (1894) T.L.R. 213 and 447 (statement by landlord that house was well built did not amount to a collateral contract); *De Lassalle v. Guildford* [1901] 2 K.B. 15

The landlord under a secure tenancy is obliged to supply the tenant with, *inter alia*, a written statement of terms which are neither express nor implied by law.[13]

Variation of the agreement

Even deeds can be varied orally: *Mitas v. Hyams*[14] (dates for payment of rent varied orally to the usual quarter days); *Plymouth Corporation v. Harvey*[15] (oral extension of time for compliance with covenants in lease varied the lease and made the forfeiture proceedings premature); *Brikom Investments v. Carr*[16] (landlord agreed that tenants' covenant to repair roof would not bind them but that the landlord would repair the roof). It should be noted that agreements subject to s.2 of the Law of Property (Miscellaneous Provisions) Act 1989 cannot be varied orally: *McCausland v. Duncan Lawrie*.[16a] The broader rule is that contracts required by statute to comply with formalities if they are to be effective (*e.g.* to be by deed) will not be effectively varied if the variation does not equally comply with the relevant formalities: *Morris v. Baron & Co.*[16b] It is not easy to reconcile this principle with *Mitas v. Hyams, Plymouth Corporation v. Harvey* and *Brikom Investments v. Carr*.   **2–05**

Variation of secure tenancies

Secure tenancies granted under the Housing Act 1985 can be and often are formally varied. It is essential to positively ascertain whether a variation has taken place.   **2–06**

Like any other tenancy, a secure tenancy can be varied by mutual agreement.[17] Unlike any other tenancy, a secure tenancy can be varied unilaterally by the landlord. The landlord is entitled to vary terms as to repair, except, of course, terms implied by statute.[18]

(collateral contract created by landlord's assurance that the drains were in good order); *Walker Property Investments (Brighton) v. Walker* (1947) 177 L.T.R. 204 (oral agreement permitting use by tenant of garden and basement was collateral contract or ground for rectification); *City of Westminster v. Mudd* [1959] Ch. 129 (oral representation by agent that tenant could sleep on the premises bound landlord so long as tenant owned the term personally despite express prohibition in the lease).

[13] s.104 Housing Act 1985.
[14] [1951] 2 T.L.R. 1215.
[15] [1971] 1 W.L.R. 549.
[16] *Supra.*
[16a] *The Times*, June 18, 1996.
[16b] [1918] A.C. 1.
[17] s.102(a) Housing Act 1985.
[18] s.102 Housing Act 1985; *R. v. Brent L.B.C., ex p. Blatt* (1991) 24 H.L.R. 319 (variation effective despite term in contract that landlord would not vary).

It is a condition precedent to the variation being effective that the landlord complies with the procedure set out in section 103 of the Housing Act 1985. The landlord has to serve each tenant affected with a preliminary notice which sets out the proposed variation and its effect and invites comment which the landlord is obliged to consider. The landlord then has to serve a notice of variation specifying the variation and the date it takes effect (which must be at least four weeks or a rental period later, whichever is the longer). The notice must be accompanied by all the information the landlord considers is necessary to inform the tenant of the nature and effect of the variation.

The tenancy agreement will be varied if the landlord complies strictly with the requirements of section 103 of the Housing Act 1985. If the landlord does not comply strictly with those requirements, difficult questions can arise. In *Palmer v. Sandwell Metropolitan Borough Council*[19] the landlord purported to vary the terms of its secure tenancies by increasing its own repairing obligations. Upon being sued by one of its tenants, however, it argued successfully that the purported variation had been ineffective and that accordingly it was not liable for failing to carry out the relevant works. The Court of Appeal held that:

(1) The tenant might if it were to his or her advantage be able to waive service of the preliminary notice under what is now section 103(2) of the Housing Act 1985.

(2) It is not possible for the tenant to waive the requirements in section 103(4) (relating to the contents of the notice of variation and in particular the specification of the date on which the variation is to take effect) even if it is to his or her advantage to do so (*e.g.* because the new terms would have obliged the landlord to carry out more extensive repairs).

(3) There had been no consensual agreement to vary the terms of the tenancy. Service of the details of the proposed variation did not on the facts of that case amount to a contractual offer because the terms were not sufficiently certain and the offer was not sufficiently unqualified. Further, the tenant did not in law accept the offer, since remaining in possession and paying rent is conduct which is equally consistent with acceptance and non-acceptance of a contractual offer.

Different cases on different facts might produce different results, in particular if the proposed variation is certain in its terms and is accompanied by a related rent increase, or if the tenant is able to run an argument based upon estoppel.

[19] (1987) 20 H.L.R. 74, C.A.

The case of *Palmer v. Sandwell Metropolitan Borough Council*[20] shows how important it can be in the case of secure tenancies to correctly identify the terms of the tenancy as to repair for the period of the claim in question. It may well be that different sets of terms will be found to apply to different periods of claim.

Suspension or creation of obligations to repair by estoppel

Estoppel can both suspend or, at least temporarily, create repairing obligations. **2–07**

Suspension of repairing obligation as a result of estoppel. In *Hughes* **2–08** *v. Metropolitan Railway Company Limited*[21] the landlord led the tenant to believe that he would not be required to comply with a repairs notice whilst he was negotiating to buy the landlord's interest. The landlord was as a result estopped from forfeiting the lease on account of the tenant's failure to comply with that notice while those negotiations were continuing.

In *Brikom Investments Limited v. Carr*[22] the landlord had assured sitting tenants that if they acquired long leases of their flats it would not enforce repairing covenants in the leases which would require them to repair the roof, but carry out the immediately necessary repairs itself. Lord Denning M.R., relying on the principle of promissory estoppel in *Central London Property Trust Limited v. High Tree House Limited,*[23] held that the landlord was as a result estopped from claiming the cost of the repairs by way of the service charge. He further held that the estoppel benefited assignees of the term and would have burdened assignees of the reversion. The majority regarded the case as one of collateral contract or as a variation of strict contractual rights.

Creation of repairing liability by operation of estoppel. In *Brikom* **2–09** *Investments Limited v. Seaford*[24] the Court of Appeal held that the landlord was to be treated as liable to repair in accordance with s.11 of the Landlord and Tenant Act 1985 even though the tenancies exceeded seven years. The reason was that fair rents had been registered and accepted by the landlord on the basis that they were in fact liable to repair in accordance with the 1985 Act. The rents would have been lower if the parties and the Rent Officer had appreciated that the landlord was not liable to repair. The landlords were however said to be entitled to apply to have the rent registers corrected to reflect their true repairing liability, at which

[20] *Supra.*
[21] (1877) 2 App. Cas. 439.
[22] *Supra.*
[23] [1947] K.B. 130.
[24] [1981] 1 W.L.R. 863.

point the estoppel would cease to operate. The form of the dispute was as to whether the tenant was entitled to set-off against rent sums expended on repairs because of the landlord's failure to repair: it could therefore be said that the use of the estoppel principle remained essentially defensive.

In *Industrial Properties (Barton Hill) Limited v. Associated Electrical Industries Limited*[25] it was determined that the tenant's repairing obligations in a tenancy by estoppel continued to bind the parties for the whole of the term and after the term comes to an end, unless the true owner dispossesses or brings some other claim against the tenant by estoppel.

In *Credit Suisse v. Beegas Nominees Limited*,[26] Lindsay J. held:

"The tenant submits that the landlord is estopped, by way of an estoppel by convention, from denying that it has been and still is liable to remedy such defects as have caused the ingress of water. Mr Gaunt relies on *Amalgamated Investment & Property Co. Limited (In Liquidation) v. Texas Commerce International Bank*[27] and *The Vistafjord*,[28] where [Lord Justice Bingham] said[29]:

I do not propose to essay a definition of estoppel by convention. It is sufficient for the purposes of this case to adopt the description given by the Court of Appeal in *Keen v. Holland*,[30] of the essential nature of the *Amalgamated* case, and to say that it applies where (a) parties have established by their construction of their agreement or their apprehension of its legal effect a conventional basis, (b) on that basis they have regulated their subsequent dealings, to which I would add (c) it would be unjust or unconscionable if one of the parties resiled from that convention.

In the light of my earlier conclusions I may take this further argument in the tenant's favour fairly shortly . . . In the context that a landlord may indicate a willingness to do works outside his strict obligation and in a context, as here, in which the landlord believes he may have a good case to get others to do works or to recover the expense of works

[25] [1977] Q.B. 580.
[26] [1994] 1 EGLR 76.
[27] [1982] Q.B. 84 at p. 121C, *per* Lord Denning M.R.
[28] [1988] 2 Lloyd's Rep 343, C.A., *per* Bingham L.J.
[29] at pp. 351–352.
[30] [1984] 1 W.L.R. 251 *supra* at p. 261.

from others, merely to point to a landlord's apparent willingness to do works or have them done is not, of itself, material sufficient to show a convention as to the effect of the underlease . . . ."

CHAPTER THREE

General Principles of Construction

In principle repairing obligations are construed in the same way as any other type of contractual provision. This subject is dealt with extensively, and with a particular eye on tenancy agreements, in *The Interpretation of Contracts* (1989) by Mr Kim Lewison Q.C.[1]

This is an area of law in which common sense is paramount: the lawyer's sense, that is, for the natural or most likely meaning of the words used as they appear in their context. Cannons of construction can be a guide, but one does not need a guide to walk from one's house to the shops, and one does not always want a guide that leads one away from the shops and into the bazaar.

Objective ascertainment of intention

3–01   The court seeks to ascertain the intention of the parties objectively by interpreting what the words of the contract in their context mean and not what either, or indeed, both parties say the words were intended to mean: *Reardon-Smith Line v. Yngver Hanson-Tangen*,[2] *Wickman Machine Tools Limited v. L. A. Schuler A.G.*[3] If a party or both parties intended to achieve a different result then the remedy may be rectification.[4]

Ordinary meaning of words

3–02   Words are given their ordinary meaning unless the context shows that a special or technical meaning was intended or some other

---

[1] For detailed assistance the reader is advised to consult that work.
[2] [1976] 1 W.L.R. 989 at p. 996E.
[3] [1974] A.C. 235 at p. 263F.
[4] *Ibid.* at p. 236G.

meaning is required to avoid absurdity: *Grey v. Pearson*[5]; *Post Office v. Aquarius Properties Limited*[6]; *Norwich Union Life Assurance Society Limited v. British Railways Board.*[7]

Context sensitive meaning

Words are construed in their factual context, objectively   **3–03** assessed, at the time of the agreement. That context can include objective evidence of the purpose of the contract (*e.g.* "what reasonable persons would have in mind in the situation of the parties") but not evidence of negotiations *per se* or of a party's subjective intentions: *Reardon-Smith Line v. Yngver Hanson-Tangen*[8]; *Prenn v. Simmonds.*[9] For example, a covenant to repair the "main timbers" in a lease of a steel-framed building requires the tenant to repair the steel frame: *Plough Investments Limited v. Manchester City Council.*[10] In *Norwich Union Life Insurance Society v. British Railways Board*[11] Hoffmann J. held that, in the context of a lease of commercial premises for 150 years, a covenant to "rebuild, reconstruct or replace" could and did extend beyond works to subsidiary parts of the premises (repairs) and required the tenant to rebuild the entire premises should they reach the end of their natural life. He distinguished *Lister v. Lane*[12] in which a similar covenant (to "repair, uphold, sustain, maintain, amend and keep") had been held to require works only to subsidiary parts (repairs) and not the rebuilding of the whole. A ground of distinction was that the context in *Lister v. Lane* was a seven year lease of a dwelling house: the parties might however be expected to intend rebuilding in the context of a 150 year commercial lease.

Rest of the document as context

Words are construed in the context of the document read as a   **3–04** whole: *Granada Theatres Limited v. Freehold Investments (Leytonstone) Limited.*[13] It may be apparent from reading the document as a whole that the word or phrase in question was intended to have a special meaning, or, for example, that it should be contrasted with a concept clearly indicated by some other word.

---

[5] (1857) 6 H.L.C. 61.
[6] [1985] 2 E.G.L.R. 105.
[7] [1987] 2 E.G.L.R. 137.
[8] *Supra.*
[9] [1971] 1 W.L.R. 1381.
[10] [1989] 1 E.G.L.R. 244.
[11] *Supra.*
[12] [1893] 2 Q.B. 212.
[13] [1959] Ch. 592, C.A.

Commercial purpose

3–05   Words are construed in the context of the commercial purpose of the transaction, but only if such a commercial purpose can be clearly discerned and only if the agreement is ambiguous: *Philpots (Woking) Limited v. Southern Conveyancers Limited*[14]; *Credit Suisse v. Beegas Nominees Limited.*[15]

Matter of impression

3–06   Having considered the words in such parts of their context as are relevant, one is left with an impression of meaning, as described by Hoffmann J. in *Post Office v. Aquarius Properties Limited*[16]:

> "One therefore returns to the language of the covenant. The use of ordinary language to convey meaning often involves subtle discriminations which for most people are intuitive rather than capable of lucid explanation. An explanation of why ordinary English words in a particular context convey a given meaning is frequently more likely to confuse than to enlighten. Perhaps this is what judges mean when they say that questions of construction are often matters of impression."

Previous definition by judges

3–07   Judges define words in cases. The rest of the book is concerned with such definitions. One must however bear in mind that judges rarely define words absolutely or for all purposes (see para. 3–03 above and *Brew Bros Ltd v. Snax (Ross) Ltd*[17]).

---

[14] [1986] 1 E.G.L.R. 97.
[15] [1994] 1 E.G.L.R. 76 at p. 85.
[16] *Supra.*
[17] [1970] 1 Q.B. 612 at 640.

PART TWO

REPAIR

CHAPTER FOUR

The Obligation to Repair

Introduction

The most common obligation is to repair. It occupies the middle **4–01** ground between terms which prevent deliberate damage to the premises, by waste or alteration, for example, and terms which require the landlord or the tenant to improve, maintain fit for their purpose or even rebuild premises.

In the commercial sphere at least, the essential character of repair as a compromise or middle course obligation is part of the commercial balance between landlord and tenant. An example of this can be found in *Norwich Union Life Insurance Society v. British Railways Board.*[1] In that case, Hoffmann J. upheld the decision of an arbitrator in rent review proceedings who made a downward adjustment of 27.5 per cent in the rent of commercial premises because the lease required the tenant not merely to repair, but also to "rebuild, reconstruct or replace".

Perhaps that kind of balance is reflected by the common, voluntary use of the repairing obligation in the residential context and its adoption by Parliament in section 11 of the Landlord and Tenant Act 1985. It seems incomprehensible, however, that Parliament has not gone further and intervened to require at least social landlords such as housing associations and local authorities to keep dwelling houses fit for human habitation. The Law Commission Report *Landlord and Tenant: Responsibility for State and Condition of Property*[2] proposes legislation imposing such a requirement in the

---

[1] [1987] 2 E.G.L.R. 137.
[2] Law Com. No. 238.

case of tenancies of all dwelling houses for under seven years. (See Parts VIII and IX). Extensive consideration of the political and theoretical issues raised can be found at chapter 7.2 of *The Nature of Tenancies* (1995) by Bright and Gilbert.

Meaning of repair and disrepair

4–02   The meaning of repair and disrepair is given in *Woodfall* as follows:

"The concept of repair is the converse of disrepair. Accordingly before liability can arise under a covenant to repair, the subject-matter of the covenant must be out of repair: *Post Office v. Aquarius Properties.*[3] Disrepair cannot exist unless the subject-matter of the covenant is in a condition worse than it was at some earlier time: *Quick v. Taff-Ely Borough Council,*[4] for disrepair connotes a deterioration from some previous physical condition: *Post Office v. Aquarius Properties.*[5] There must be damage to the subject-matter of the covenant, for repair connotes the idea of making good damage so as to leave the subject so far as possible as though it had not been damaged: *Anstruther-Gough-Calthorpe v. McOscar.*[6]"

In *Brew Bros Ltd v. Snax (Ross) Ltd,*[6a] Sachs L.J. said:

"the correct approach is to look at the particular building, to look at the state in which it is in at the date of the lease, to look at the precise terms of the lease, and to come to a conclusion as to whether, on a fair interpretation of those terms in relation to that state, the requisite work can fairly be termed repair. However large the covenant it must not be looked at *in vacuo.*"

Disrepair irrelevant unless to a building element covered by a repairing obligation

4–03   There is no breach of an obligation to repair if there is no deterioration to a part of the premises covered by an obligation to repair, even though there is damage to other parts of the premises, or the premises become unpleasant or unfit for their purpose.

---

[3] [1987] 1 All E.R. 1055.
[4] [1986] Q.B. 809, 821.
[5] *Supra.*
[6] [1924] 1 K.B. 716, 734, *per* Atkin L.J.
[6a] [1970] 1 Q.B. 612 at 640.

The local authority was not in breach of its obligation to repair the structure and exterior of the dwelling house even though the decorations and furnishings in the house were ruined by severe condensation, there was widespread mould and damp and during the winter the house was unfit for human habitation: *Quick v. Taff-Ely B.C.*[7] The decorations and furnishings were in disrepair but the landlord was only obliged by the terms of the tenancy agreement to repair the structure and exterior of the premises, which had not been damaged. The premises were unfit for human habitation, damaged the tenant's property and posed a serious health risk but that was irrelevant: the landlord's liability was only to repair, and only to repair (damage to) the structure or exterior.

The tenant was not in breach of its obligation to "keep in good repair and condition the demised premises and every part thereof" when a defective kicker joint allowed water to penetrate laterally into the basement up to ankle height because neither the joint nor any other part of the premises had actually deteriorated. The joint was defective and was not fit for its purpose: it was not in disrepair because it had not deteriorated: *Post Office Properties Limited v. Aquarius Properties Limited.*[8]

On the other hand, the courts can and do approach the question whether there has been damage or deterioration in a broad manner. In *Staves v. Leeds City Council*[9] the Court of Appeal held that plaster which had become damp as the result of condensation and required renewal was in disrepair. The plaster required renewal because: (a) its moisture content had increased; (b) the fine particles in the mix were dissolving, leaving hollow areas; and (c) the gypsum portion was re-crystallising causing the plaster to start to break up. It was no defence that the damp was caused by condensation, itself not caused by any disrepair to the structure of the building but by its inherently poor construction.[9a]

No disrepair despite failure to perform function

A door which simply fails to perform its function of keeping out **4–04** the rain is not for that reason in disrepair: *Stent v. Monmouth D.C.*[10] Once the water ingress causes the wood to rot, however, the door is in disrepair. Furthermore, the court may then decide that the

---

[7] *Supra.*
[8] *Supra.*
[9] (1991) 23 H.L.R. 107.
[9a] See also *Postel Properties Ltd v. Boots the Chemist* [1996] 41 E.G. 164.
[10] [1987] 1 E.G.L.R. 59. Compare the kicker joint in *Post Office Properties Limited v. Aquarius Properties Limited, supra.*

only "sensible", "practicable" or "necessary" repair involves making the door functionally effective for the future.

Disrepair despite functional effectiveness

4–05   A building element may remain functionally effective and yet be in disrepair. In *Sheldon v. West Bromwich Corporation*[11] the landlord was on notice that the water tank was in disrepair because it knew that the metal was discoloured and accordingly probably corroded, given the age of the tank.

In *Re Mayor and Corporation of London*[12] the tenant was obliged to repair rusting and weakened girders even though they remained fit for their purpose (supporting Smithfield meat market above). On the other hand, in *Camden L.B.C. v. Civil Aviation Authority*[13] works to deteriorating high alumina cement concrete beams were not "repairs". The principle reason was that as a matter of fact and degree the works were too extensive to qualify as repairs[14] but it was relevant to that conclusion that the building would be fit for its purpose as offices for the foreseeable future even if the works were not done.

Blockage of conduits is disrepair

4–06   Conduits are in disrepair if they are blocked. In *Bishop v. Consolidated London Properties Ltd*[15] a gutter blocked by a dead pigeon was in disrepair. In *Melles & Co. v. Holme*[16] a gutter blocked by ash from the chimney was in disrepair. In *Greg v. Planque*[17] cleaning a flue was held to be a repair.

Obligation to repair includes obligation to prevent future damage

4–07   Where some damage covered by the repairing obligation has occurred the obligation and right to repair can include the obligation and right to repair as yet undamaged elements of the premises if further disrepair is likely and it is reasonable for further repair work to be carried out in advance: *Ravenseft Properties Limited v. Davstone (Holdings) Limited*[18] (removal of entirety of stone cladding around building and its replacement with new cladding

---

[11] (1973) 13 H.L.R. 23.
[12] [1910] 2 Ch. 314.
[13] (1980) 257 E.G. 273.
[14] See below paras. 6–02, 6–03.
[15] (1933) 102 L.J.K.B. 257.
[16] [1918] 2 K.B. 100.
[17] [1936] 1 K.B. 669.
[18] [1980] Q.B. 12.

properly fixed was repair. Large areas of cladding had not yet fallen off, although they were likely to); *Holding & Management Limited v. Property Holding & Investment Trust Plc*[19] (replacement of complete cladding was not repair because works were too extensive: but in principle works to as yet undamaged building elements are capable of being repairs if future damage is likely); *McDougall v. Easington D.C.*[20] (prophylactic measures to prevent further water penetration through roof were repairs); *Reston v. Hudson*[21] (the landlord was entitled to recover as the cost of repairs by way of service charge the cost of replacing all of the windows in the block even when many were undamaged, when it would be cheaper and more sensible to replace the lot); *Postel Properties Ltd v. Boots the Chemist*[21a] (replacement of roof more economic than patch repairs so cost allowed as service charge; repairs to all windows in shopping centre more economic than to repair in batches only when the (inevitable) signs of rust became apparent): see also *London & North Eastern Railway Co. Ltd v. Berriman*[22] (routine oiling and cleaning of railway track equipment was "repairs"); *Day v. Harland & Wolff Limited*[23] (antifouling work to ship was "repairs": "to repair is to remedy defects, but it can also properly include an element of the 'stitch in time saves nine' ").

Obligation to repair includes obligation to decorate

An obligation to repair includes an obligation to paint or **4–08** otherwise decorate where such work is reasonably required in order to prevent disrepair, *e.g.* painting the exterior woodwork to prevent rot: *Proudfoot v. Hart*[24]; *Crawford v. Newton*[25]; *Irvine v. Moran.*[26]

Additionally, although purely decorative work is not required, nor is it required that the decorations are maintained in the same condition as when the agreement was made, neither the premises nor any subsidiary part affected by an obligation to repair is in repair if the decoration has deteriorated to the point which makes it no longer "reasonably fit for [the occupation of] a reasonably minded tenant of the class who would be likely to take it": *Proudfoot*

[19] (1989) 21 H.L.R. 596.
[20] (1989) 58 P. & C.R. 201.
[21] [1990] 37 E.G. 86.
[21a] [1996] 41 E.G. 164.
[22] [1946] A.C. 301.
[23] [1953] 2 All E.R. 387.
[24] (1890) 25 Q.B.D. 42.
[25] (1886) 36 W.R. 54.
[26] [1991] 1 E.G.L.R. 261.

v. Hart[27]; *Monk v. Noyes*[28]; *Gemmell v. Galsworthy.*[29] In other words, an obligation to keep windows in repair will require the inside parts to be decorated, even though the decoration is not required for protection, if the decoration has deteriorated to the point at which a reasonably minded tenant of the type likely to rent would have cause for complaint.

Obligation to repair includes obligation to put into repair

4–09   An obligation to repair implies and includes an obligation to put premises into repair if they are not in repair at the time of the agreement: *Payne v. Haine*[30]; *Proudfoot v. Hart.*[31] In *Payne v. Haine* Parke B. said: "If, at the time of the demise, the premises were old and in bad repair, the lessee was bound to put them in good repair as old premises; for he cannot keep them in good repair without putting them into it."

The *general* condition of the premises at the date of the agreement remains of some relevance to the construction of the standard of repair required: *Payne v. Haine*[32] (which reviews a number of earlier authorities); *Walker v. Hatton*[33]; *Pontifex v. Foord*[34]; *Credit Suisse v. Beegas Nominees Ltd.*[35] It is however of limited relevance because the obligation to repair includes an obligation to put into repair.

---

[27] *Supra.*
[28] (1824) 1 C.& P. 265.
[29] (1942) S.A.S.R. 55.
[30] (1847) 16 M.&W. 451.
[31] *Supra.*
[32] *Supra.*
[33] (1842) 10 M.&W. 249.
[34] (1884) 12 Q.B.D. 152.
[35] (1994) 11 E.G. 151.

CHAPTER FIVE

Implied Pre-Condition of Notice

Pre-condition affects landlord, not tenants

In certain circumstances the common law implies a term that a **5–01** landlord is not liable for failing to repair unless he or she has notice of the disrepair and fails to carry out repairs within a reasonable period of time thereafter. There is no such implied pre-condition where it is the tenant who is liable to repair.

The general rule as to notice

The requirement of notice applies to premises or parts thereof **5–02** which have been let to the tenant. The landlord is not liable for failing to repair until he or she has been put on notice of the existence of disrepair and failed to carry out repairs within a reasonable period of time thereafter: *Makin v. Watkinson*[1]; *Torrens v. Walker*[2]; *McCarrick v. Liverpool Corporation*[3]; *O'Brien v. Robinson*[4]; *Calabar Properties Ltd v. Stitcher*[5]; *Morris v. Liverpool Corporation.*[6]

The origin of the rule lies in the practical consideration that only the tenant and not the landlord can be expected to have knowledge

---

[1] (1870) L.R. 6 Ex 24.
[2] [1906] 2 Ch. 166.
[3] [1947] A.C. 219.
[4] [1973] A.C. 912.
[5] [1984] 1 W.L.R. 287.
[6] [1988] 1 E.G.L.R. 47.

of damage to premises let to the tenant. As it was put by Collins M.R. in *Redway v. Machin*[7]:

> "[The] rule rests upon the principle that the landlord is not the occupier of the premises, and has no means of knowing what is the condition of the premises unless he is told, because he has no right of access to the demised premises, whereas the occupier has the best means of knowing of any want of repair."

Over the years the rule has become formalised and lost its essentially fair basis. For example, the requirement of notice has been held to apply to disrepair which existed and which the landlord could have discovered before the premises were let (*Uniproducts (Manchester) v. Rose Furnishers*[8]: rotten joists collapsing and causing personal injury); to disrepair which was latent and could not have been identified by the tenant any more than by the landlord (*O'Brien v. Robinson*[9]: defective ceiling which collapsed causing personal injury); to disrepair which only the landlord and not the tenant had the means of identifying (*Hugall v. M'Lean*[10]: flooding as a result of defective drains); and in cases in which the landlord has the right to enter and inspect the premises (*Morgan v. Liverpool Corporation*[11]: sash cord broke and window fell injuring plaintiff's hand; *McCarrick v. Liverpool Corporation*[12]: defective steps causing a fall and personal injury).

The result has been criticised, particularly in relation to the implied repairing obligations in respect of dwelling houses arising under section 11 of the Landlord and Tenant Act 1985, by Lord Donaldson M.R.:

> "It is, as we think, unfortunate that the House of Lords felt impelled in *O'Brien v. Robinson*[13] to hold that liability under this covenant only arises when the landlord learns, or perhaps is put on inquiry, that there is a need for such repairs, because such a construction penalises the conscientious landlord and rewards the absentee. Furthermore a covenant to 'keep in repair' would appear to be much more onerous than one to 'repair on notice', yet this is how the section has been construed, notwithstanding that by s.30(3) the landlord is given power to enter the house to inspect its condition."

[7] (1904) 91 L.T. 310.
[8] [1956] 1 W.L.R. 45.
[9] *Supra.*
[10] (1885) 53 L.T. 94.
[11] [1927] 2 K.B. 131.
[12] *Supra.*
[13] [1972] A.C. 912.

Sufficiency of notice

To compensate, the courts adopt a relatively broad approach to   **5–03**
evidence of notice. In *Hussein v. Mehlman*[14] Mr Stephen Sedley
Q.C. whilst sitting as an assistant recorder at Wood Green Trial
Centre held that:

> "I do not understand the decision in *O'Brien v. Robinson* to
> require formal notice: it reflects the common-sense proposi-
> tion that a person cannot take steps to remedy a defect of
> which he knows nothing. This is turn requires that he should
> not be permitted to claim to be ignorant of things to which he
> has shut his eyes where a prudent property owner would have
> taken notice."

The tenant need not specify the disrepair, merely supply the
landlord with such information as would place a reasonable
landlord on inquiry: *O'Brien v. Robinson*[15]; *British Telecommunica-
tions plc v. Sun Life Assurance Society plc.*[15a]
Accordingly:

(1) Notice can come from a source other than the tenant
providing it is a "responsible source" and need not include
an express request that the landlord carry out repairs:
Dinefwr B.C. v. Jones[16] (district valuer's right to buy survey);
Hall v. Howard[17] (tenant's surveyor's valuation report).

(2) Notice will be sufficient if the landlord's builder notices the
defect (providing he actually notices it): *Griffin v. Pillett*.[18]

(3) A repairs notice served by the local authority can be
sufficient: *McGreal v. Wake*,[19] as can valuation reports.

(4) The landlord was sufficiently put on notice when made
aware of a bulging ceiling (which later collapsed): *Porter v.
Jones*.[20] But not when the tenant merely complained of
"banging and jumping" upstairs which might cause the
ceiling to collapse when there was no visible defect in the
ceiling: *O'Brien v. Robinson*.[21]

(5) The landlord was sufficiently on notice of disrepair by
knowing that a water tank (which later burst) was corroded,
even though, in the absence of weeping, corrosion did not

---

[14] [1992] 32 E.G. 59.
[15] *Supra* at p. 926B.
[15a] [1995] 3 W.L.R. 622.
[16] (1987) 19 H.L.R. 445.
[17] (1988) 57 P.&C.R. 226.
[18] [1926] 1 K.B. 117;
[19] (1984) 13 H.L.R. 107.
[20] (1942) 112 L.J.K.B. 113.
[21] *Supra*.

indicate that works of repair were immediately necessary: *Sheldon v. West Bromwich Corporation*.[22]

(6) A counterclaim can not constitute notice for the purposes of proceedings on the counterclaim because no cause of action arises until the expiry of a reasonable period of time after notice: *Al-Hassani v. Merrigan*.[23]

Exceptions to requirement of notice

5–04   The requirement of notice does not apply to parts of the premises or land which the landlord has retained in his or her possession as a matter of law.

Where the landlord agrees to repair, for example, the roof or walls of a building, but lets only the interior of the building to the tenant, retaining possession of the roof or walls, the landlord is liable on his or her covenant to repair immediately disrepair arises: *Melles & Co v. Holme*[24]; *Bishop v. Consolidated London Properties Ltd*[25]; *Loria v. Hammer*[26]; *British Telecom v. Sun Life Assurance Society*.[27]

Further, it may be that even where part of premises is demised, the requirement of notice will not apply, providing evidence shows that as a matter of practice the landlord retained possession and control of the relevant part of the demised premises for the benefit of the tenant and other tenants: as in the case of the sea wall in *Murphy v. Hurley*.[28] The case was cited to their Lordships in argument in *O'Brien v. Robinson*[29] but was neither approved nor disapproved in any of the judgments.

Notice and section 4 of the Defective Premises Act 1972

5–05   Section 4 of the Defective Premises Act 1972 makes landlords liable in some circumstances when there is an implied precondition of notice but the landlord does not have actual notice of disrepair.

Section 4(1) of the Defective Premises Act 1972 places landlords under a duty to take such care as is reasonable in all the circumstances to prevent personal injury or damage to the property of all persons (including tenants) who might reasonably expect to be affected by a failure on the part of the landlord to perform an

---

[22] (1973) 25 P.&C.R. 360.
[23] (1988) 20 H.L.R. 238.
[24] [1918] 2 K.B. 100.
[25] (1933) 102 L.J.K.B. 257.
[26] [1989] 2 E.G.L.R. 249.
[27] [1995] 4 All E.R. 44.
[28] [1922] 1 A.C. 369.
[29] *Supra.*

obligation to repair or maintain premises. Section 4(2) Defective Premises Act 1972 provides that: "The said duty is owed if the landlord knows (whether as the result of being notified by the tenant or otherwise) or if he ought in all the circumstances to have known of the relevant defect."

The effect is that, even in cases where the common law imposes a pre-condition of notice on liability, the landlord will be liable if he or she ought in all the circumstances to have known of the defect, at least when personal injury or property damage ensues. In every case, factual issues will arise as to what a responsible landlord ought to have known or discovered. The cases do however establish that landlords are generally expected to take positive steps to inspect for latent defects when aware that a problem might exist.

(1) In *Kathleen Clarke v. Taff Ely B.C.*[30] the plaintiff suffered personal injury when rotten floorboards collapsed beneath her. The court accepted that such collapse was foreseeable by the local authority, which knew that the floorboards of a large number of houses in the area were susceptible to damp and therefore to rot and possible collapse. The presence of rot could have been detected by simple visual inspection or by applying pressure to the floorboards. The court held that the landlord ought to have known of the defect by inspecting positively for it on one of the occasions on which it carried out other repairs to the subject premises, alternatively, that the landlord ought to have arranged a scheme of positive inspection.

(2) Landlords are not however expected to discover unforeseeable dangers: in *Preston B.C. v. Fairclough*[31] the Court of Appeal held that there was no breach of duty, the risk of an infant being trapped and scalded by un-insulated hot water pipes not being foreseeable.[32]

The Gas Safety (Installation and Use) Regulations 1994[33]

The Gas Safety (Installation and Use) Regulations 1994 requires **5–06** landlords to positively ensure that gas appliances are "maintained in a safe condition so as to prevent risk of injury to any person" (reg. 35(2)) and also requires them to undertake yearly inspections (reg. 35(3)). Failure to undertake sufficient inspections is likely to result in a finding that, for the purposes of section 4 of the

---

[30] (1980) 10 H.L.R. 44.
[31] (1982) 8 H.L.R. 75.
[32] For further information on s.4 of the Defective Premises Act 1972 see paras. 11–13 to 11–20 below.
[33] S.I. 1994 No. 1886.

Defective Premises Act 1972, the landlord "ought to have" known of a relevant defect.

Failure to complain when notice not required

5–07   In circumstances where the landlord is liable to repair irrespective of notice, the tenant who is aware of disrepair but fails to complain may find his or her award of general damages reduced on the ground of failure to mitigate: *Minchburn v. Peck.*[34]

---

[34] [1988] 1 E.G.L.R. 53. See below at para. 21–01.

CHAPTER SIX:

Damage Which is Either too Small or too Large is Not Disrepair

Breach of obligation to repair only when damage unacceptable

It is not sufficient to point to some deterioration, however slight, to   **6–01**
the premises. There is no breach of an obligation to repair until
there is unacceptable damage.

General considerations. The court decides whether deterioration is
unacceptable in the context primarily of the age of the premises at
the date of letting, but also their character and locality and the
expectations of the reasonably-minded hypothetical tenant likely to
rent: *Proudfoot v. Hart*[1]; *Anstruther-Gough-Calthorpe v. McOscar.*[2]
Proudfoot v. Hart[3] and *Belcher v. M'Intosh*[4] were approved by Lord
Atkin in *Summers v. Salford Corporation*[5] and have been followed in
a number of subsequent cases, *e.g. Lurcott v. Wakely*[6]; *Elmcroft
Developments Ltd v. Tankersley-Sawyer.*[7]

Age of premises. The age of the premises as at the date of letting is
of importance because "nobody could reasonably expect that a

[1] (1890) 25 Q.B.D. 42.
[2] [1924] 1 K.B. 716.
[3] *Supra.*
[4] (1829) 2 M.&Rob. 186.
[5] [1943] A.C. 283.
[6] [1911] 1 K.B.905.
[7] (1984) 270 E.G. 140.

house 200 years old should be in the same condition of repair as a house lately built".[8] The age of the premises as at the date of the letting agreement or lease is the "dominant feature" of the context in which the standard of repair is determined: *Anstruther-Gough-Calthorpe v. McOscar.*[9] Express words may however require the premises to be kept in such repair as is appropriate from time to time, for example, for a modern high-class office building in the City of London: *Gooderham & Worts Limited v. Canadian Broadcasting Corporation.*[10]

Character of premises. The character of the premises is of importance "because the same class of repairs as would be necessary to a palace would be wholly unnecessary to a cottage": *Proudfoot v. Hart.*[11] The general condition of the premises at the date of the agreement is relevant although not detailed evidence as to condition: *Payne v. Haine.*[12] The character of the premises at the time of the letting agreement or lease is what is important and any subsequent deterioration or improvement is irrelevant: *Anstruther-Gough-Calthorpe.*[13] This is in accordance with the general principle in construing contracts that the court may have regard to the factual context at the time of the agreement but not subsequent changes.

Locality of premises. The locality is of relevance "because the state of repair necessary for a house in Grosvenor Square would be wholly different from the state of repair necessary for a house in Spitalfields": *Proudfoot v. Hart.*[14] Again, changes in the character of the locality subsequent to the date of the agreement are not relevant: *Anstruther-Gough-Calthorpe.*[15]

Suitability for likely tenants. The condition of the premises must be such as to be "reasonably fit for occupation of a reasonably minded tenant of the class who would be likely to take it": *Proudfoot v. Hart.*[16] By close analogy, the condition of any subsidiary element of the building must be "reasonably fit" having regard to the reasonable expectations of the likely type of tenant. Again, changes in the type of tenant likely to rent the premises occurring after the date of the agreement are of no relevance: *Anstruther-Gough-Calthorpe.*[17]

---

[8] *per* Lord Esher M.R. in *Proudfoot v. Hart, supra.*
[9] *Supra, per* Bankes L.J.
[10] [1947] A.C. 66.
[11] *Supra, per* Lord Esher M.R.
[12] (1847) 16 M.&W. 451.
[13] *Supra.*
[14] *Supra, per* Lord Esher M.R.
[15] *Supra.*
[16] *Supra, per* Lord Esher M.R.
[17] *Supra.*

Damage which is too small

It follows from the general principles set out above that there can **6–02**
be a certain degree of deterioration without disrepair. If the
deterioration does not exceed what a reasonably minded tenant of
the type likely to rent the premises would consider reasonable,
having regard to the age, character and locality of the premises as
at the date of letting, then there is no disrepair.

Trivial damage. Repair means substantial repair and not perfect
repair: *Harris v. Jones*[18]; *Proudfoot v. Hart*[19] ("The house need not
be put into the same condition as when the tenant took it; it need
not be put into perfect repair . . . ", *per* Lord Esher M.R.). It would
take additional and very clear language for a repairing obligation to
be construed as requiring all defects however small to be made
good: *Harris v. Jones.*[20] Defects which, in the context of the
tenancy agreement or lease in question, have been held to be too
trivial to fall within the terms of a repairing obligation are: a "mere
crack in a pane of glass" (*Stanley v. Towgood*[21]) and nails in the wall
of a house and the holes made by them (*Perry v. Chotzner*[22]).

Damage which is acceptable. As a general principle, there is no
breach of an obligation to repair until the premises or the subject-
matter of the obligation has deteriorated unacceptably, having
regard primarily to the age of the premises, but also to their
character and locality and the expectations of the reasonably-
minded hypothetical tenant likely to rent as at the date of letting:
Proudfoot v. Hart[23]; *Anstruther-Gough-Calthorpe v. McOscar.*[24]

In *Plough Investments Limited v. Manchester City Council*[25] Scott J.
held that a wall was not in disrepair although some of the bricks
surrounding the steel frame were cracked:

> "Nor, in my opinion, would [the obligation to repair] include
> the removal and replacement of every cracked brick or block,
> no matter how small the crack. There were cracks when the
> leases were granted. A building of this sort, over 60 years old,
> is bound, in my view, to have some cracks in the bricks or
> blocks. . . . The same approach of degree justifies, in my
> judgment, a distinction being drawn between bricks or blocks

---

[18] (1832) 1 Moo. & R. 173.
[19] *Supra.*
[20] *Supra.*
[21] (1836) 3 Bing. N.C. 4.
[22] (1893) 9 T.L.R. 477.
[23] *Supra.*
[24] *Supra.*
[25] [1989] 1 E.G.L.R. 244.

suffering only hairline or minimal cracks and bricks or blocks which are more severely cracked or have become displaced."

In some cases, deterioration can be treated as acceptable, in part because the remedial works required are unusually extensive and costly. An obligation to repair office premises did not require remedial works to concrete beams even when expert evidence showed that the strength of some of the beams had deteriorated and that there was a serious risk of the concrete being defective. The reason was that the beams would continue to function effectively for the foreseeable future and a prudent landlord could well decide to carry out strengthening work some time in the future: *Camden L.B.C. v. Civil Aviation Authority*.[26] A similar decision in relation to rusting steel frames causing some deterioration to the exterior cladding was reached in *Plough Investments Ltd v. Manchester City Council*.[27]

In *Staves & Staves v. Leeds City Council*[28] however the Court of Appeal dismissed the argument that four areas of plaster which were saturated by damp and perishing and which were "inches rather than feet" were *de minimis*. Lloyd L.J. indeed said that "We need not inquire how much of the plaster was 'damaged'. If the plaster required to be renewed as a result of saturation, then it seems to me that, as a matter of ordinary language, what was done was a repair."

In the county court case of *Hallet v. Camden L.B.C.*[29] the Recorder held that cracks to the plaster of walls and ceilings was not sufficiently serious as to amount to a failure to repair. But in another county court case, *Windever v. Liverpool C.C.*[30] the Recorder held that floors which had sunk due to settlement so as to cause furniture to wobble and some floorboards to rise did not provide an adequate surface for seating and other normal uses and were in disrepair.

Damage which is too large

6–03 Conversely, there are cases in which, although the condition of the premises has deteriorated, the problem is so serious that the works necessary are considered to be too extensive to be repairs.

In *Holding & Management Limited v. Property Holding & Investment Ltd*[31] Nicholls L.J. emphasised the practical nature of the

[26] (1981) 257 E.G. 273.
[27] [1989] 1 E.G.L.R. 244.
[28] (1991) 23 H.L.R. 107.
[29] *Legal Action*, August 1994, p. 17.
[30] *Legal Action*, December 1994, p. 17.
[31] (1989) 21 H.L.R. 596.

investigation, reflecting the fact that the decision is ultimately one of fact and degree and not law:

" . . . the exercise involves considering the context in which the word 'repair' appears in a particular lease and also the defect and remedial works proposed. Accordingly, the circumstances to be taken into account in a particular case under one or other of these heads will include some or all of the following: the nature of the building; the terms of the lease; the state of the building at the date of the lease; the nature and extent of the proposed remedial works, at whose expense the proposed remedial works are to be done; the value of the building and its expected lifespan; the effect of the works on such value and lifespan; current building practice; the likelihood of a recurrence if one remedy rather than another is adopted; and the comparative cost of alternative remedial works and their impact on the use and enjoyment of the building by the occupants. The weight to be attached to these circumstances will vary from case to case.

This is not a comprehensive list. In some cases there will be other matters properly to be taken into account. For example, as in the present case, where a design or construction fault has led to part of the building falling into a state of disrepair, and the proposed remedial works extend to other parts of the building, an important consideration will be the likelihood of similar disrepair arising in other parts of the building, if the remedial work is not undertaken there also, and how soon such further disrepair is likely to arise."

There are similar statements of principle in *Ravenseft Properties v. Davstone (Holdings)*[32]; *Lurcott v. Wakely*[33]; *Brew Bros Ltd v. Snax (Ross) Limited*[34]; *Wates v. Rowland*[35]; *Post Office v. Aquarius Properties Limited*[36]; and *McDougall v. Easington D.C.*[37]

Inherent defects generally

The fact that disrepair is caused by defective design or construction does not of itself mean that remedial work can not be required under the terms of a repairing obligation:

---

[32] [1980] Q.B. 12.
[33] [1911] 1 K.B. 905.
[34] [1970] 1 Q.B. 612.
[35] [1952] 2 Q.B. 12.
[36] [1985] 2 E.G.L.R. 105.
[37] (1989) 58 P.&C.R. 210.

(1) If the defective design or construction causes disrepair (or other damage involving a breach of the agreement) the disrepair must be remedied.

(2) If the work to cure the underlying cause of the disrepair (the defective design or construction of the building itself) is not too large to be classified as repair, and if it is the only practical, sensible or necessary course, the courts will order work to cure the underlying inherent defect.

Ravenseft Properties Limited v. Davstone (Holdings) Limited[38]; *Halliard Property Co. Limited v. Nicholas Clarke Investments Limited*[39]; *Quick v. Taff-Ely B.C.*[40]

In his seminal judgment in *Ravenseft*, approved by the Court of Appeal in *Elmcroft Developments Limited v. Tankersley-Sawyer*[41]; *Quick v. Taff-Ely B.C.*[42]; and *Stent v. Monmouth D.C.*[43] Forbes J. held that:

"the explanation of the ratio of *Lister v. Lane*[44] as giving the tenant a complete defence, if the cause of any want of reparation is an inherent defect, has never been adopted by any court but on the contrary ... the court, when dealing with wants of reparation caused by an inherent defect, chose to treat the matter as one of degree, while in *Brew Brothers Ltd v. Snax (Ross) Ltd*[45] the court effectively said that every case, whatever the causation, must be treated as one of degree.

I find myself, therefore, unable to accept Mr. Colyer's contention that a doctrine such as he enunciates has any place in the law of landlord and tenant. The true test is, as the cases show, that it is always a question of degree whether that which the tenant is being asked to do can properly be described as repair, or whether on the contrary it would involve giving back to the landlord a wholly different thing from that which he demised.

In deciding this question, the proportion which the cost of the disputed work bears to the value or cost of the whole premises, may sometimes be helpful as a guide ... the cost [of inserting expansion joints] would have been in the region of £5,000. The total cost of the remedial works was around £55,000 ... For comparison, the cost of building a structure of this kind in 1973 would have been in the region of £3

---

[38] [1980] Q.B. 12.
[39] [1984] 1 E.G.L.R. 45.
[40] [1986] Q.B. 809.
[41] (1984) 270 E.G. 140.
[42] [1986] Q.B. 805.
[43] (1987) P.&C.R. 193.
[44] [1983] 2 Q.B. 212.
[45] [1970] 1 Q.B. 612.

million, or rather more . . . The expansion joints form but a trivial part of this whole building and looking at it as a question of degree, I do not consider that they amount to such a change in the character of the building as to take them out of the covenant to repair."

It is explicit in the approach taken by the courts that works which go beyond the meaning of repair in one context might be treated as repairs in another context. Nonetheless, the following examples may be of assistance.

Underpinning. The tenant under a seven-year lease of an old   **6–04** dwelling house was not liable under a repairing covenant to underpin the entire house to a depth of 17 feet, the house having been defectively constructed upon a wooden platform over boggy soil: *Lister v. Lane.*[46] In that case Kay L.J. held:

"Underpinning", as I understand, means digging down through the mud until you reach the solid gravel, and then building up from that to the brickwork of the house. Would that be repairing, or upholding, or maintaining the house? To my mind, it would not; it would be making an entirely new and different house. It might be just as costly to underpin as to pull the house down and rebuild it.

The tenant under a 99-year lease in *Sotheby v. Grundy*[47] was not liable to underpin an old dwelling house to prevent structural collapse due to the absence of any, or any proper, foundations (the court indicating, by contrast, that replacement of defective floor joists would be a repair and remarking that the tenant was being asked to carry out works which would lead to a building with an expected life, as constructed, of 80 years obtaining a further life of 100 years).

The tenant under a long lease was also not liable to underpin in *Collins v. Flynn.*[48]

Underpinning where subsidence was caused by a combination of drought and inadequate foundations was neither repair nor maintenance in *ACT Construction Limited v. Commissioners for Customs & Excise.*[49]

The landlord under a 21-year lease of restaurant premises was held liable to carry out underpinning works in *Smedley v. Chumley & Hawke Limited*[50] in order to comply with a covenant to keep the

---

[46] *Supra.*
[47] [1947] 2 All E.R. 761.
[48] [1963] 2 All E.R. 1068.
[49] [1981] 1 W.L.R. 49, [1982] 1 W.L.R. 1542.
[50] [1982] 1 E.G.L.R. 47.

walls and roof in repair. The Court of Appeal distinguished *Lister v. Lane*,[51] *Sotheby v. Grundy*[52] and similar cases on the ground that they concerned lettings of houses which had deteriorated over time, whilst the restaurant had been newly constructed, and on the ground that the repairing obligation in relation to the roof and walls was, on a true construction of this particular lease, unqualified (and also coupled with an obligation to keep the premises in good structural condition). In particular, the court held that the underpinning in this particular case gave back to the tenant no more than the type of premises contemplated by the parties at the date of the agreement.

A small amount of underpinning was treated as falling within a repairing covenant in *Rich Investments Limited v. Camgate Litho Limited*.[53]

In *Brew Bros Ltd v. Snax (Ross) Ltd*[54] the Court of Appeal held by a majority that works were not repairs when the lease was of a shop with a flat above for 14 years and cost almost as much as rebuilding the house would cost. The works involved rebuilding the flank wall and parts of the front and back walls, repairs to the drains and new foundations for the flank wall. Harman L.J., dissenting, was of the view that all the works other than the new foundations, which were of an entirely different character, fell within the repairing covenant.

In *Wates v. Rowland*[55] the Court of Appeal held in the case of a Rent Act tenancy that work carried out by the landlord involving the insertion of an additional concrete raft under the joists in order to prevent rotting of the joists caused by a rise in the water table was not work of repair but of improvement.

In *Halliard Property Co. Limited v. Nicholas Clarke Investments Limited*[56] in a case he described as "borderline" the judge held that the tenant of commercial, single storey premises held under a 14-year lease was not obliged under its repairing covenants to demolish a jerry-built utility room at the rear, which had (unknown to the parties) been in danger of collapse since prior to the lease, having been constructed very poorly; dig new foundations and rebuild the walls, with insulation, according to current building practice. The cost was to be £3,500, more than a third of the cost of rebuilding the entire premises and considerably more than a third of the sale value of the entire premises. French J. concluded by saying:

[51] *Supra.*
[52] *Supra.*
[53] (1989) E.G.C.S. 142.
[54] *Supra.*
[55] [1952] 2 Q.B. 12.
[56] (1983) 269 E.G. 1257.

"Regarding, as I do, this matter as a borderline case, the conclusion that I come to is that the reinstatement or rebuilding of this utility room is not covered by the obligations imposed upon the defendants by the repairing covenant. In my judgment, that which would be involved in rebuilding the utility room could not properly be described as a repair. While, of course, that which would be handed back on the expiry of the demise would include the intact 'two thirds in area' front part of the premises, it would involve handing back to them, so far as the utility room was concerned, an edifice entirely different from the unstable and jerry-built structure of which the defendants took possession at the start of this lease."

In *Minchburn v. Peck*[57] the Court of Appeal held that "drastic work by way of underpinning" would have been within a covenant to "maintain, repair, redecorate and renew the main structure and foundations", which covenant, according to Dillon L.J., was "as wide a covenant as there could be imposed on the lessor".

Damp proof courses. In *Pembery v. Lamdin*[58] the Court of Appeal   **6–05** considered a lease of 16 years of old premises containing a wine bar on the ground floor. The tenant to the knowledge of the landlord had intended to open a cocktail bar in the basement but could not do so as a result of severe lateral earth water penetration into the basement. The basement had been constructed at a time when damp proofing was unheard of. The work required involved asphalting the basement walls, constructing internal 4.5 inch thick walls and a new 4 inch concrete floor. The Court of Appeal held that the premises were not in disrepair, since there had been no deterioration in their condition and that the repairs proposed would have involved the creation of " 'a different thing' from that which [the tenant] took when she entered into the covenant".

The basement flats in *Elmcroft Developments Ltd v. Tankersley-Sawyer*[59] also suffered from severe lateral earth water penetration, which saturated the plaster, and which arose as a result of the horizontal slate damp proof course having been laid below ground level. The landlord conceded it was liable to repair the plaster. The Court of Appeal held that the landlord's obligation to keep "in good and tenantable repair and condition" the exterior and main walls required it not just to renew the saturated plaster but also to install a silicone injection damp proof course costing about £500

[57] [1988] 1 E.G.L.R. 53.
[58] [1940] 2 All E.R. 434.
[59] *Supra.*

(the value of the flats was about £40,000). Ackner L.J. referred to *Pembery v. Lamdin*[60] and said:

> "I personally find this case of no assistance at all. It does not involve the letting of a flat. It involved letting of premises that contained this cellar in a building which was built some 100 years before the court considered the problems. That must be round about 1840. We are concerned about the letting a few years ago of what was built as a separate self-contained flat and a flat in a high-class fashionable residential area in the centre of London. I entirely agree with what Forbes J. said in the *Ravenseft* case,[61] that this was a decision arrived at by considering the question as one of degree. That view was followed by the learned county court judge, and I consider that he was wholly right in so doing."

A differently constituted Court of Appeal reached a different result on similar facts in *Wainwright v. Leeds City Council*,[62] after *Elmcroft Developments Ltd v. Tankersley-Sawyer*[63] had been decided but not reported. The decision in *Wainwright* was on the basis that *Pembery v. Lamdin*[64] could not be distinguished on its facts; there was apparently no argument before the court similar to that in *Elmcroft Developments Ltd* and the decision is to be treated with caution.

6–06   *Roofs.* In *Elite Investments Limited v. T. I. Bainbridge (Silencers) Limited*[65] it was held that the installation of a new roof made of modern material did fall within the tenant's repairing obligation, when the old roof had deteriorated beyond patching. The cost using the new materials was about the same as using the old materials which were still available and was about £140,000, whereas the cost of rebuilding the entire factory would have been nearly £1 million. A similar conclusion was reached in *New England Properties Limited v. Portsmouth New Shops Limited*,[66] and in *Postel Properties Ltd v. Boots the Chemist*.[66a]

6–07   *Cladding.* In *Ravenseft Properties Limited v. Davstone (Holdings) Limited*[67] the cladding to a 16-storey block of maisonettes became loose and was in danger of falling because it had been fixed without

---

[60] *Supra.*
[61] at p. 939.
[62] (1984) 13 H.L.R. 117.
[63] *Supra.*
[64] [1940] 2 All E.R. 434.
[65] [1986] 2 E.G.L.R. 43.
[66] [1993] 1 E.G.L.R. 84.
[66a] [1996] 41 E.G. 164.
[67] *Supra.*

expansion joints, the necessity for which had not been appreciated at the date of construction. There had in addition been some defective workmanship in the fixing of the cladding. The landlord removed all the cladding from the worst affected elevation and refixed it according to current building practice. It also re-fixed two thirds of the cladding on one of the other elevations. Forbes J. held that such work was not too extensive to be a repair.

In *Holding & Management Limited v. Property Holding & Investment Trust Limited*[68] the Court of Appeal held that the complete removal of cladding to a 12-storey block of flats went beyond the obligation to repair: but that was really because on the facts the cladding did not require complete replacement, only more limited works.

Lindsay J. held in *Credit Suisse v. Beegas Nominees Limited*[69] that replacement of all of the cladding over four floors at a cost of £1.2 million went beyond a repair. The cladding appears, however, to have been of an unusually expensive type.

Steel frames. In *Plough Investments Limited v. Manchester City Council*[70] Scott J. held that: **6–08**

"If, in the present case, the degree of rusting had so reduced the strength of the steel frame as to require the substantial reinforcement of the whole of the external steel frame in the manner contemplated by . . . the remedial works proposed by the plaintiff, I would have been of the opinion that the remedial works went, as a matter of degree, beyond 'repair'. But if one section only, say the section at or around location A, required strengthening, by being surrounded with reinforced concrete, I would not regard that work as going beyond repair. At some point between those two extremes a line would, in my opinion, need to be drawn."

Plant. In *Morcom v. Campbell-Johnson*[71] the Court of Appeal   **6–09** held that the replacement of cold water storage tanks in individual flats by a centralised cold water tank with associated pipework and the replacement of separate pipes from toilets and basins with single waste water pipes, when that plumbing had reached the end of its life, were works of repair, albeit that a substantial amount of improvement was involved.

In *Roper v. Prudential Assurance Co. Limited*[72] an obligation to repair, maintain and keep in good and substantial repair order and

---

[68] *Supra.*
[69] [1994] 4 All E.R. 803.
[70] [1989] 1 E.G.L.R. 244.
[71] [1956] 1 Q.B. 106.
[72] [1992] 1 E.G.L.R. 5.

condition was held to recover replacing electrical wiring in a farm house.

Works necessary to comply with the law or good practice

6–10   Generally speaking, an obligation to repair carries with it an obligation to repair in accordance with current legislation or building regulations and this may involve a degree of improvement: *Lurcott v. Wakely*[73]; *Halliard Property Co. Limited v. Nicholas Clarke Investments Limited.*[74] It may require that the work is carried out according to current good practice: *Ravenseft Properties Limited v. Davstone (Holdings) Limited,*[75] *Postel Properties Ltd v. Boots the Chemist,*[75a] *Stent v. Monmouth D.C.*[75b] This does not of itself mean that the works involved become too extensive to be described as repairs: *Wright v. Lawson*[76]; *Halliard Property Co. Limited v. Nicholas Clarke Investments Limited.*[77]

Repair including renewal

6–11   It is wrong to assume that repair is the antithesis of renewal or improvement. Repair work always involves a degree of renewal and often involves a degree of improvement, in the sense that the building element repaired is objectively somewhat better in one aspect or another than the element it replaces. As Buckley L.J. said in *Lurcott v. Wakely*[78]: " 'Repair' and 'renewal' are not words expressive of a clear contrast. Repair always involves renewal; renewal of a part; of a subsidiary part."

The question is not whether the work involves an element of renewal or improvement, but whether, as a matter of fact and degree, the works go beyond the type of work envisaged by the particular obligation to repair in question.

Complete renewal rather than patching up

6–12   Generally, there is a range of different repair options which a reasonable person might wish to pursue. The choice might lie between effecting a patch repair and completely renewing a damaged element. Or the choice might lie between a relatively cheap and a relatively expensive material. Within reason the choice

[73] *Supra.*
[74] *Supra.*
[75] *Supra.*
[75a] *Supra.*
[75b] (1987) 54 P. & C.R. 193.
[76] (1903) 19 T.L.R. 203.
[77] *Supra.*
[78] *Supra.*

of method is for the party who has to repair, whether it be landlord or tenant: *Murray v. Birmingham City Council*[79]; *Dame Margaret Hungerford Charity Trustees v. Beaseley*[80]; *Fox v. Jolly*[81]; *Plough Investments Limited v. Manchester City Council*[82]; *McDougall v. Easington District Council*,[83] *Postel Properties Ltd v. Boots the Chemist.*[83a]

There are limits, however. Examples have already been given[84] of cases in which the courts have required landlords and tenants to remedy underlying defects of construction or design which have caused disrepair to a building element the landlord or tenant is responsible for repairing. In *Elmcroft Developments Limited v. Tankersley-Sawyer*,[85] for example, Ackner L.J. held that:

"the learned judge was wholly right in the decision which he made as to the failure by the appellants to comply with the repairing covenant and their obligation in regard to curing the damp by using the only practical method at this price, namely, injecting silicone into the wall. Mr Whittaker was at one stage prepared to concede that, as the plaster became saturated (which, of course, it was) his clients had the obligation to do the necessary patching—that is removing—the perished plaster and renewing it. I am bound to say that concession made the resistance to inserting the damp-proof course a strange one. The damp-proof course, once inserted, would on the expert evidence cure the damp. The patching work would have to go on and on and on, because, as the plaster absorbed (as it would) the rising damp, it would have to be renewed, and the cost to the appellants in constantly being involved with this sort of work, one would have thought, would have outweighed easily the cost in doing the job properly. I have no hesitation in rejecting the submission that the appellant's obligation was repetitively to carry out futile work instead of doing the job properly once and for all."

In *Murray v. Birmingham City Council*[86] Slade L.J. held:

" . . . in any case where the landlord, or the tenant for that matter, is under an obligation to keep in repair an old roof, the stage may come where the only practicable way of performing

[79] [1987] 2 E.G.L.R. 53.
[80] [1993] 2 E.G.L.R. 144.
[81] [1916] 1 A.C. 1.
[82] *Supra.*
[83] *Supra.*
[83a] *Supra.*
[84] Paras. 6–03 to 6–09.
[85] *Supra.*
[86] *Supra.*

that covenant is to replace the roof altogether . . . [there was] no evidence to suggest that a piecemeal repair of the roof in 1976 right up to 1982 was not a perfectly practicable proposition. I, for my part, am quite unable to accept the submission that, merely because there had been some half a dozen, no doubt troublesome, incidents of disrepair occurring during those six years, it necessarily followed from that the roof was incapable of repair by any way other than replacement."

In that case, had the roof been part of the demise with the result that the obligation to repair was breached only after notice of disrepair and delay in repairing, the landlord would only have been liable in the event that he delayed in carrying out the works of patching that became necessary from time to time. If the roof was not demised but subject to a repairing covenant, then the landlord of course would have been liable every time and immediately disrepair occurred.

In *Stent v. Monmouth District Council*[87] Stocker L.J. said:

"If the only defect in the door was that it did not perform its primary function of keeping out the rain, and the door was otherwise undamaged and in a condition which it or its predecessors had been at the time of the letting, then it seems to me, on the authorities of *Quick* and *Aquarius*, this cannot amount to a defect for the purpose of a repairing covenant even though, as it seems to me in layman's terms, that a door which does not keep out the rain is a defective door, and one which is in need of some form of repair or modification or replacement. . . . In this case, however, the factual position is that the damage undoubtedly did occur. The appellant's own documents illustrate that clearly and graphically. There was damage such as to require the replacement of the door. . . . Accordingly, applying the reasoning of this court from the cases cited, and in particular *Ravenseft Properties Ltd v. Davstone (Holdings) Ltd* and *Elmcroft Developments Ltd v. Tankersley-Sawyer*, the former having been specifically approved by this court, in my judgment the replacement of a wooden door by a self-sealing aluminium door was a mode of repair which a sensible person would have adopted; and the same reasoning applies if for the words 'sensible' there is substituted some such word as 'practicable' or 'necessary'. . . . Of course, it does not follow that the self-sealing door is the only sensible way in which that object could be achieved. There may well have been others, but in my view the obligation under the covenant in this case was one which called upon the appellants

[87] *Supra.*

to carry out repairs which not only effected the repair of the manifestly damaged parts but also achieved the object of rendering it unnecessary in the future for the continual repair of this door."

PART THREE

OTHER TYPES OF OBLIGATION
TO CARRY OUT WORK

CHAPTER SEVEN

Other Types of Obligation to Carry Out Work

The torrential drafting style

Covenants in leases, which are broadly recognisable as "repairing   **7–01**
covenants", may be drafted in a "torrential" style. Practitioners will
be familiar with covenants such as "well, sufficiently and substantially [to] repair, uphold, sustain, maintain, glaze, pave . . .
amend and keep all and singular the said premises . . . ": *Lister v.
Lane.*[1]

The question of construction that arises is whether the draftsman included the additional words in order to impose additional
obligations beyond repair, or in order merely to illustrate or express
the many diverse obligations which the courts have over many years
held to be inherent in the obligation to repair.

Hoffmann J. said in *Norwich Union Life Assurance Society Limited
v. British Railways Board*[2]:

> "Now I accept that in the construction of covenants such as
> this one cannot, for the reasons I have already given, insist
> upon giving each word in a series a distinct meaning. Drafts-
> men frequently use many words either because it is traditional
> to do so or out of a sense of caution so that nothing which
> could conceivably fall within the general concept which they
> have in mind should be left out."

[1] [1893] 2 Q.B. 212.
[2] [1987] 2 E.G.L.R. 137.

Hoffmann J. does not appear to have been expressly referred to *Lurcott v. Wakely*[3] in which Fletcher-Moulton L.J. said: "I think it is our duty to give the full meaning to each word in the covenant." He nonetheless decided on the facts of the case before him that the words in the obligation to "repair, rebuild, reconstruct and replace" should be given separate meanings. In the context of a 150-year lease: "the draftsman had two separate concepts in mind: first, that of repair and, second, that of rebuilding, reconstructing or replacing the entire premises". As Lindsay J. held in *Credit Suisse v. Beegas Nominees Limited*[4]: "Even where there is a torrent, each stream of which it is comprised can be expected to have added to the flow."

Redundant adjectives

7–02   When the word "repair" is prefaced by an adjective such as "good", "tenantable" or "habitable" the court is likely to find that nothing is added to the concept of "repair": *Proudfoot v. Hart*[5]; *Anstruther-Gough-Calthorpe v. McOscar.*[6]

The same normally applies to phrases such as "good tenantable repair": *Proudfoot v. Hart,*[7] "in good tenantable repair and condition": *Pembery v. Lamdin*[8] or "thorough repair and good condition": *Lurcott v. Wakely*[9] (although one of the three Court of Appeal judges, Fletcher-Moulton L.J., would have given an independent and broader meaning to the phrase "good condition").

The same result will not necessarily follow in every case. That is because in each case, the meaning of the individual words comprised in the repairing covenant, and their meaning in combination, is to be construed in the context of the whole document and in the context of the particular factual matrix at the time of the agreement. In *Anstruther-Gough-Calthorpe v. McOscar,*[10] for example, Atkin L.J. followed Fletcher-Moulton L.J. in *Lurcott v. Wakely*[11] and held that:

"I see no reason for construing the words of covenants in leases dealing with obligations to repair in any other way that one would construe any other covenant. Effect should be given if possible to every word used by the parties: see *per* Fletcher--

---

[3] [1911] 1 K.B. 905.
[4] [1994] 1 E.G.L.R. 76.
[5] (1890) 25 Q.B.D. 42.
[6] [1924] 1 K.B. 716.
[7] *Supra.*
[8] [1940] 2 All E.R. 434.
[9] *Supra.*
[10] *Supra.*
[11] *Supra.*

Moulton L.J. in *Lurcott v. Wakely.* It does not appear to me to be useful to refer to such covenants as the usual covenants to repair, or general repairing covenants, and then consider only what is the meaning of 'repair'. It appears to me still less useful to take a number of terms which may be found in different leases, treat them all as synonymous, and so impute to all of them a special meaning attached by authority to one of them."

Bankes L.J. in the same case held that:

"I attach no importance to the particular form of words used in the covenant. The effect is the same in my opinion whatever words the parties used, provided they plainly express the intention that the premises are to be repaired, kept in repair and yielded up in repair."

When one considers however what Bankes L.J. meant by the words "provided they plainly express the intention", the extent of any disagreement with Atkin L.J. is by no means clear.

Obligation to renew

All repairs involve renewing a subsidiary part of the building: "if **7–03** window frames become rotten and decayed, you cannot repair them except by renewing"—*Lurcott v. Wakely.*[12] The addition of an obligation to renew adds nothing to the obligation to repair, unless it was the intention of the parties that there should be a liability to renew the whole building and not merely one or more of its subsidiary parts.

That would involve a liability to carry out works which are normally regarded as too large to be repairs.[13]

If that is alleged to be the contention, then, generally, "much stronger and more specific words would have to be used", *e.g.* than merely the inclusion of the word "renew" among the relevant obligations: *Collins v. Flynn.*[14]

The majority of the Court of Appeal in *Anstruther-Gough-Calthorpe v. McOscar*[15] saw no obligation more extensive than an obligation to repair in the expression "well and sufficiently repair support uphold maintain paint pave empty scour cleanse amend and keep . . . ".

In the context of a very differently worded lease, however, of a new architect-designed office building, the word "renew" was held

---

[12] *Supra,* at p. 912.
[13] See para. 6–03.
[14] [1963] 2 All E.R. 1068.
[15] *Supra.*

to extend beyond repair and to include major works of a kind which would not normally be included as part of a repairing obligation: *Credit Suisse v. Beegas Nominees Limited.*[16]

Obligation to keep in good or tenantable condition

7–04   In *Lurcott v. Wakely*[17] Fletcher-Moulton L.J. held that the covenant to keep the premises in good condition was wider than the covenant to keep the premises in repair. He said

> "I have dwelt by preference on the covenant to keep in good condition because it seems to me that it is entirely free from any consideration of the means that have to be employed by the lessee to do the work . . . they covenanted to keep the house in good condition, besides covenanting to do repairs . . . and therefore they could not plead that they had performed their contract if they allowed the house to come into a condition in which it was no longer habitable as a house."

Cozens-Hardy M.R. and Buckley L.J. decided the case only on the basis that there had been a breach of the covenant to repair.

In *Smedley v. Chumley and Hawke Limited*[18] Cumming-Bruce L.J., with whom Templeman L.J. and Dame Elizabeth Lane agreed said that "I . . . derive much assistance from the judgment of Fletcher-Moulton L.J. in *Lurcott v. Wakely*. . . ." He held that the covenant "To keep the main walls and roof in good structural repair and condition throughout the term" required that walls be underpinned:

> "in order to discover whether there is an obligation to do work made necessary in order to correct the effect of defects in design, it is necessary to examine carefully the whole lease and to decide the intention to be collected therefrom, and in this lease the intention was to place upon the landlords an unqualified obligation to keep the walls and roof in good structural condition."

In *Post Office v. Aquarius Properties Limited*[19] both Hoffmann J. and that Court of Appeal, considering the expression "well and substantially to repair . . . amend . . . renew and keep in good and substantial repair and condition" held that the phrase "keep in good and substantial repair and condition" added nothing to the obligation to repair. That, however, was on the basis, as the Court

---

[16] *Supra.*
[17] *Supra.*
[18] [1981] 45 P.&C.R. 50.
[19] [1987] 1 All E.R. 1055.

of Appeal was careful to indicate, that no reliance had been placed on the additional words in the course of argument.

In *Credit Suisse v. Beegas Nominees Limited*[20] Lindsay J. again followed Fletcher-Moulton L.J. in *Lurcott v. Wakely*.[21] He held that "the duty of the court is to give a proper and full effect to each word used in repairing covenants" and that, accordingly, there was a clear distinction between an obligation to "repair" and an obligation "*otherwise* to keep in good and tenantable condition":

"while I accept the inevitability of the conclusion of the Court of Appeal in *Post Office v. Aquarius Properties Limited*[22] that one cannot have an existing obligation to repair unless and until there is disrepair, that reasoning does not apply to a covenant to keep (and put) into good and tenantable condition . . . all that is needed, in general terms, to trigger a need for activity under an obligation to keep in (and put into) a given condition is that the subject-matter is out of that condition . . . where, as here, one has not only the verbs other than 'repair' but also a context showing that 'defects' in express contradistinction to 'repairs' are within the covenant, the great body of law debating whether a given shortcoming is or is not a repair or is or is not an inherent defect such that remedying it goes beyond repair does not, in my judgment, apply. Of course, as with covenants to repair, questions as to the age and nature and class of the subject matter to be put and kept in the specified condition have to be borne in mind . . . but, as I see it, it is no necessary escape from liability under a covenant to put and keep in a specified condition that the work needed in order that that condition should be achieved is not a repair strictly so called. Nor do I see as important on this part of the landlord's covenant that the work required to achieve the given condition is of a particular great cost. I can see that that may well affect and has been frequently taken to affect whether the work is one of 'repair', but I do not see it as material to an obligation to put and keep in a given condition . . . . It may be . . . that a proper limitation on the obligation to put and keep in good and tenantable condition is that the landlord cannot be required to provide the tenant with something 'of a wholly different character from that which had been let': see *McDougall v. Easington District Council*.[23] I thus say nothing as to that."

---

[20] *Supra.*
[21] *Supra.*
[22] *Supra.*
[23] [1989] 1 E.G.L.R. 93 at p. 96 (C.A.).

In *Jones v. Joseph*[24] the obligation was to keep and deliver up the premises "in as good repair and condition" as at the commencement of the tenancy. That covenant in so far as it referred to "good condition" was broken when the premises became infested with bugs.

In *Belcher v. Mackintosh*[25] a covenant to put premises into "tenantable repair" and "habitable repair" required that the premises could be occupied "not only with safety, but with reasonable comfort, by the class of persons by whom, and for the sort of purposes for which, they were to be occupied".

In *Summers v. Salford Corporation*[26] Lord Atkin held that:

> I am bound to say that I find it difficult to draw a distinction between an obligation to put premises into habitable repair and so deliver them up, and to keep premises "in all respects reasonably fit for human habitation".

Obligation to rebuild, reconstruct or replace

7–05   The lease in *Norwich Union Life Assurance Co. Limited v. British Railways Board*[27] imposed an obligation to repair, rebuild, reconstruct and replace. Hoffmann J. held that the obligation was not limited to an obligation to rebuild, reconstruct or replace subsidiary parts (*e.g.* it was not merely an obligation to repair). He held that in the context of a 150-year lease: "the draftsman had two separate concepts in mind: first, that of repair and, second, that of rebuilding, reconstructing or replacing the entire premises".[28]

Obligation to maintain

7–06   This obligation is highly ambiguous. Its construction is very much context-sensitive. It can refer to works of day-to-day maintenance, imposing an obligation significantly less onerous than a repairing obligation[29]: *ACT Construction Limited v. Customs & Excise Commissioners.*[30] It can be treated as including obligations which are more extensive than repair, shading into an obligation to "maintain" in "good condition" (compare *Credit Suisse* above): *Day v. Harland & Wolff Limited.*[31] It can include "replace":

---

[24] [1918] K.B. 510.
[25] (1839) 2 Moo. & R. 186.
[26] [1943] A.C. 283.
[27] [1987] 2 E.G.L.R. 137.
[28] See also *New England Properties Limited v. Portsmouth New Shops Limited* [1993] 1 E.G.L.R. 94.
[29] See damage which is too small at para. 6–02 above.
[30] [1981] 1 W.L.R. 59.
[31] [1953] 1 W.L.R. 906.

Greetings Oxford Kola Hotel Property Limited v. Oxford Squar
Investments Property Limited.[31a]

Obligation to decorate at specified intervals

Obligations to decorate at specified intervals are binding whether   **7–07**
or not the premises actually require decoration: *Gemmell v. Gold-*
sworthy.[32]

Obligation to maintain in accordance with a schedule of condition

The parties can agree that one of them will keep the premises in   **7–08**
no worse condition than at the start of the lease, in which case a
schedule of condition will normally be attached to the lease.

By a variety of express contract provisions the parties can agree
to obligations requiring detailed attention to aspects of the decoration, furnishings and fittings and so forth.

Obligation to supply services or maintain in proper working order

An obligation to supply a service such as hot water or heating is   **7–09**
a strict one and can require works which are too large to be
described as repairs: *Yorkbrook Investments Limited v. Batten*[33]
(landlord obliged to replace antiquated and unserviceable communal hot water and central heating system). In *Morcom v. Campbell-*
Johnson [1956] 1 Q.B. 106 the replacement of a drainage system
and a cold water system in a block of flats was a repair not an
improvement. The complete re-wiring of a farmhouse was a repair
in *Roper v. Prudential Assurance Co. Ltd* [1992] 1 E.G.L.R. 5.

The obligation to keep in proper working order (found, in
relation to specified installations in section 11 of the Landlord and
Tenant Act 1985) requires more than repair. The installation
concerned has to be in such condition that it performs its intended
function adequately. The obligation therefore requires that installations which have always been defective are remedied: *Liverpool City*
Council v. Irwin.[34]

Other obligations

There are no limitations on what the parties can agree (except   **7–10**
that where the Landlord and Tenant Act 1985 applies the landlord

---

[31a] (1989) 18 N.S.W.L.R. 33.
[32] [1942] S.A.S.R. 55.
[33] (1986) 52 P.&C.R. 51.
[34] [1977] A.C. 239.

out of his obligations under that Act). The parties sly stipulate that one of them is to be obliged to r construction defects in the premises let. They provements and/or specified building works are to the case of commercial premises they can agree ill keep the premises in a condition which makes them fit for their specified purpose; in a residential lease they could agree that the landlord will keep the premises fit for human habitation and/or abate statutory nuisances within the meaning of the Environmental Protection Act 1990. All such clauses fall to be construed carefully, to ascertain whether the parties did in fact intend to create obligations going beyond repair.

PART FOUR

IMPLIED TERMS OF THE CONTRACT

CHAPTER EIGHT

Terms Implied by Common Law or by the Express Terms of the Contract Itself

General rule: caveat emptor

The basic rule is summarised by Lord Atkinson in *Cavalier v.* **8–01**
Pope[1]:

> "It is well established that no duty is, at law, cast upon a landlord not to let a house in a dangerous or dilapidated condition, and further, that if he does let it while in such a condition, he is not thereby rendered liable in damages for injuries which may be sustained by the tenant, his (the tenant's) servants, guests, customers or others invited by him to enter the premises by reason of this defective condition."

Lord McNaghten, agreeing with Lord Atkinson, approved the statement of Erle C.J. in *Robbins v. Jones*[2] that:

> "A landlord who lets a house in a dangerous state is not liable to the tenant's customers or guests for accidents happening during the term: for, fraud apart, there is no law against letting a tumble-down house; and the tenant's remedy is upon his contract, if any."

The Court of Appeal in *Rimmer v. Liverpool City Council*[3] held that "*Cavalier v. Pope* must be kept in close confinement". The

---

[1] [1906] A.C. 428.
[2] (1863) 15 C.B. (N.S.) 221.
[3] [1985] Q.B. 1.

Court of Appeal in *McNerny v. Lambeth B.C.*[4] held however that the principles expressed in *Cavalier v. Pope* remain good law where they apply.

The strictness of the common law rule has been modified principally by statute, which implies terms into some leases and, in particular, implies basic repairing covenants into dwellings rented for less than seven years.[5] The common law does countenance implied terms in restricted circumstances.[6]

No covenant of fitness for purpose or to repair

8–02   At common law the landlord does not impliedly covenant that premises are fit for occupation or for their purpose: *Hart v. Windsor*[7]; *Lynch v. Thorne*[8]; *Sleafer v. Lambeth Borough Council*[9]; *Duke of Westminster v. Guild*[10]; *Sutton v. Temple*[11]; *Manchester Bonded Warehouse v. Carr*.[12] The result, for example, is that there was no liability at common law for death as a result of carbon monoxide poisoning from a defective gas boiler: *Bottomley v. Bannister*.[13]

There is no implied obligation at common law that the landlord will carry out any repairs at all: *Robbins v. Jones*[14]; *Colebeck v. The Girdlers & Co.*[15]; *Cockburn v. Smith*[16]; *Ayling v. Wade*[17]; *Duke of Westminster v. Guild*.[18]

The landlord does not warrant that the premises will last for the term of the lease: *Arden v. Pullen*.[19]

Cases in which terms will be implied: general principles

8–03   There is a range of narrowly defined situations in which terms as to repair will be implied. The range goes from elucidating what is implicit but not spelt out in the express terms of the contract, to implying standard terms into recognisable types of contract. In

---

[4] (1989) 21 H.L.R. 106.
[5] See Chapter 11.
[6] See paras. 8–04 to 8–10 below.
[7] (1844) 12 M. & W. 68.
[8] [1956] 1 All E.R. 744.
[9] [1960] 1 Q.B. 43.
[10] [1985] Q.B. 688.
[11] (1843) 12 M. & W. 52.
[12] (1880) 5 C.P.D. 507.
[13] [1932] 1 K.B. 458.
[14] (1863) 15 C.B. (N.S.) 221.
[15] (1876) 1 Q.B.D. 234.
[16] [1924] 2 K.B. 119.
[17] [1961] 2 Q.B. 228.
[18] *Supra.*
[19] (1842) 1 M. & W. 321.

Liverpool City Council v. Irwin,[20] Lord Wilberforce held as follows:

"There are many varieties of implications which the courts think fit to make and they do not necessarily involve the same process. Where there is, on the face of it, a complete, bilateral contract, the courts are sometimes willing to add terms to it, as implied terms; this is very common in mercantile contracts where there is an established usage: in that case the courts are spelling out what both parties know and would, if asked, unhesitatingly agree to be part of the bargain. In other cases, where there is an apparently complete bargain, the courts are willing to add a term on the ground that without it the contract will not work—this is the case, if not of *The Moorcock*[21] itself on its facts, at least the doctrine of *The Moorcock* as usually applied. This is, as was pointed out by the majority in the Court of Appeal, a strict test—though the degree of strictness seems to vary with the current legal trend—and I think that they were right not to accept it as applicable here. There is a third variety of implication, that which I think Lord Denning M.R. favours, or at least did favour in this case, and that is the implication of reasonable terms. But although I agree with many of his instances, which in fact fall under one or other of the preceding heads, I cannot go so far as to endorse his principle; indeed, it seems to me, with respect, to extend a long and undesirable way beyond sound authority.

The present case, in my opinion, represents a fourth category, or I would rather say a fourth shade on a continuous spectrum. The court here is simply concerned to establish what the contract is, the parties not having themselves fully stated its terms."

Lord Cross held:

"When it implies a term in a contract the court is sometimes laying down a general rule that in all contracts of a certain type—sale of goods, master and servant, landlord and tenant and so on—some provision is to be implied unless the parties have expressly excluded it. In deciding whether or not to lay down such a prima facie rule the court will naturally ask itself whether in the general run of such cases the term in question would be one which it would be reasonable to insert. Sometimes, however, there is no question of laying down any prima facie rule applicable to all cases of a defined type but what the

[20] [1977] A.C. 239.
[21] (1889) 14 P.D. 64.

court is being in effect asked to do is to rectify a particular
—often very detailed—contract by inserting in it a term which
the parties have not expressed. Here it is not enough for the
court to say that the suggested term is a reasonable one the
presence of which would make the contract a better or fairer
one: it must be able to say that the insertion of the terms
necessary to give—as it is put—'business efficacy' to the
contract and that if its absence had been pointed out at the
time both parties—assuming them to have been reasonable
men—would have agreed without hesitation to its insertion."

It is important to seek to apply the fundamental principles,
summarised by the judgments in *Liverpool City Council v. Irwin*,[22]
carefully and pragmatically to the tenancy agreement under consideration, in the context of facts known to the parties at the date
of the agreement, without being led too far astray by decisions and
dicta in the many cases in which such an exercise has been
undertaken in the past. Such cases can only be useful guides.

8–03A *Implied rights to enter.* Rights to enter premises are considered fully
below.[23] They are of obvious importance to landlords who wish to
maintain the capital value of their property, and also to tenants,
because of the effect of section 4(4) of the Defective Premises Act
1972, which converts rights to enter to carry out repairs into
duties.[24] The only point made here is that the principles which
govern the implication of duties to repair also govern the implication of rights to repair. In *McAuley v. Bristol City Council*[25] Ralph
Gibson L.J. held:

"There is no doubt of the principles applicable to the implying
of an obligation to do repairs. They were considered and
explained by the House of Lords in *Liverpool City Council v.
Irwin*[26] . . . [there are] two classes of case where the courts are
prepared to imply terms in contracts: the first is where the
court lays down a general rule of law that, as a legal incident
of all contracts of a certain type (sale of goods, master and
servant, landlord and tenant and so on), some provision is to
be implied. The second class is where there is no question of
laying down any prima facie rule applicable to all cases of a
defined type, but the court is being asked in effect to rectify a
particular contract by inserting in it a term which the parties

[22] *Supra.*
[23] See paras. 10–02, 10–03.
[24] See paras. 11–13 to 11–19.
[25] [1992] Q.B. 134.
[26] *Supra.*

have not expressed. In that second class the court must be able to say that the insertion of the term is necessary to give 'business efficacy' to the contract and that, if its absence had been pointed out, both parties, assuming them to have been reasonable men, would have agreed without hesitation to its insertion . . . . I see no reason why the principles by reference to which the court determines whether a right can be implied in favour of a landlord, which he may assert against the tenant, should differ from those applicable for implying an obligation to be imposed upon a landlord which the tenant may assert against the landlord."

Terms generally implied into certain types of tenancy

Lettings of furnished dwelling-houses: implied covenant of fitness for human habitation

A landlord who lets a *furnished* dwelling-house for immediate occupation impliedly covenants that the premises are fit for occupation as a dwelling at the start of the letting: *Wilson v. Finch-Hatton*[27]; *Collings v. Hopkins*[28]; *Smith v. Marrable*[29]; *Hart v. Windsor*.[30]   **8–04**

The landlord does not covenant that the premises will remain fit for occupation as a dwelling: *Sarson v. Roberts*.[31] The covenant is broken, however, if the premises are initially unfit even though this is only discovered later: *Harrison v. Malet*.[32]

There is no such implied covenant in the case of lettings of *unfurnished* dwelling-houses, even if newly decorated and let on the basis that the tenant will take up immediate residence: *Hart v. Windsor*[33]; *McNerny v. Lambeth Borough Council*.[34]

The distinction may be explicable on the basis that the doctrine of *stare decisis* simply perpetuates an irrational distinction between lettings of furnished and lettings of unfurnished dwelling-houses. Consideration of the cases cited, however, suggests that the really important distinction is between fully furnished short rentals and longer term unfurnished lettings. In other words, that the implied term really only exists in relation to fully furnished accommodation where there is to be an immediate, but short-term letting.

---

[27] (1877) 2 Ex. D 336.
[28] [1923] 2 K.B. 617.
[29] (1843) 11 M. & W. 5.
[30] *Supra.*
[31] [1895] 2 Q.B. 395.
[32] (1886) 3 T.L.R. 58.
[33] *Supra.*
[34] *Supra.*

Licenses of dwelling-houses: implied covenant of fitness for human habitation and repair

8–05   Licensors of dwelling-houses may retain sufficient control so as to be liable to occupiers in negligence or so as to justify an implied term as to repair or fitness for purpose: it depends on all of the facts of the case.

In *Greene v. Chelsea Borough Council*[35] the council exercised statutory powers to requisition housing accommodation for persons made homeless as a result of enemy action. Those powers made it impossible for the council to grant a tenancy: the plaintiff's husband was accordingly a licensee. The plaintiff was injured when part of the kitchen ceiling collapsed. The council was held liable in negligence, having been put on notice of the bulging condition of the ceiling and having failed to repair it. The action was brought in negligence because the plaintiff was not the licensee and therefore had no implied contractual right to exercise (even if one could have been implied). The Court of Appeal distinguished cases in which it had been held that there is no implied term that a landlord will carry out any repairs or even take care to ensure that a dwelling, if unfurnished, is fit for human habitation at the start of the tenancy. Denning L.J. said:

> "This is not a landlord and tenant case. It is a requisitioning case. The duty of the defendants here arose not out of contract, but because they, as the requisitioning authority, were in law in possession of the house, and were in practice responsible for the repairs. This practical responsibility meant that they had control of the house for the purpose of repairs: and this control imposed upon them a duty to every person lawfully on the premises to take reasonable care to prevent damage through want of repair."

In *Wettern Electric Ltd v. Welsh Development Agency*[36] the Official Referee, His Honour Judge Newey, sitting as a judge of the High Court, held that a commercial licence of a factory unit was subject to an implied term that the building was structurally sound and reasonably fit for its purpose, either because the term was necessary to give the contract business efficacy (*The Moorcock*[37]) or to complete the contract as the parties must have intended (*Liverpool City Council v. Irwin*[38]).

[35] [1954] 2 Q.B. 127.
[36] [1983] 1 Q.B. 796.
[37] *Supra.*
[38] *Supra.*

In *Morris-Thomas v. Petticoat Lane Rentals*[39] the Court of Appeal neither approved nor disapproved of *Wettern Electric Limited v. Welsh Development Agency*[40] (although the result was doubted by Ralph Gibson L.J.). In *Morris-Thomas v. Petticoat Lane Rentals*[41] the Court of Appeal held that there was no implied term in the licence of a unit in an antiques market that the unit was fit for the sale and storage of antiques. The different result primarily arises out of the different facts of the two cases. In *Wettern* the licence of the factory unit was granted for a short period to accommodate the plaintiff's expanding business whilst the defendants built an extension to the plaintiff's existing factory (which was let to the plaintiffs by the defendants). In *Morris-Thomas* the licence was drafted by counsel as part of a settlement of proceedings between the parties and contained no repairing obligations either way, although there was no reason why it should not have done if that was what was intended.

The current position remains, therefore, that it is possible to argue that, on the facts of the case, there is an implied term in a licence (but not in a tenancy or lease) that premises will be fit for their purpose and that, accordingly, such a term can be implied in the unfurnished licence of a dwelling-house. The result will depend on the facts of such a hypothetical licence, taken as a whole. It may continue to be arguable that a duty of care can arise to prevent personal injury or property damage in licence cases, as in *Greene v. Chelsea L.B.C.*[42]

In principle, of course, there can be concurrent liability in contract and tort: *Henderson v. Merett Syndicates Limited.*[43] The courts will only very rarely, however, be prepared to fill gaps in contracts or extend contractual duties by reference to the law of tort: *Tai Hing Cotton Mill Ltd v. Liu Chong Hing Bank Ltd*[44]; *Henderson v. Merett Syndicates Limited.*[45] Despite dicta in *Rimmer v. Liverpool City Council*,[46] influenced by *Greene v. Chelsea Borough Council*[47] (and really relating only to the continued existence of the landlord's pre-existing tortious liability as builder which had not become excluded by the letting contract) the intrusion of negligence concepts into relations between landlord and tenant is

---

[39] [1986] 53 P. & C.R. 238.
[40] *Supra.*
[41] *Supra.*
[42] *Supra.*
[43] [1994] 3 All E.R. 506.
[44] [1985] 2 All E.R. 947.
[45] *Supra.*
[46] *Supra.*
[47] *Supra.*

rightly regarded as anathema: *Gordon v. Selico Co. Ltd*[48]; *Smith v. Scott.*[49]

What is unfit?

8–06   Premises are unfit for human habitation if they are "incumbered with a nuisance of so serious a nature that no person can reasonably be expected to live in them": *Smith v. Marrable.*[50] Premises have been held to be unfit when infested with bugs (*Smith v. Marrable*[51]), have defective drains and filth in the cellar (*Wilson v. Finch-Hatton*[52]), have defective sewers (*Harrison v. Malet*[53]) or are infectious (*Wilson v. Finch-Hatton,*[54] *Collins v. Hopkins*[55]).

Premises are not unfit merely because they are in ordinary disrepair, for example, with cracked and fallen ceiling plaster (*Maclean v. Currie*[56]).

If premises are in breach of an implied term as to fitness at the start of the letting, the tenant is entitled to rescind the letting and is not liable for rent or damages for use and occupation: *Wilson v. Finch-Hatton*[57]; *Bird v. Greville (Lord).*[58]

Where the landlord retains essential means of access or facilities: implied covenant to keep in repair and proper working order

8–07   Tenants have an implied easement over essential means of access to their dwelling-houses. At common law, generally speaking, in the absence of express agreement to the contrary it is the dominant and not the servient owner who is bound to repair land over which the easement passes: *Holden v. White*[59]; *Miller v. Hancock.*[60] In *Liverpool City Council v. Irwin*[61] both Lord Wilberforce and Lord Cross saw no reason why that general implied term should not apply to lettings when the owner of a house merely lets the top floor to a tenant. The House of Lords held unanimously, however, that where a landlord lets a building to a number of tenants and retains in his or her ownership the stairs, lifts, corridors (and rubbish

---

[48] [1985] 2 E.G.L.R. 79 at p. 84B.
[49] [1972] 3 All E.R. 645 at p. 650c.
[50] *Supra.*
[51] *Supra.*
[52] *Supra.*
[53] *Supra.*
[54] *Supra.*
[55] *Supra.*
[56] (1844) Cab. & El. 361.
[57] *Supra.*
[58] (1844) C. & E. 317.
[59] [1982] Q.B. 679.
[60] [1893] 2 Q.B. 177.
[61] *Supra.*

chutes) without imposing any obligation on the tenants to repair the same, there must be an implied term of the contract that the landlord will take reasonable care to ensure that the means of access (and rubbish chutes) are kept in reasonable repair and efficacy. There is a similar obligation in relation to lighting, providing lighting is essential for the safe use of the means of access.

It is notable that "essential" means of access was not intended to mean "only" means of access because the lifts as well as the staircases were included. In *King v. South Northamptonshire District Council*[62] the Court of Appeal implied an obligation on the landlord to maintain a rear access path to the premises even though the premises had a front access path. The Court of Appeal rejected a submission that the rear access path was not sufficiently "essential", on the ground that the purpose of the rear access path was for the removal of refuse and that it was "essential" if the dwelling was to be enjoyed in accordance with its function and design. It was part of the reasoning that the letting agreement was incomplete and imposed no repairing obligations at all on the landlord and that the dwelling in question was part of a small estate in which all houses were served by such rear access paths.

The decision would appear to apply to all lettings including commercial lettings where there are essential common facilities and an incomplete contract: see *Liverpool City Council v. Irwin*.[63] Both Lord Wilberforce[64] with whom Lord Fraser agreed and Lord Cross[65] treated *Liverpool City Council v. Irwin*[66] as identifying a prima facie term implied into such contracts: see also *Duke of Westminster v. Guild*.[67]

The Court of Appeal in *Duke of Westminster v. Guild*[68] was concerned with a case in which drains serving only the demised premises had become defective but were not subject to an express repairing obligation binding upon landlord or tenant. The Court of Appeal refused to imply a term into the lease which would have imposed an absolute or a qualified obligation to repair the relevant section of drain upon the landlord. The reasoning was that this case did not fall within the general type of case considered in *Liverpool City Council v. Irwin* in which landlords had retained ownership of essential amenities benefiting a number of tenants without imposing any repairing obligation on the tenants. It was

---

[62] [1992] 1 E.G.L.R. 53.
[63] [1977] A.C. 239 *per* Lord Cross at pp. 259E–260D.
[64] at p. 256F.
[65] at p. 259E.
[66] *Supra.*
[67] *Supra.* at p. 698D–H.
[68] *Supra.*

the second type of case referred to by Lord Cross, in which "the court is being in effect asked . . . to rectify a particular—often a very detailed—contract by inserting in it a term which the parties have not expressed". The test, accordingly, was strictly one of necessity. The term sought to be implied failed this test because: (a) there was a lease containing detailed repairing obligations, suggesting that the parties had not left out any term which they intended to put in; (b) the term sought to be implied was onerous and conflicted to an extent with other parts of the lease; and (c) the lease worked perfectly well without the term, the tenant being entitled as the owner of an easement through the drain to repair it at his own expense.

Where the landlord retains ownership of ancillary property: duty to take reasonable care not to let that property deteriorate so as to cause personal injury or damage

8–08   In particular when a landlord lets out parts of a building to a number of tenants, he or she frequently retains ownership of residual parts of the building: a common roof, for example, cold and/or hot water tanks, plant for space and/or water heating, gutters and/or drains, lifts, staircases and halls, perhaps even the main walls of the building. Such residual elements ought to be the subject of an express repairing obligation, but sometimes are not. When nothing is said, the courts will not normally imply a term that the landlord will keep those elements of the building in repair. The courts will, however, apply the principle set out in *Woodfall*[69] approved by the Court of Appeal in *Duke of Westminster v. Guild*[70]:

> "Where the landlord retains in his possession and control something ancillary to the premises demised, such as a roof or staircase, the maintenance of which in proper repair is necessary for the protection of the demised premises or the safe enjoyment of them by the tenant, the landlord is under an obligation to take reasonable care that the premises retained in his occupation are not in such a condition as to cause damage to the tenant or to the premises demised."

The landlord was accordingly liable for water penetration resulting from leaky gutters retained in his ownership even though he had not expressly contracted to keep the gutters in repair: *Cockburn*

---

[69] at para. 13.004.
[70] *Supra.*

v. Smith[71]; see also *Hargroves, Aronson & Co. v. Hartopp* (another rainwater gutter).[72]

The landlord can be liable under this principle even though the damage is caused in part by the tenant's failure to comply with his or her repairing obligations: *Tennant Radiant Heat v. Warrington Development Corporation*[73] (landlord liable in nuisance for failing to clear rainwater outlets on the main part of the roof, retained in its ownership; tenant 10 per cent responsible for failing to keep clear the rainwater outlet on the roof immediately above the tenant's premises, demised to the tenant subject to a tenant's repairing covenant).

In principle, it might be argued that this duty should require the landlord to carry out works which would normally be considered too major to be repairs, properly so called, providing such work was necessary to prevent personal injury, damage to the premises demised or to the tenant's possessions. It might be argued, however, that a duty that extensive went beyond "reasonable" care.

The principle only applies when there has been damage to the premises, the tenant or the tenant's property. It was held not to apply in a case in which a drain retained in the landlord's ownership became blocked and defective with the result only that the tenant was not able to discharge foul water from his premises: *Duke of Westminster v. Guild*.[74] If the Court of Appeal had been prepared to adopt a broader notion of what damage to a property was then the tenant might have succeeded.

The duty is not a tort duty but arises because a term has been implied into the particular contract: *Gordon v. Selico Co.*,[75] affirmed on appeal without express consideration of this particular point.[76] The duty will not, therefore, necessarily be implied where consideration of the particular lease in its factual context indicates that it ought not to be. The duty was held to be applicable in *Gordon v. Selico* because as Slade L.J. held:

"The repair and maintenance scheme provided by this lease is a very cumbersome one and we agree with the learned judge that, even if the lessors and their agents were duly to carry out their obligations, the scheme might not always suffice to give the lessees necessary and timely protection . . . . Nevertheless, on a reading of the lease, we feel little doubt that it was

---

[71] [1924] 2 K.B. 119.
[72] [1905] 1 K.B. 472.
[73] [1988] 1 E.G.L.R. 71.
[74] *Supra.*
[75] [1985] 2 E.G.L.R. 79.
[76] (1986) 18 H.L.R. 219.

intended, by all the parties, to provide a comprehensive code
in regard to repair and maintenance of the block. We are by no
means satisfied that the implication of any further terms in this
respect is necessary to give the lease business efficacy, or that
the lessor, assuming it to have been a reasonable person,
would have agreed without hesitation to the insertion of the
suggested additional implied terms relating to the maintenance and repair of the block."

It is, however, arguable that this reasoning is not consistent with
the reasoning of Bankes L.J. in *Cockburn v. Smith*[77] in which he
held that:

"In my opinion, express agreements concerning premises
demised or granted do not exclude tacit agreements concerning matters which are neither demised nor granted, and I
cannot think either party contemplated that because the
landlords had agreed to keep the entrance hall, staircases,
passages and landings sufficiently lighted and in good repair,
they should therefore be relieved of all duty to take reasonable
care that the roof and gutters should not be in such a state as
to render the demised premises uninhabitable."

Where the landlord expressly agrees to repair an ancillary part of
the building retained in his ownership his liability arises as soon as
damage occurs and irrespective of notice: *Melles & Co. v. Holme*[78];
Bishop v. Consolidated London Properties Limited[79]; *Loria v. Hammer.*[80]

Where there is no express agreement to repair, however, the
obligation is to take "reasonable care". Where the landlord
inspected regularly but damage occurred as a result of an unforsee-
able accident the landlord was not liable: *Carstairs v. Taylor.*[81] The
clearest way of establishing want of reasonable care is to notify the
landlord of the need for works: *Cockburn v. Smith.*[82]

In many circumstances the tenant may be better off relying on
nuisance.[83]

The implication of terms into particular agreements

The acid test for all implied terms, whether their genesis is trade
custom, necessity, or decisions of the courts that "in all contracts of

[77] *Supra.*
[78] [1918] 2 K.B. 100.
[79] (1933) 102 L.J.K.B. 257.
[80] [1989] 2 E.G.L.R. 249.
[81] (1871) L.R. 6 Ex. 217.
[82] *Supra.*
[83] See Chapter 12.

a certain type . . . some provision is to be implied unless the parties have expressly excluded it",[84] is what the parties actually intended, objectively speaking, having regard to express terms in their factual context.

All terms that would normally be implied on the ground of trade custom, typicality or even necessity are capable of being excluded by an express term or indeed by a view that the implied term is incompatible with the true intentions of the parties as gathered from the letting agreement in its factual context.

General rule

The general rule is summarised by Lord Simon of Glaisdale **8–09** giving judgment for the Privy Council in *B. P. Refinery (Westenport) Limited v. Shire of Hastings*[85]:

"In their [Lordship's] view, for a term to be implied, the following conditions (which may overlap) must be satisfied: (1) it must be reasonable and equitable; (2) it must be necessary to give business efficacy to the contract, so that no term will be implied if the contract is effective without it; (3) it must be so obvious that 'it goes without saying'; (4) it must be capable of clear expression; (5) it must not contradict any express term of the contract."

The second term summarises the effect of *The Moorcock*[86] while the third term summarises the effect of equally famous dicta in *Shirlaw v. Southern Foundries (1926) Limited.*[87]

If the tenancy agreement or lease already contains detailed provision as to repairs, rather than being patently incomplete, the courts can decide that the parties did not intend any further obligations to be entered into by either side and on that basis refuse to endeavour to complete any gap in the repairing obligations: *Duke of Westminster v. Guild*[88]; *Gordon v. Selico Co Limited*[89]; *Hafton Properties Limited v. Camp.*[90]

Cases such as these last three do not, however, sit comfortably with dicta of both Lord Wilberforce and Lord Cross in *Liverpool City Council v. Irwin*,[91] which contemplate without difficulty the implication of terms into contracts which are apparently complete

---

[84] *per* Lord Cross in *Liverpool City Council v. Irwin* at p. 257H.
[85] (1978) A.L.J. 20.
[86] *Supra.*
[87] [1939] 2 K.B. 206.
[88] *Supra.*
[89] *Supra.*
[90] [1994] 3 E.G. 129.
[91] *Supra.*

and detailed where the implication of the term is "necessary" to make the contract work.[92] See also *Cockburn v. Smith*.[92a]

The inconsistency is probably explicable, however, on the basis that English judges as a breed, probably because they are English, have a very relaxed notion of what "business efficacy" actually is, particularly when it comes to dwelling-houses. While it is considered quite unacceptable that the home (or, in technical language, wharf) of a ship was not safe and caused it damage (*The Moorcock*[93]) or that the couches in a Turkish bath for reclining on were contaminated with vermin (*Silverman v. Imperial London Hotels Limited*[94]), one arrived at the position at common law that the landlord was not liable for death as a result of carbon monoxide poisoning from a defective gas boiler: *Bottomley v. Bannister*,[95] or for substantial property damage or personal injury as a result of condensation and mould growth caused by the inherently defective condition of the premises: *McNerny v. Lambeth L.B.C.*[96]

It is trite law that where a lease is silent as to repairs or as to particular types of repair, the correct inference might well be that neither party was intended to carry out the repair: *Demetriou v. Robert Andrews (Estate Agents) Limited*[97]; *Demetriou v. Poolaction Limited*[98] in which it was said:

> "It is a phenomenon, certainly known at common law, that there may be situations in which there is no repairing obligation imposed either expressly or impliedly on anyone in relation to a lease."

Thus, where a landlord fails to covenant to repair, even an important part of the premises, even when he could have required all the tenants to pay for the cost by way of a service charge, it will not ordinarily be implied that the landlord has the duty or the right to repair, or that the tenant or tenants have the duty to repair: *Tennant Radiant Heat Limited v. Warrington Development Corporation*.[99] In the case of a dwelling-house, it is not enough that the provisions of the lease contemplate that the landlord will carry out repairs, confer rights on him to enter for that purpose and require the tenant to occupy the premises as his or her home nor is it enough that the landlord has in the past in practice carried out

---

[92] at p. 253F-G, 258B.
[92a] *Supra.*
[93] *Supra.*
[94] (1927) 137 L.T. 57.
[95] *Supra.*
[96] *Supra.*
[97] (1990) 62 P. & C.R. 526.
[98] [1991] 1 E.G.L.R. 100.
[99] *Supra.*

repairs for any implied repairing obligation binding on the landlord to arise: *Sleafer v. Lambeth L.B.C.*[1]; see also *London Hospital Board of Governors v. Jacobs*[2]; *Demetriou v. Poolaction Limited*[3]; *Duke of Westminster v. Guild*[4]; *Gordon v. Selico Co. Limited*[5]; *Hafton Properties Limited v. Camp.*[6] The Law Commission proposes, however, that where the parties make no express provision as to repairs there shall be a default term that the landlord will repair the premises. This provision would apply to both residential and commercial tenancies commencing after legislation was enacted except where s. 11 Landlord and Tenant Act 1985 applies.[6a]

Correlative obligations

The concept of "correlative obligations" is the most common method by which terms are implied into contracts which are regarded as only partially complete. **8–10**

Where the tenant covenants to pay for works or services. In *Barnes v. City of London Real Property Co. Limited*[7] the tenant covenanted to pay a weekly sum for the cleaning of the premises by a housekeeper: the landlord was held to be bound by a correlative obligation to provide a housekeeper to carry out such cleaning. In *Russell v. Laimond Properties Limited*,[8] however, the true construction of the lease was merely that *if* the landlord supplied a resident porter then he was entitled to recover the cost from the tenant. **8–11**

In *Edmonston Corporation v. Knowles*[9] the tenant covenanted to pay the landlord the cost of redecorating in every third year of the term: the landlord was subject to an implied correlative obligation to redecorate accordingly. In *Duke of Westminster v. Guild*,[10] however, the tenant also covenanted to pay for the cost of repairing the drain: that covenant did not give rise to any implied correlative obligation on the part of the landlord, because: (a) such an implied term would have been inconsistent with other express provisions in the lease; (b) the lease contained a prima facie complete repairing code; (c) if such a term were implied there were a number of further correlative terms which by parity of reasoning would have been implied and that would have been onerous for the landlord on

[1] [1960] 1 Q.B. 43.
[2] [1956] 2 All E.R. 603.
[3] *Supra.*
[4] *Supra.*
[5] *Supra.*
[6] *Supra.* New Law Reform Paper.
[6a] Law Com. No. 238.
[7] [1918] 2 Ch. 18.
[8] (1984) 269 E.G. 946.
[9] [1962] 60 L.G.R. 124.
[10] *Supra.*

the facts of the case; (d) implication of the term was not necessary for business efficacy because the tenant had the right to repair the drains at his own expense.

8–12   *Where the tenant's obligations imply corresponding obligations on the part of the landlord.* In *Barrett v. Lounova (1982) Limited*[11] there was a tenancy of a dwelling-house for one year and thereafter month by month. The tenant contracted "to do all inside repairs (if any) now required and to keep and at the expiration of the tenancy to leave the inside of the said premises and fixtures in good repair order and condition but fair wear and tear to be allowed at the end of the tenancy". The tenant also agreed "To permit the landlord and his agents to enter at all reasonable times upon the said premises and for all reasonable purposes." There was no express agreement relating to responsibility for repairs to the structure and exterior of the premises and section 11 of the Landlord and Tenant Act 1985 did not apply because the tenancy began before October 24, 1961. The structure and the exterior of the premises had not been maintained for years and had deteriorated to the extent that there was extensive water penetration, causing damage to the internal plaster and timbers. It was common ground that the work required to the structure and exterior would cost about £10,000. The issue was whether there was an implied term that the landlord would keep the structure and exterior in repair.

Kerr L.J. accepted the formulation of Mr Recorder Keane Q.C. in the County Court that the issue was whether such a term should be implied because it was "not merely desirable but necessary to give business efficacy or in other words necessary to make the contract workable". He went on to recognise that cases such as *Hart v. Windsor*[12] and *Cockburn v. Smith*[13] established that as a general proposition there was no implied term arising out of the relationship of landlord and tenant *per se* that the landlord would keep a dwelling-house fit for habitation, but then added, citing *Liverpool City Council v. Irwin*[14] that the "implication of a landlord's repairing covenant is a permissible approach if the terms of the agreement and circumstances justify it".

Although in *Sleafer v. Lambeth L.B.C.*[15] the Court of Appeal did not consider it possible, on the facts, to identify any implied term as to fitness or repair, Kerr L.J. noted that Ormrod L.J. had in that case said:

---

[11] [1990] 1 Q.B. 348.
[12] *Supra.*
[13] *Supra.*
[14] *Supra.*
[15] *Supra.*

"A tenancy agreement, like any other agreement, must be read as a whole, and it may very well be that in construing the agreement it is possible to imply an obligation on the landlord to do repairs."

Wilmer L.J. had said:

"I think there is much to be said for the view that clause 2 of the agreement, which requires the tenant to reside in the dwelling-house does, by implication, require the landlords to do such repairs as may make it possible for the tenant to carry out that obligation. At least it seems to me that that is a possible view."

More recently, in *Duke of Westminster v. Guild*,[16] Slade L.J. had   **8–13**
said:

"We do not doubt . . . that in some circumstances it will be proper for the court to imply an obligation against a landlord, on whom an obligation is not in terms imposed by the relevant lease, to match a correlative obligation thereby expressly imposed on the other party."

There are similar dicta in *Churchward v. R.*,[17] not cited in *Barret v. Lounova (1982) Limited*.
Kerr L.J. accordingly concluded that:

"It is obvious, as shown by this case itself, that sooner or later the covenant imposed on the tenant in respect of the inside can no longer be complied with unless the outside has been kept in repair. Moreover, it is also clear that the covenant imposed on the tenant was intended to be enforceable throughout the tenancy. For instance, it could not possibly be contended that it would cease to be enforceable if the outside fell into disrepair. In my view it is therefore necessary, as a matter of business efficacy, to make this agreement workable, that an obligation to keep the outside in repair must be imposed on someone. For myself, I would reject the persuasive submission of Mr Pryor on behalf of the landlord, that both parties may have thought that in practice the landlord—or possibly the tenant—would do the necessary repairs, so that no problem would arise. In my view that is not a businesslike construction of the tenancy agreement."

The decision has been criticised by the editors of *Woodfall* and by Dowding and Reynolds in *Dilapidations: The Modern Law and Practice*.

---

[16] *Supra.*
[17] [1865] L.R. 1 Q.B. 173.

It is said that the implication of the repairing term was not necessary to give business efficacy to the contract, which having created a monthly tenancy, could be determined on one month's notice by the tenant, *i.e.* the tenant was not "locked in" to the agreement indefinitely. As a matter of common sense, however, a contract is hardly to be characterised as "efficacious" or "workable" when the only way of making it work sensibly is for one party to terminate it.

It is also said that it remained *possible* for the tenant to comply with his internal decorating and repairing covenants: it would just be substantially more expensive for him to do so. It is clear from *Liverpool City Council v. Irwin*[18] and *King v. South Northamptonshire District Council*[19] that the threshold is not so low. The test is not whether the contract will be "impossible" to perform without the implied term, but whether the implied term is necessary to make the contract work efficaciously, or as the parties must plainly have intended it to. As it was put by Lord Evershed M.R. in *Re Webb's Lease, Sandom v. Webb*[20]:

> "If the court were satisfied that, in order to make the transaction between landlord and tenant sensible and effective according to its terms, they must have intended some particular right to be reserved to the landlord, it might be possible to imply an appropriate reservation."

The Court of Appeal was entirely correct to regard a contract as not working efficaciously when it involves periodic tenants, of modest means, in dwelling-houses without roofs or water tight walls, spending their days and relatively scant resources endlessly patching up the internal components of the dwelling and its decorations, which were being endlessly ruined by the wind and rain.

The principle does, however, have inherent limitations. In *Demetriou v. Poolaction Limited,*[21] for example, a case in which the tenant had undertaken no repairing obligation, the court held that it was not possible to imply any correlative repairing obligation on the part of the landlord. Stuart-Smith L.J. pointed out:

> " . . . it is a phenomenon, certainly known at common law, that there may be situations in which there is no repairing obligation imposed either expressly or impliedly on anyone in relation to a lease."

[18] *Supra.*
[19] *Supra.*
[20] [1951] 1 Ch. 808 at p. 816.
[21] *Supra.*

CHAPTER NINE

Special Cases of Liability

*Where the landlord is also the builder: common law duty and
section 1 of the Defective Premises Act 1972*

Landlords who build and/or design premises owe tenants a com-   **9–01**
mon law duty as builders which is quite separate from any
contractual duty *qua* landlord. It is a duty to take reasonable care
in the building or design not to cause personal injury or damage to
property other than the premises itself: *Rimmer v. Liverpool City
Council*[1]; *Targett v. Torfaen Borough Council*[2]; *Murphy v. Brentwood
District Council*[3]; *D&F Estates v. Church Commissioners*[4]; *Department
of the Environment v. Thomas Bates & Son.*[5]

Section 1 of the Defective Premises Act 1972 imposes a duty of
care on any person "taking on work for or in connection with the
provision of a dwelling (whether the dwelling is provided by the
erection or by the conversion of enlargement of a dwelling" owes a
duty "to see that the works which he takes on is done in a
workman-like or, as the case may be, professional manner, with
proper materials and so that as regards that work the dwelling will
be fit for habitation when completed".

The duty is owed to all persons who may acquire an interest in
the dwelling, *e.g.* the landlord, the original and subsequent tenants:
section 1(1) DPA 1972.

[1] [1985] Q.B. 1.
[2] [1992] 3 All E.R. 27.
[3] [1991] A.C. 398.
[4] [1989] A.C. 177.
[5] [1990] 2 All E.R. 908.

The duty, being tortious, will extend to personal injury, physical discomfort and damage to property only and not to pure economic loss or damage to the dwelling itself: *Murphy v. Brentwood District Council*[6]; *D&F Estates v. Church Commissioners*[7]; *Department of the Environment v. Thomas Bates & Son.*[8]

The duty is excluded in cases in which the NHBC scheme applies: section 2 DPA 1972.

The duty applies only to work carried out or lettings entered into after January 1, 1974. Any cause of action is deemed to have accrued, for the purposes of the limitation acts, at the time when the dwelling was completed (or, when the cause of action arises out of defective post-completion work, the time when such work was completed): section 1(5) DPA 1972; *Alexander v. Mercouris.*[9] The duty is not abated by subsequent disposals: section 3 DPA 1972.

The duty applies to non-feasance as well as misfeasance: *Andrews v. Schooling.*[10] It is not enough however that the premises are defective for a breach to arise. They must be unfit for human habitation: *Thompson v. Clive Alexander.*[11]

Lettings of premises in the course of construction

9–02   If a letting is entered into while the premises are in the course of construction there is an implied warranty in the letting agreement that the premises will be built in a good and workman-like manner with good and proper materials: *Lawrence v. Cassel*[12]; *Miller v. Cannon Hill Estates*[13]; *Hancock v. Brazier (BW) (Anerly).*[14] It is further implied that the premises, if a dwelling house, will be fit for human habitation on completion: *Perry v. Sharon Development Co.*[15]; *Billyack v. Leyland Construction Co. Ltd*[16]; *King v. Victor Parsons & Co.*[17] No doubt it would be implied also that commercial premises would be fit for their purposes when built. These duties, again, arise out of the liability of builders and are quite distinct from liabilities owed by landlords.

[6] *Supra.*
[7] *Supra.*
[8] [1990] 2 All E.R. 908.
[9] [1979] 1 W.L.R. 1270.
[10] (1991) 23 H.L.R. 317.
[11] (1992) 59 B.L.R. 77.
[12] [1930] 2 K.B. 83.
[13] [1931] 2 K.B. 113.
[14] [1966] 1 W.L.R. 1317.
[15] [1937] 4 All E.R. 390.
[16] [1968] 1 W.L.R. 471.
[17] [1972] 1 W.L.R. 801.

CHAPTER TEN

Implied Terms for the Benefit of the Landlord

The implied pre-condition of notice before liability arises

As a general rule, landlords are not liable under express or implied **10–01**
repairing covenants (even when implied by section 11 of the
Landlord and Tenant Act 1985) unless and until they have notice
of the disrepair and fail to take action within a reasonable period of
time: *Makin v. Watkinson*[1]; *Torrens v. Walker*[2]; *McCarrick v. Liverpool Corporation*[3]; *O'Brien v. Robinson*[4]; *Calabar Properties Ltd v.
Stitcher*[5]; *Morris v. Liverpool Corporation*.[6] This rule and the exceptions to it are considered above.[7]

The only point made here is that the requirement of notice is no
more and no less than an implied term, as appears from the
judgement of Bramwell B. in *Makin v. Watkinson*[8]:

"I have the strongest objection to interpolate words into a
contract, and think we ought never to do so unless there is
some cogent and almost irresistible reason for it, arising from
the absurdity of the contract if it is read without them. Does
such a reason exist here? I think it does. I think that we are

---

[1] (1870) L.R. 6 Ex 24.
[2] [1906] 2 Ch. 166.
[3] [1947] A.C. 219.
[4] [1973] A.C. 912.
[5] [1984] 1 W.L.R. 287.
[6] [1988] 1 E.G.L.R. 47.
[7] Paras. 5–01 to 5–07.
[8] *Supra.*

irresistibly driven to say that the parties cannot have intended so preposterous a covenant as that the defendant should keep in repair that of which he has no means of ascertaining the condition . . . . This is so preposterous that we ought to hold that the parties intended the covenant to be read with the qualification suggested."

As it appears, however, from the cases considered,[9] the implied pre-condition of notice has become the type of implication described by Lord Cross in *Liverpool City Council v. Irwin*[10] as follows:

"When it implies a term in a contract the court is sometimes laying down a general rule that in all contracts of a certain type—sale of goods, master and servant, landlord and tenant and so on—some provision is to be implied unless the parties have expressly excluded it."

There may be an exception in cases where, whether or not the particular building element has been demised, the circumstances show that the landlord intended to retain control over it: *Murphy v. Hurley.*[11] It is possible that other exceptions might arise from time to time in unusual circumstances.

Right of entry to inspect and carry out works

10–02   Absent an express or implied right of entry, the landlord has no such right. Ownership of the reversion is not sufficient by itself: *Stocker v. Planet Building Society.*[12]

There is, however, an implied right to enter to carry out repairs which the landlord has covenanted to carry out: *Edmonston Corporation v. W. M. Knowles & Son.*[13] Such a right has to be exercised reasonably and the tenant informed of the nature of the work (although not entitled to a specification): *Granada Theatres Limited v. Freehold Investments (Leytonstone) Limited.*[14]

In the case of periodic tenancies of dwelling-houses there is an implied right to enter to repair defects which might cause personal injury: *McAuley v. Bristol City Council.*[15]

In tenancies to which sections 8 and 11 of the Landlord and Tenant Act 1985 apply the landlord has the right "at reasonable times of the day and on giving 24 hours' notice in writing" to enter

[9] Paras. 5–01 to 5–03.
[10] [1977] A.C. 239.
[11] [1922] 1 A.C. 369.
[12] (1879) 27 W.R. 877.
[13] (1962) 60 L.G.R. 124.
[14] [1959] Ch. 592.
[15] [1992] Q.B. 134.

premises to view "their condition and state of repair": sections 8(2) and 11(6) of the Landlord and Tenant Act 1985.

Further rights of entry in the cases of Rent Act and Assured tenants are provided by section 148 of the Rent Act 1977 and section 16 of the Housing Act 1988.

Right to repair and right to have vacant possession to repair

The landlord's duty to repair is also a right, capable of being **10–03** enforced against a reluctant tenant. If vacant possession is strictly necessary in order for the landlord to be able to perform the works he or she is obliged or entitled to perform, then the landlord is entitled to vacant possession: *Saner v. Bilton*.[16]

Where vacant possession is not strictly necessary, but merely desirable so that the landlord is not put to the extra expense involved in having to work around the tenant, the landlord is not entitled to vacant possession: *McGreal v. Wake*.[17] If the landlord desires vacant possession, he or she has to negotiate for it.[18]

Tenants' implied obligations and waste

There is, first, an implied term as to tenant-like user, described **10–04** by Denning L.J. in *Warren v. Keen*[19] as follows:

"[The tenant] must take proper care of the place. He must, if he is going away for the winter, turn off the water and empty the boiler. He must clean the chimneys, where necessary, and also the windows. He must mend the electric light when it fuses. He must unstop the sink when it is blocked by his waste. In short, he must do the little jobs about the place which a reasonable tenant would do. In addition, he must, of course, not damage the house wilfully or negligently; and he must see that his family and guests do not damage it; and if they do, he must repair it."

The duty is not one of repair but of conduct and user: *Regis Property Co. Ltd v. Dudley*.[19a]

The tenant is not liable for burst pipes caused by failing to drain the water system when leaving the premises for a short period: *Wycombe Health Authority v. Barnett*,[20] but may be liable if he or she leaves the premises for a long period: *Mickel v. M'Coard*.[21]

---

[16] (1878) 7 Ch.D. 815.
[17] (1984) 13 H.L.R. 134.
[18] See para. 21–02.
[19] [1954] 1 Q.B. 15.
[19a] [1959] A.C. 370.
[20] (1982) 264 E.G. 619.
[21] (1913) S.C. 896.

The tenant owes a duty not to commit voluntary waste, *i.e.* not to deliberately damage the premises: *Mancetter Developments Limited v. Garmanson.*[22] Small defects are not waste (*e.g.* holes caused by nails or screws) nor is damage in the course of ordinary and reasonable use. The damage has to be such as to affect the value of the landlord's interest: *Doe & Grubb v. Earl of Burlington*[23]; *Mancetter Developments Limited v. Gamanson.*[24]

There is no liability for permissive waste (except in certain cases where there is a fixed term tenancy) and the continued existence of the alleged duty to keep the premises wind- and watertight is doubtful: *Warren v. Keen.*[25]

One potentially useful feature of the law of waste is that action lies against the tenant not merely for the tenant's own acts but for those of any other person (*e.g.* visitors): *Attersoll v. Stevens.*[26] Directors may become personally liable for waste by their company: *Mancetter Developments Limited v. Garmanson.*[27] Waste is a tort; it may or may not apply to licensees: *Mancetter Developments Ltd.*

The Law Commission proposes the replacement of the tort of waste and the implied term as to tenant-like user by the statutory creation of implied obligations on the part of both tenants and licensees (subject to any express contractual terms), (a) to take proper care of premises which they occupy; (b) to make good damage caused wilfully to the premises by occupiers or visitors; (c) not to carry out works which are likely to affect the character of the premises to the landlord's detriment. The obligations are intended to cover common parts.[28]

---

[22] [1986] 1 All E.R. 449.
[23] (1833) 5 B. & D. 507.
[24] *Supra.*
[25] *Supra.*
[26] (1808) 1 Taunt. 183, 198.
[27] *Supra.*
[28] *Landlord and Tenant: Responsibility for State and Condition of Property* (Law Com. No. 238).

CHAPTER ELEVEN

Terms Implied by Statute

Section 8 of the Landlord and Tenant Act 1985

The statutory obligation

Section 8 of the Landlord and Tenant Act 1985 provides as **11–01**
follows:

> **8.—(1) In a contract to which section applies for the letting
> of a house for human habitation there is implied, notwith-
> standing any stipulation to the contrary—**
> **(a) a condition that the house is fit for human habitation
> at the commencement of the tenancy, and**
> **(b) an undertaking that the house will be kept by the
> landlord fit for human habitation during the ten-
> ancy.**

The section applies when:

(1) There is a contract for the letting of a house for human
habitation: section 8(1) of the Act;
(2) The rent does not exceed the annual limit: sections 8(3)(a)
and (4) of the Act;
(3) The letting is not a letting which is (a) for a term of three
years or more and which (b) is upon terms obliging the
tenant to put the premises into a state fit for human
habitation: section 8(5) of the Act.

Statutory fitness

Section 10 of the Act sets out a number of matters to which the **11–02**
court is enjoined to have regard in determining whether any

particular premises are fit for human habitation: repair, stability, freedom from damp, internal arrangement, natural lighting, ventilation, water supply, drainage and sanitary conveniences, facilities for preparation and cooking of food and for the disposal of waste water.

A dwelling is to be regarded as not fit for human habitation only if it is defective in one or more of the specified respects and "it is not reasonably suitable for occupation in that condition": see *Hall v. Manchester Corporation*,[1] *Daly v. Elstree Rural District Council*,[2] *Morgan v. Liverpool Corporation*[3] (general approach); *Estate and Trust Agencies Ltd v. Singapore Improvements Trust*,[4] *Wyse v. Secretary of State for the Environment*[4a] (general approach); *Jones v. Green*[4b] (basic standard); *Summers v. Salford Corporation*[4c] (broken sash cord sufficient, general observations); *Walker v. Hobbs*[5] (falling plaster sufficient); *Fisher v. Walters*[6] (falling plaster sufficient); *Porter v. Jones*[7] (falling plaster sufficient); *Horrex v. Pidwell*[8] (defective toilet and guttering sufficient); *Daly v. Elstree RDC*[9] (defective hot water heating system not sufficient on the facts); *Stanton v. Southwick*[10] (occasional invasions by rats not sufficient, but strongly criticised in *Summers v. Salford Corporation*).

The landlord is required to ensure that the house is "reasonably suitable for occupation" and to fulfill that requirement he or she must "carry out such work upon the premises during the continuance of the tenancy as might from time to time be needed to keep them reasonably fit for human habitation": *O'Brien v. Robinson*.[11] The purpose of the Act was to reverse the common law rule that there is no implied term that an unfurnished dwelling house would be fit for habitation. The then prime minister, the Marquess of Salisbury, said during the Second Reading Debate in the House of Lords:

"At present, under the law, a man who lets a furnished house is compelled to enter into a contract that the house is healthy; but, by a curious peculiarity of the law, that does not extend to

---

[1] (1915) 84 L.J.Ch. 732.
[2] [1948] 2 All E.R. 13.
[3] [1927] 2 K.B. 131.
[4] [1937] A.C. 898.
[4a] [1984] J.P.L. 256.
[4b] [1925] 1 K.B. 659.
[4c] [1943] A.C. 283.
[5] (1889) 23 Q.B.D. 458.
[6] [1926] 2 K.B. 315.
[7] (1942) 112 L.J.K.B. 173.
[8] [1958] C.L.Y. 1461.
[9] [1948] 2 All E.R. 13.
[10] [1920] 2 K.B. 642.
[11] [1973] A.C. 912, at 927.

an unfurnished house. By the provisions of this Bill that anomaly will be removed and the evil will be met . . . I look to this clause more than to any other to diminish the death-rate that is caused by insanitary dwellings."

Implied pre-condition of notice

The terms contained in section 8 of the Act take effect on **11–03** implied terms of the letting agreement: *O'Brien v. Robinson.*[11a] The section is actionable only after notice in so far as the defect arises on parts demised to the tenant: *McCarrick v. Liverpool Corporation.*[11b] The section does not apply to the common parts, only the premises themselves: *Dunster v. Hollis.*[12] It does not apply where the premises can not be made fit at reasonable expense: *Buswell v. Goodwin*[13] (see also *Kenny v. Kingston upon Thames Borough Council*[14] and other cases on "reasonable expense" under what is now section 206 of the Housing Act 1985).

Rent limits

The rent limits are, in relation to contracts made before July 31, **11–04** 1923, £40 in London and £26 or £16 elsewhere; for contracts made on or after July 31, 1923 and before July 31, 1957, £40 in London and £26 elsewhere; and for contracts made on or after July 31, 1957, £80 in London and £52 elsewhere.

These annual rental limits are so low (remaining unchanged since 1957) that the section applies to no-one or hardly anyone these days. Until the rental limits are increased there is little point in considering the section any further. The failure by Parliament to update the rent limits was regretted by Lawton L.J. in *Quick v. Taff-Ely Borough Council*[15] who said "This case would seem to indicate that a new definition of a low rent is needed."

The Law Commission has reported[15a] that, subject to certain **11–04A** exceptions, legislation should impose a term on leases of dwelling-houses for less than 7 years that the landlord will keep the dwelling-house fit for human habitation, applying the criteria in section 604 of the Housing Act 1985. There will be no contracting-out.

[11a] *Supra.*
[11b] [1947] A.C. 219.
[12] [1918] 2 K.B. 795.
[13] [1971] 1 W.L.R. 92.
[14] (1985) 17 H.L.R. 344.
[15] [1986] Q.B. 809.
[15a] Law Com. 238.

Section 11 of the Landlord and Tenant Act 1985

Text of the section

11–05   The section (as amended by the Housing Act 1988 with effect only in relation to new tenancies entered into on or after January 15, 1989) provides as follows:

> 11.—(1) In a lease to which this section applies (as to which, see sections 13 and 14) there is implied a covenant by the lessor—
>
> (a) to keep in repair the structure and exterior of the dwelling-house (including drains, gutters and external pipes),
>
> (b) to keep in repair and proper working order the installations in the dwelling-house for the supply of water, gas and electricity and for sanitation (including basins, sinks, baths and sanitary conveniences, but not other fixtures, fittings and appliances for making use of the supply of water, gas or electricity), and
>
> (c) to keep in repair and proper working order the installations in the dwelling-house for space heating and heating water.
>
> (1A) If a lease to which this section applies is a lease of a dwelling-house which forms part only of a building, then, subject to subsection (1B), the covenant implied by subsection (1) shall effect as if—
>
> (a) the reference in paragraph (a) of that subsection to the dwelling-house included a reference to any part of the building in which the lessor has an estate or interest; and
>
> (b) any reference in paragraphs (b) and (c) of that subsection to an installation in the dwelling-house included a reference to an installation which, directly or indirectly, serves the dwelling-house and which either—
>
> > (i) forms part of any part of a building in which the lessor has an estate or interest; or
> >
> > (ii) is owned by the lessor or under his control.
>
> (1B) Nothing in subsection (1A) shall be construed as requiring the lessor to carry out any works or repairs unless the disrepair (or failure to maintain in working order) is such as to affect the lessee's enjoyment of the dwelling-house or of any common parts, as defined in section 60(1) of the Landlord and Tenant Act 1987, which the lessee, as such, is entitled to use.
>
> (2) The covenant implied by subsection (1) ("the lessor's

repairing covenant") shall not be construed as requiring the lessor—

(a) to carry out works or repairs for which the lessee is liable by virtue of his duty to use the premises in a tenant-like manner, or would be so liable but for an express covenant on his part,

(b) to rebuild or reinstate the premises in the case of destruction or damage by fire, or by tempest, flood or other inevitable accident, or

(c) to keep in repair or maintain anything which the lessee is entitled to remove from the dwelling-house.

(3) In determining the standard of repair required by the lessor's repairing covenant, regard shall be had to the age, character and prospective life of the dwelling-house and the locality in which it is situated.

(3A) In any case where—

(a) the lessor's repairing covenant has effect as mentioned in sub-section (1A), and

(b) in order to comply with the covenant the lessor needs to carry out works or repairs otherwise than in, or to an installation in, the dwelling-house, and

(c) the lessor does not have a sufficient right in the part of the building or the installation concerned to enable him to carry out the required works or repairs,

then, in any proceedings relating to a failure to comply with the lessor's repairing covenant, so far as it requires the lessor to carry out the works or repairs in question, it shall be a defence for the lessor to prove that he used all reasonable endeavours to obtain, but was unable to obtain, such rights as would be adequate to enable him to carry out the works or repairs.

(4) A covenant by the lessee for the repair of premises is of no effect so far as it relates to matters mentioned in subsection (1)(a) to (c), except in so far as it imposes on the lessee any of the requirements mentioned in subsection (2)(a) or (c).

(5) The reference in subsection (4) to a covenant by the lessee for the repair of premises includes a covenant—

(a) to put in repair or deliver up in repair,

(b) to paint, point or render,

(c) to pay money in lieu of repairs by the lessee, or

(d) to pay money on account of repairs by the lessor.

(6) In a lease in which the lessor's repairing covenant is implied there is also implied a covenant by the lessee that the lessor, or any person authorised by him in writing, may at reasonable times of the day and giving 24 hours'

notice in writing to the occupier, enter the premises comprised in the lease for the purpose of viewing their condition and state of repair.

Cases to which the section applies

11–06   Subject to exceptions where the tenancy is granted by the Crown, is an agricultural tenancy or was granted to a specified public body, section 11 of the Landlord and Tenant Act 1985 applies to any lease of a building or part of building for the purposes wholly or mainly as a private residence granted on or after October 24, 1961 for a term of less than 7 years[15b]: sections 13 and 14 of the Act contain further elaboration. The section plainly applies to periodic tenancies of dwelling houses granted after October 24, 1961.[15c]

Amendments introduced by the Housing Act 1988

11–07   Prior to the amendments introduced by the Housing Act 1988, there were serious gaps in the protection which section 11 was able to afford to tenants of flats.

The phrase "structure and exterior of the dwelling-house" in section 11(1)(a) had in one sense been defined broadly, obliging landlords to repair elements of the building which in point of fact physically were part of the structure or exterior of the flat, even though not included in the demise (*e.g.* walls in the case of an eggshell demise). The phrase had also, however, been defined narrowly as obliging landlords to repair only the immediate structure and exterior of the flat and not other structural or external parts of the building even though such parts might be damaging the flat: *Campden Hill Towers v. Gardner*[16]; *Douglas-Scott v. Scorgie.*[17]

The tenant had no remedy under section 11(1)(a) if, for example, his flat suffered water penetration as the result of leaks from gutters which were not situated on the immediate exterior of his or her flat but on the exterior of one of the upstairs flats; or as the result of leaks from the roof when the tenant was not the top floor tenant, or if he was the top floor tenant but the roof was not as a matter of surveying fact actually part of the structure or exterior of his flat.

[15b] ss.13, 14 and 16 Landlord and Tenant Act 1985.
[15c] A lease of three floors for the purpose of residential sub-letting was not itself within section 11 of the Act: *Demetriou v. Robert Andrews (Estate Agencies) Ltd* (1990) 62 P. & C.R. 536.
[16] [1977] Q.B. 823.
[17] [1984] 1 W.L.R. 716.

It can just as easily be seen that there was no remedy under section 11(1)(b) and (c) for tenants who were the victims of defective communal hot water or heating systems, when the defects arose outside the dwelling house itself.

These gaps have now been substantially filled by the amendments included in the text of the section set out above, but only in respect of tenancies entered into on or after January 15, 1989 which are not entered into pursuant to a contract made before that date: section 116(4) Housing Act 1988. Tenants of flats under tenancies entered into before that date still face the difficulties set out above. Where the tenancy is entered into before January 15, 1989, tenants have to seek to rely on the implied terms considered at paras. 8–07, 8–08 and 8–10 above.

Obligation to keep the structure and exterior of the dwelling house in repair

The expression "structure and exterior" was defined in *Campden Hill Towers Limited v. Gardner*[18]: **11–08**

"Anything which, in the ordinary use of words, would be regarded as part of the structure, or of the exterior . . . the outside wall or walls of the flat; the outside of inner party walls of the flat; the outer side of horizontal divisions between [the flat] and flats above and below; the structural framework and beams directly supporting floors, ceilings and walls of the flat."

For a full consideration of which parts of buildings have been treated as part of the structure and/or exterior of a dwelling-house, see below.[19]

Obligation to keep installations in repair and proper working order

As the terms of section 11(1)(b) suggest, not all installations for the supply of water, gas and electricity and for sanitation are included: the obligation extends to "basins, sinks, baths, and sanitary conveniences but not other fixtures, fittings and appliances for making use of the supply of water, gas and electricity". Installations such as cookers and refrigerators are not included, for example, even though included in the tenancy; but gas and electric fires, boilers and radiators are included by virtue of section 11(1)(c). **11–09**

[18] *Supra.*
[19] Chapters 17 and 18.

The important point about this obligation is that it requires the landlord to do more than repair: he or she has to keep the relevant installation both in repair and in "proper working order". This means that the landlord has to ensure that the relevant installation is and remains functional, even in cases in which it has never functioned properly and there has been no identifiable deterioration to its physical condition. In *Liverpool City Council v. Irwin*,[20] for example, Lord Edmund-Davies said:

"It is clear that [the] section . . . imposes an *absolute* duty upon the landlord 'to keep in repair and proper working order the installations in the dwelling-house'. It can be said that the opening words ('to keep . . . ') apparently limit the landlord's obligations to preserving the *existing* plant in its original state and create no obligation to improve plant which was, by its very design, at all times defective and inefficient. But the phrase has to be read as a whole, and as I think, it presupposes that at the inception of the letting the installation was 'in proper working order' and that if its design was such that it did not work 'properly' the landlord is in breach."

The obligation has been held:

(1) To require the landlord to remedy a cistern which as a result of bad design flooded the floor when used: *Liverpool City Council v. Irwin*[21];

(2) To extend to rusting water pipes or insulation on wiring which was wearing out: *Wycombe Health Authority v. Barnett.*[22]

The obligation has been held:

(1) Not to require landlords to lag water pipes to prevent bursting as " 'proper working order' in its context relates to the physical or mechanical condition of the installation as such and involves that it shall be capable of working properly as an installation"[23]: *Wycombe Health Authority v. Barnett*[24];

(2) Not to require the landlord to replace fuses or washers: *Wycombe Health Authority v. Barnett.*[25]

---

[20] [1977] A.C. 239.
[21] *Supra.*
[22] (1982) 5 H.L.R. 84.
[23] *per* May L.J. at p. 92.
[24] *Supra.*
[25] *Supra.*

Contracting out/in

Unless approved in advance by the court upon a consent **11–10** application any provision in a letting agreement purporting to limit the application of section 11 of the Landlord and Tenant Act 1985 or impose any penalty on the tenant who invokes it is void: section 12.

Covenants which purport to place any landlord's obligation contained in section 11 of the Landlord and Tenant Act 1985 upon the tenant are also void: section 11(4). A covenant on the part of the tenant to carry out external painting is accordingly void because such decoration, being protective of structural or external elements, is part of the obligation to repair: *Irvine v. Moran.*[26]

A landlord who demands and accepts rent which has been registered on the basis that section 11 of the Landlord and Tenant Act 1985 applies will be estopped from denying liability under that section: at least until the rent register has been rectified: *Brikom Investments Limited v. Seaford.*[27]

In general, there is no reason parties cannot contract on the basis that a statute applies, so that analogous rights are conferred: *Daejan Properties v. Mahoney.*[28]

Requirement of notice

In so far as relevant disrepair affects the demised premises, the **11–11** position under section 11 is the same as the position at common law: there is an implied condition precedent to any liability on the part of the landlord that the landlord has notice of the disrepair and fails to remedy it within a reasonable period of time: *O'Brien v. Robinson.*[29]

Section 11 of the Landlord and Tenant Act (and, in particular, by definition, the sections added by the Housing Act 1988) can, however, also apply so as to require the landlord to repair elements of the building which are not included in the demise. The common law rule, if applied to section 11 cases in a straightforward manner, would mean that no such implied condition precedent existed in relation to such disrepair: *Melles & Co. v. Holme*[30]; *Bishop v. Consolidated London Properties Ltd*[31]; *Loria v. Hammer*[32]; *British Telecom v. Sun Life Assurance Society.*[33]

---

[26] [1991] 1 E.G.L.R. 261.
[27] [1981] 1 W.L.R. 863.
[28] [1995] 45 E.G. 128.
[29] [1973] A.C. 912. See also Chapter 5 generally.
[30] [1918] 2 K.B. 100.
[31] (1933) 102 L.J.K.B. 257.
[32] [1989] 2 E.G.L.R. 249.
[33] [1995] 4 All E.R. 44 (see generally para. 5–04).

Standard of repair

11–12   In determining the standard of repair, section 11(3) requires that regard is had to the age, character and locality of the dwelling-house. This adds nothing to what is in any event required when construing express and implied repairing obligations at common law.[34]

Section 11(3) also requires regard to be had to the "prospective life of the dwelling-house". This is arguably a new consideration: see *Newham L.B.C. v. Patel*[35]:

> "In subsection (3) the crucially important addition is the phrase 'prospective life of the dwelling-house'. In my judgment that is an exceedingly important qualification. If the prospective life of the dwelling-house, as in this case, is short, then it is perfectly proper, sensible and reasonable to adjust the landlord's obligations accordingly and not to seek to impose a construction on the statute, which can only be described as pedantic."

In that case the landlord was held to be not liable to repair or pay compensation in respect of, *inter alia*, dilapidated roofs and windows, leaking gutters, areas of perished plaster, ill-fitting doors, rising damp in two ground-floor rooms and penetrating damp in four rooms. It had been let to the tenant in 1973 and he was still there in 1977, although the local authority was trying to rehouse him. The rent had been very low: £2.83 per week (as against the norm for that time and for a house of that type in reasonable repair of £7.53 per week). Templeman L.J. held that the local authority "were not bound to carry out repairs which would be wholly useless" given the imminent redevelopment of the property. There appears to have been no proof that the premises were in the poor condition described in the survey report for any lengthy period, or that the landlord had been put on notice of the condition of the premises any appreciable time before it offered to rehouse the tenant.

The Court of Appeal in *McClean v. Liverpool City Council*[36] distinguished *Newham L.B.C. v. Patel*[37] in an important and decisive manner. Nourse L.J. did not find the case "at all comparable" with *Newham L.B.C. v. Patel* when the highest the landlord's case was put was that the future life of the house was "extremely limited" and there was no evidence that "the property was actually at the end of its life" or, as Templeman L.J. had put it in *Newham*

---

[34] See para. 6–01.
[35] (1978) 13 H.L.R. 77 *per* Ormrod L.J. at p. 85.
[36] (1987) 20 H.L.R. 25.
[37] (1978) 13 H.L.R. 77.

L.B.C. v. Patel that repairs would be "wholly useless". The house was unfit for human habitation but there was no suggestion that it should be demolished. As Nourse L.J. said: "it will. . . . have some form of life, albeit only for a matter of a few years".

Where the landlord proposed to reconstruct the entire property with vacant possession then that may be a factor in determining that it is reasonable to carry out running repairs to rather than completely replace a roof: *Dame Margaret Hungerford Charity Trustees v. Beazeley.*[38]

The standard of repair is no higher for local authorities than for private sector landlords: *Wainwright v. Leeds City Council.*[39]

Section 4 of the Defective Premises Act 1972

Text of the section

Section 4 of the Defective Premises Act 1972 provides as **11–13** follows:

> **4.—(1) Where premises are let under a tenancy which puts on the landlord an obligation to the tenant for the maintenance or repair of the premises, the landlord owes to all persons who might reasonably be expected to be affected by defects in the state of the premises a duty to take such care as is reasonable in all the circumstances to see that they are reasonably safe from personal injury or from damage to their property caused by a relevant defect.**
>
> **(2) The said duty is owed if the landlord knows (whether as the result of being notified by the tenant or otherwise) or if he ought in all the circumstances to have known of the relevant defect.**
>
> **(3) In this section "relevant defect" means a defect in the state of the premises existing at or after the material time and arising from, or continuing because of, an act or omission by the landlord which constitutes or would if he had had notice of the defect, have constituted a failure by him to carry out his obligation to the tenant for the maintenance or repair of the premises; and for the purposes of the foregoing provision "the material time" means—**
>
> **(a) where the tenancy commenced before this Act, the commencement of this Act; and**
>
> **(b) in all other cases, the earliest of the following times, that is to say—**

---

[38] [1993] 2 E.G.L.R. 143.
[39] (1984) 270 E.G. 1289.

(i) the time when the tenancy commences;
(ii) the time when the tenancy agreement is entered into;
(iii) the time when possession is taken of the premises in contemplation of the letting.

(4) Where premises are let under a tenancy which expressly or impliedly gives the landlord the right to enter the premises to carry out any description of maintenance or repairs of the premises, then, as from time to time when he first is, or by notice or otherwise can put himself, in a position to exercise the right and for so long as he is or can put himself in that position, he shall be treated for the purposes of subsections (1) to (3) above (but for no other purposes) as if he were under an obligation to the tenant for that description of maintenance or repair of the premises; but the landlord shall not owe the tenant any duty by virtue of this subsection in respect of any defect in the state of the premises arising from, or continuing because of, a failure to carry out an obligation expressly imposed on the tenant by the tenancy.

(5) For the purposes of this section obligations imposed or rights given by any enactment in virtue of a tenancy shall be treated as imposed or given by the tenancy.

(6) This section applies to a right of occupation given by contract or any enactment and not amounting to a tenancy as if the right were a tenancy and "tenancy" and cognate expression shall be construed accordingly.

Cases to which the section applies

11–14   The Act applies to commercial premises as well as dwelling-houses. It applies as from January 1, 1974 where the tenancy began before that date: section 4(3).

The Act applies to the whole of the land let, not just the dwelling-house itself, *e.g.* it applies to a patio at the rear of a dwelling-house: *Smith v. Bradford Metropolitan Council.*[40] It does not apply to land not let, *e.g.* the common parts (but similar duties covering the common parts can be found in the Occupiers Liability Act 1957).

"Tenancy" and cognate expressions are further defined by section 6 of the Act. Of particular interest is section 4(6) of the Act, which applies the Act to licenses (*cf.* sections 13 and 16 of the Landlord and Tenant Act 1985, which applies section 11 of that Act only to lettings).

---

[40] (1982) 44 P. & C.R. 171.

The nature of the duty owed

The duty is to "take such care as is reasonable in all the **11–15** circumstances" to see that persons to whom the duty is owed are reasonably safe from (a) personal injury, and (b) damage to their property, caused by a relevant defect of which the landlord knows or ought to have known.

The scope of the duty is restricted in such a way that the landlord would not appear liable for physical discomfort or inconvenience, as if he or she had failed to comply with a repairing obligation. The liability is only for property damage or for personal injury, which is defined as "any disease and any impairment of a person's physical or mental condition".[41]

The Act creates a statutory duty of care, rather than an implied repairing obligation. Its effect can be, however, to create new repairing obligations: see para. 11–20 below.

To whom the duty is owed

The duty is owed to "all persons who might reasonably be **11–16** expected to be affected by defects in the state of the premises". This includes the tenant: *Smith v. Bradford Metropolitan Borough Council,*[42] *Barrett v. Lounova (1982) Ltd.*[43] It should also include family members of the tenant, arguably whether or not the landlord had actual knowledge of their occupation.

Duty only arises in relation to "relevant defects"

A "relevant defect", as is apparent from the wording of section **11–17** 4(1), is restricted to a defect to the premises demised, *e.g.* does not include defects to ancillary property retained in the ownership of the landlord or let to other tenants.

A "relevant defect" is a defect which:

(1) The landlord is obliged to repair or deal with by maintenance under the express or implied terms of the tenancy agreement or as the result of any obligation imposed by statute, *e.g.* section 11 of the Landlord and Tenant Act 1985;

(2) The landlord is obliged to repair or deal with by way of maintenance by virtue of section 4 (4) of the Act.

---

[41] S.6(1).
[42] *Ibid.*
[43] [1990] 1 Q.B. 348.

Sections 4(1)–(3) of the 1972 Act create no new repairing obligations

11–18   In *McNerny v. Lambeth L.B.C.*[44] Dillon L.J. remarked, in relation to sections 4(1)–(3) of the Defective Premises Act 1972 that:

> "The important point is that that statutory protection for those in occupation of defective premises is geared to the landlord's obligation to repair the premises. It goes no wider than the repair covenant."

In fact, the protection afforded by sections 4(1)–(3) of the 1972 Act will be in three respects *less* wide than the repairing covenant to which it attaches:

(1) First, the duty applies only to the demised premises and not to the common parts;
(2) secondly, the duty is not absolute, it is only a duty to take reasonable care;
(3) thirdly, the duty is only breached when relevant defects cause personal injury or damage to property.

The advantages of sections 4(1)–(3) of the 1972 are, however, that:

(1) The Act creates an independent duty owed to family members and guests.
(2) There is no need to prove that the landlord had notice of the defect, where notice is required as an implied condition precedent to liability providing the tenant can prove that the landlord "ought in all the circumstances to have known of the relevant defect".

When a landlord "ought to have known" about a relevant defect
Normally, there is no reason why, absent a complaint from the tenant, a landlord "ought to have known of" a relevant defect. If the central heating system breaks down, the roof starts to leak, or the damp proof course starts to break down, there is much to be said for the proposition that, in the absence of special circumstances, the landlord can expect his or her tenant who actually resides at the premises to inform him or her of any defects.

In *Kathleen Clarke v. Taff Ely Borough Council*,[45] however, the tenant could not possibly have complained to her landlord about the condition of the floorboards at her home because their defective condition was latent. She was injured when they collapsed beneath

[44] (1988) 21 H.L.R. 188.
[45] (1980) 10 H.L.R. 47.

her and successfully sued her landlord under sections 4(1)–(3) of the 1972 Act. On the facts, it was proven (indeed, it was not even in dispute) that due to the unusual construction of the premises:

> "with knowledge of the age of the house, the type of construction of the floorboards and the presence of damp, one could foresee that rot was likely to occur. Secondly, it was foreseeable that, if rot did occur, then the floors would be likely to give way . . . ."

The landlord "ought to have known" that these particular floorboards were in disrepair because (a) the landlord was aware of the problem with floorboards prevalent in the area, (b) could and should have tested the floorboards (by jumping) when attending the premises to carry out other routine repairs, (c) alternatively should have carried out a planned programme of checks (on the facts such a programme was economically feasible). Further cases are considered at para. 5–05 above.

The duty-creating role of section 4(4)

This is a remarkable piece of legislation. The effect is to convert **11–19** a landlord's *entitlement* to carry out specified works of repair or maintenance into a *duty* to carry out such works.

When the landlord is "expressly or impliedly" entitled to enter the premises to carry out "any description of maintenance or repair" then the landlord is treated as being under a positive duty to carry out that description of maintenance or repair for the purposes of section 4(1)–(3), *i.e.* he or she has a duty to take reasonable care to ensure that his or her failure to repair or maintain in that respect does not cause personal injury or property damage. For example, if the tenancy agreement, although not containing any express repairing obligations, reserves a right to the landlord to enter the premises upon 24 hours written notice to repair the roof, walls and foundations, section 4(4) converts that right into a duty to take reasonable care to ensure that disrepair to the roof, walls and foundations does not cause personal injury to or damage to the property of any person who might reasonably be expected to be affected by the failure.

The duty arises as soon as the landlord is, or by notice is able to put himself or herself, in a position to exercise the right of entry to repair: section 4(4). In the case of the above example, the duty would arise 24 hours after the tenancy began.

The duty created by section 4(4) is not an absolute obligation to repair, comparable with express repairing covenants or the terms implied by section 11 of the Landlord and Tenant Act 1985. It is no more than the duty under section 4(1)–(3), *i.e.* a duty to take

reasonable care to prevent personal injury or property damage
when the landlord knew or ought to have known of a defect he or
she had the right to repair.

The sting in the tail of section 4(4) of the 1972 Act is that it
creates duties out of implied as well as express rights to enter and
repair or maintain. In *McAuley v. Bristol City Council*[46] Ralph
Gibson L.J. held:

> "In imposing the obligations stated in section 4 of the 1972
> Act, where there is no obligation to repair, whether con-
> tractual or statutory, Parliament required proof of a tenancy
> which 'expressly or impliedly gives the landlord the right to
> enter the premises to carry out any description of maintenance
> or repair'. If such a right is proved, the landlord is, if the other
> conditions are satisfied, to be treated as under an obligation to
> the tenant for that description of repair. Parliament thus
> legislated by reference to the common law. If the common law
> says that the right to repair is implied, the statute imposes the
> obligation."

In *Smith v. Bradford Metropolitan Borough Council*[47] the agreement provided that the tenant would "give the Council officers . . .
reasonable facilities for inspecting the premises and their state of
repair and for carrying out repairs". The Court of Appeal held that
the premises as defined included a rear patio, that this clause gave
the landlord the right to repair the patio and that, accordingly,
section 4(4) of the 1972 Act applied to convert that right into a
duty to take reasonable care that disrepair to the patio did not
cause personal injury. The landlord had had notice of the dangerous condition of the patio as a result of complaints by the tenant
and was therefore liable for injury suffered by the tenant when the
patio gave way.

In *McAuley v. Bristol City Council*[48] the Court of Appeal went yet
further. The tenancy agreement required the tenant to give the
landlord access "for any purpose which may from time to time be
required by the council". The Court of Appeal held that the clause
should be construed as limited to purposes which the landlord
could lawfully carry out. The landlord was subject to the terms
implied by section 11 of the Landlord and Tenant Act 1985 and the
tenant was obliged to decorate the interior and tend the gardens.
The Court of Appeal held that it was necessary, in order to give
business efficacy to the tenancy agreement, to imply a term
entitling the landlord to enter the premises to repair defects likely

[46] [1992] Q.B. 134.
[47] *Supra.*
[48] *Supra.*

to cause personal injury to the tenant or her family. Section 4(4) of the 1972 Act turned that right into a duty and the landlord was, accordingly, liable when the tenant broke her ankle on an unstable step in the garden: the landlord knew about the unstable step as a result of complaints made by the tenant but had refused to repair it because (as the landlord rightly contended) it was not obliged to do so by virtue of any express repairing obligation or by virtue of section 11 of the Landlord and Tenant Act 1985, the step not forming part of the structure or exterior of the dwelling-house itself).

There are dicta in *Smith v. Bradford Metropolitan Council*[49] to the effect that "there must be an implied right in the council to repair any part of their property which they wish to repair".[50] There are similar dicta in *Mint v. Good*.[51] If that were so, then landlords would potentially be subject to wide-ranging duties by virtue of section 4(4) of the Defective Premises Act 1972. The more wide-ranging the implied rights of entry to repair (and an implied right to "repair any part of their property which they wish to repair" is fairly wide-ranging) the more extensive the duties owed under the Act.

11–20

The potential effect of such dicta was effectively nullified by *McAuley v. Bristol City Council*.[52] Ralph Gibson L.J. said that:

"There is, I think, no warrant for a wide construction of the words of the section. They apply to all landlords, and not merely to local authorities, and can operate so as to impose a substantial burden upon a landlord in respect of premises under the immediate control of the tenant and in respect of which the landlord has assumed no contractual obligation."

For that reason the court held that the landlord's powers of entry were restricted to entry for lawful purposes (and that that was what was meant by a contractual provision permitting entry for "any purpose which may from time to time be required by the council").

The right of entry to carry out repairs to prevent "a significant risk of injury" was implied because it was necessary to give business efficacy to this particular agreement rather than because it was the type of provision that should be a legal incident of this type of contract. There are, however, many periodic tenancies of dwelling-houses which are in fact similar to the tenancy in *McAuley v. Bristol City Council*. The court is likely to imply into all such

---

[49] *Supra.*
[50] *per* Lord Donaldson at p. 177.
[51] [1951] 1 K.B. 517.
[52] *Supra.*

contracts—as a matter of business efficacy—the right to enter to repair or maintain to remove a significant risk of personal injury.

The as yet unanswered question is what scope of works is likely to be included in the notion of "repair" and "maintenance"?

PART FIVE

OTHER RELEVANT OBLIGATIONS
OWED BY LANDLORDS TO TENANTS

CHAPTER TWELVE

Nuisance

General principles

A private nuisance occurs when, as a result of an act or a failure to take action, the condition of the defendant's land, or the use to which the defendant's land has been put, damages or interferes with the plaintiff's enjoyment of his or her land or some right connected with it (for example, an easement). **12–01**

There are three key features of private nuisance:

(1) The defendant's act or failure to act may be (and usually is) entirely lawful and yet be a nuisance.

(2) The tort is essentially land based: the condition of the defendant's land, or the use to which it is put, causes damage to the plaintiff's land or the plaintiff's enjoyment of his or her land. The defendant need not be the owner of the offending land, however, and can be the trespasser or other person who has caused the nuisance. On the other hand, even though he or she did not cause the nuisance, the occupier or purchaser of land will be liable for "continuing" the nuisance "if with knowledge or presumed knowledge of its existence he fails to take any reasonable means to bring it to an end though with ample time to do so": *Sedleigh-Denfield v. O'Callaghan*[1] (see also *Rowell v. Prior*[2]; *Barker v. Herbert*[3]). He or she will also be liable if he or she "adopts" the nuisance, *i.e.* "if he makes any use of the erection,

---

[1] [1940] A.C. 880.
[2] (1701) 12 Mod. 635.
[3] [1911] 2 K.B. 633.

building, bank or artificial contrivance which constitutes a nuisance": *Sedleigh-Denfield v. O'Callaghan.*[4]

(3) There must be interference to the plaintiff's enjoyment of land. But the plaintiff need not be the owner of the land. In *Hunter v. Canary Wharf Limited,*[5] the Court of Appeal held that "a substantial link between the person enjoying the use and the land on which he or she is enjoying it is essential but, in my judgment, occupation of property, as a home, does confer upon the occupant a capacity to sue in private nuisance".

The nuisance can arise by virtue of:

(1) A permanent physical encroachment (overhanging branches or subterranean roots): *Davey v. Harrow Corporation.*[6]

(2) An activity or condition which causes damage (water spilling onto the plaintiff's land from a blocked drain: *Sedleigh-Denfield & Co. v. O'Callaghan*[7]; vibrations damaging the plaintiff's buildings: *Grosvenor Hotel Co. v. Hamilton*[8]; dilapidated house with pieces falling onto plaintiff's land: *Wringe v. Cohen.*[9]

(3) An activity or condition which substantially interferes with the plaintiff's enjoyment of the land. As it was described in *St Helens Smelting Co. v. Tipping,*[10] "the personal inconvenience and interference with one's enjoyment, one's quiet, one's personal freedom, anything that discomposes or injuriously affects the senses or the nerves".

Interference with the enjoyment of land

12–02   The interference must be unreasonable. That is a question of fact. The relevant considerations were summarised by Oliver J. in *Stone v. Bolton*[11] as follows:

"Whether such an act does constitute a nuisance must be determined not merely by an abstract consideration of the act itself, but by reference to all the circumstances of the particular case, including, for example, the time of the commission of the act complained of; the place of its commission; the manner of committing it, that is, whether it is done wantonly or in the reasonable exercise of rights; and the effect of its

[4] *Supra.*
[5] [1996] 1 All E.R. 483.
[6] [1958] 1 Q.B. 60.
[7] *Supra.*
[8] [1894] 2 Q.B. 836.
[9] [1940] 1 K.B. 229.
[10] (1865) 11 H.L.C. 642.
[11] [1949] 1 All E.R. 237.

commission, that is, whether those effects are transitory or permanent, occasional or continuous; so that the question of nuisance or no nuisance is one of fact."

Examples of this type of nuisance are as follows:

(1) Smells, for example from rubbish (*Att.-Gen. v. Todd Heatley*[12]) or gas fumes (*Wood v. Conway Corporation*[13]).
(2) Dust (*Pwllbach Colliery v. Woodman*[14]; *Hunter v. Canary Wharf Limited*[15]).
(3) Noise, for example from the banging doors of a lift (*Newman v. Real Estate Debenture Corporation*[16]); a playground (*Dunton v. Dover District Council*[17]) or lorries (*Halsey v. Esso Petroleum Company Limited*[18]).
(4) Causing excessive heat to pass into adjoining premises. (*Sanders-Clark v. Grosvenor Mansions Co*[19]).

There has to be, judged objectively, a substantial interference for there to be a nuisance. As it was put in *Walter v. Selfe*[20] there must be:

"an inconvenience materially interfering with the ordinary comfort physically of human existence, not merely according to elegant and dainty modes and habits of living, but according to plain and sober and simple notions among the English people."

There is, accordingly, no nuisance when damage is caused to unusually sensitive persons or chattels, or even, it seems, to susceptible but hardly exceptional persons such as invalids or the elderly, by something which would not ordinarily be considered a nuisance: *Robinson v. Kilvert*[21] (ordinary heating damaging delicate brown paper: no liability); *Bridlington Relay Limited v. Yorkshire Electricity Board*[22] (interference with television and radio relay system no nuisance). On the other hand, it appears that once the plaintiff has established the existence of a nuisance he or she can recover for damage in fact caused to unusually sensitive chattels:

[12] [1897] 1 Ch. 560.
[13] [1914] 2 Ch. 47.
[14] [1915] A.C. 634.
[15] *Supra.*
[16] [1940] 1 All E.R. 131.
[17] (1978) 76 L.G.R. 87.
[18] [1961] 1 W.L.R. 683.
[19] [1900] 2 Ch. 373.
[20] (1851) 4 De. G. & Sm. 315.
[21] (1889) 41 Ch.D. 88.
[22] [1965] Ch. 436.

McKinnon Industries v. Walker[23] (orchids). You take your victim as you find him for the purposes of damages, not liability.

The character of the neighbourhood is taken into account: "what would be a nuisance in Belgrave Square would not necessarily be so in Bermondsey": *Sturges v. Bridgman.*[24] Issues of causation and remoteness are considered below at paras. 19–12 to 19–14.

The liability of landlords in their capacity as landlords to third parties and other tenants

12–03   Landlords can be liable in nuisance to third parties, including other tenants of the landlord who may occupy other flats in the same block or other houses in the same street.

12–04   *Nuisances in existence at the date of the letting.* Landlords remain liable to third parties in respect of nuisances present on the land at the time it is let: *Spicer v. Smee*[25] (defective electrical wiring causing a fire damaging adjoining property); *Todd v. Flight*[26] as explained in *Pretty v. Bickmore*[27] (noisy central heating system). The landlord does not escape liability merely because the tenant is liable under his or her repairing covenant to abate the nuisance and, having failed to do so, is also liable to the third party: *Brew Bros Limited v. Snax (Ross) Limited*[28] (wall collapsing onto adjoining premises). It is, however, necessary to show that the landlord knew or ought to have known of the nuisance when the tenancy was granted: *Brew Bros Limited v. Snax (Ross) Limited.*[29]

12–05   *Nuisances arising after the date of the letting.* Landlords are liable to third parties or other tenants if they have either a duty (for example, under a repairing covenant) or a power (under an express or implied term of the agreement) to enter the land to abate the nuisance: see *Payne v. Rogers,*[30] *Nelson v. Liverpool Brewery Co.*[31] (both cases in which the landlord was expressly liable under the terms of his contract with the tenant to carry out repairs which would have abated the nuisance causing damage to the third party); *Wilchick v. Marks*[32] (injury caused when defective shutter fell from dwelling-house onto pavement), *Wringe v. Cohen*[33] (gable end wall falling into adjoining shop), *Heap v. Ind Coope and Allsop*

---

[23] [1951] D.L.R. 577.
[24] (1879) 11 Ch.D. 852.
[25] [1946] 1 All E.R. 489.
[26] (1860) 9 C.B.N.S. 377.
[27] (1873) L.R. 8 C.P. 401.
[28] [1970] 1 Q.B. 612.
[29] [1970] 1 Q.B. 612.
[30] (1794) 2 Hbl. 350.
[31] (1877) 2 C.P.D. 31.
[32] [1934] 2 K.B. 56.
[33] *Supra.*

Limited[34] (person falling through light shaft cover on pavement into cellar) and *Mint v. Good*[35] (boy on highway injured by falling wall fronting dwelling-house). These are all cases in which there was an implied duty or right to repair the defects which caused damage to the third party. The basis for the decision is elegantly expressed in *Heap v. Ind Coope and Allsop Limited*[36] as follows:

"The landlord has expressly reserved to himself the right to enter and do necessary repairs: why then should he be under no duty to make [the premises] safe for passers by? . . . The proximity is there: he had the right to enter and remedy a danger. Is the injured person to be left in such a case only to a remedy against the tenant?"

It is no defence that the nuisance arose after the date of the letting. The landlord may be liable even if he or she did not know and could not have known of the nuisance, except when the nuisance is caused by the act of a trespasser or an unobservable act of nature, such as subsidence, when the landlord is only liable if he or she fails to abate the nuisance after knowledge or the means of knowledge of its existence: *Wringe v. Cohen*,[37] *cf. Caminer v. Northern & London Investment Trust Limited*[38] (landlord not liable for injury caused by apparently sound tree).

Landlords who authorise nuisance. The landlord will be liable to **12–06** third parties and other tenants if he or she lets the land for the purpose of, or authorises, an activity which causes a nuisance: *Harris v. James*[39] (burning lime); *Tetley v. Chitty*[40] (go-karting); *Sampson v. Hodson-Pressinger*[41] (walking on patio above plaintiff's premises constructed in such a way that the sound reverberated through the plaintiff's premises).

The landlord was not, however, liable merely for letting premises to a "problem family" when the letting conditions prohibited nuisance and the landlord had not actively encouraged the nuisance. The nuisance was entirely that of the family.[42]

Tenants' liabilities to third parties and other tenants

Tenants as occupiers of the land are liable to third parties and **12–07** other tenants of the landlord for nuisances emanating from the

[34] [1940] 2 K.B. 476.
[35] [1951] 1 K.B. 517.
[36] *Supra.*
[37] *Supra.*
[38] [1951] A.C. 88.
[39] (1876) 45 L.J.Q.B. 545.
[40] [1986] 1 All E.R. 663.
[41] [1981] 3 All E.R. 710.
[42] *Smith v. Scott* [1973] 1 All E.R. 314: see para. 19–09 below.

land, even though the nuisance pre-dates the letting, providing the tenant knew or ought to know of its existence: *Nelson v. Liverpool Brewery Co.*[43]; *Sedleigh-Denfield v. O'Callaghan.*[44] The tenant is liable to the third party even though the landlord has contracted to repair or otherwise carry out works which would abate the nuisance and the tenant has an action for an indemnity against the landlord: *St Anne's Well Brewery Co. v. Roberts.*[45]

Landlord's liability to tenants in capacity as adjoining occupier

12–08   As the owner of adjoining land, providing that the landlord is in actual possession of the land, he or she may become liable to a tenant in nuisance: *Sampson v. Hodson-Pressinger*[46]; *Gordon v. Selico Co. Limited*[47]; *Toff v. McDowell.*[48] The point was expressly decided in *Guppys (Bridport) Limited v. Brookling*[49]:

> "If a landlord uses his own property—it may be lawfully—in a way which unduly interferes with the enjoyment of his tenant's property . . . he falls fairly and squarely within the category of wrongdoers who commit the tort of nuisance."

Where, accordingly, the landlord has retained ownership and possession of the main walls of the building, but those walls let through water, which penetrates into the tenant's flat and causes dry rot, the landlord is liable in nuisance: *Gordon v. Selico Co. Limited.*[50] Where there was a flood into the tenant's premises as a result of blocked rainwater outlets in the roof, retained in the landlord's possession, despite clear warning, the landlord was liable in nuisance in *Tennant Radiant Heat Ltd v. Warrington Development Corporation.*[50a] The same result would follow where, for example, an adjacent flat or house owned by the landlord had become unoccupied and deteriorated so as to cause a nuisance to the tenant.

Where the landlord lets adjacent premises to another tenant for a purpose likely to cause a nuisance to the plaintiff tenant, then the landlord will be liable: *Harris v. James.*[51]

When the adjacent premises are so poorly sound insulated that noise nuisance is likely to be caused to the plaintiff tenant by

---

[43] *Supra.*
[44] *Supra.*
[45] (1929) 140 L.T. 1.
[46] *Supra.*
[47] [1985] 2 E.G.L.R. 79, [1986] 1 E.G.L.R. 71.
[48] (1993) 25 H.L.R. 650.
[49] (1983) 269 E.G. 846.
[50] *Supra.*
[50a] [1988] 1 E.G.L.R. 41.
[51] (1876) 45 L.J.Q.B. 545.

ordinary user by the adjacent tenant, both landlord and adjacent tenant are liable in nuisance: *Sampson v. Hodson-Pressinger.*[52] See also *Network Housing Association v. Westminster City Council*[52a]; *A. Lambert Flat Management Limited v. Lomas.*[52b]

A landlord who acquires the reversion is also liable, if he authorised the nuisance, for example by having knowledge of the nuisance when he or she acquires the reversion and by accepting rent: *Sampson v. Hodson-Pressinger.*[53] When the Crown acquired property as *bona vacantia* and tried to sell it instead of immediately disclaiming it, the Crown had not however authorised the nuisance of which it had been made aware: *Toff v. McDowell.*[54]

It is important to note that damages are payable and will not be reduced even though the user of the adjoining premises had been reasonable and ordinary, albeit that a nuisance had been caused: *Sampson v. Hodson-Pressinger*[55]; *Toff v. McDowell.*[56] In *Toff v. McDowell* damages against the owner of the adjoining premises were substantially increased when *unreasonable* behaviour by his sub-tenants had actually exacerbated the noise nuisance.

Nuisances caused by infestations

When cockroaches, or other vermin, enter the tenant's premises **12–09** via land or common parts (*e.g.* service ducts) retained in the ownership and control of the landlord, the landlord can be liable in nuisance: *Sharpe v. City of Manchester.*[57] When it can not be shown that the cockroaches, or other vermin, entered the tenant's premises from land owned by the landlord, the landlord will not be liable in nuisance: at least, not unless he or she retains sufficient power over the surrounding land (*e.g.* block of flats, or housing estate), from which the infestation does emanate, which would have entitled him or her to enter as of right to abate the nuisance: *Habinteg Housing Association v. James.*[58]

Nuisances caused by building works

Dust and noise caused by building works will not be a nuisance **12–10** if the defendant takes all reasonable and proper steps to ensure that

[52] *Supra.*
[52a] (1994) 27 H.L.R. 189.
[52b] [1981] 1 W.L.R. 898.
[53] *Supra.*
[54] *Supra.*
[55] *Supra.*
[56] *Supra.*
[57] (1977) 5 H.L.R. 71.
[58] (1994) 27 H.L.R. 299.

there is no undue inconvenience. In *Harrison v. Southwark &
Vauxhall Water Co.*,[59] Vaughan Williams said:

> "A man who pulls down a house for the purpose of building a
> new one no doubt causes considerable inconvenience to his
> next-door neighbours during the process of demolition; but he
> is not responsible as for a nuisance if he uses all reasonable
> skill and care to avoid annoyance to his neighbour by the
> works of demolition. Nor is he liable to an action even though
> the noise and dust and the consequent annoyance be such as
> would constitute a nuisance if the same, instead of being
> created for the purpose of demolition of the house, had been
> created in sheer wantonness, or in the execution of works for
> a purpose involving a permanent continuance of the dust and
> noise. For the law, in judging what constitutes a nuisance does
> take into consideration both the object and the duration of
> that which is said to constitute the nuisance."

If a builder fails to take all reasonable steps to minimise noise
and dust, then the employer of the builder will be liable even
though the builder is an independent contractor. That is because in
nuisance cases, defendants are liable for the actions even of
independent contractors if:

(1) If the defendant should reasonably have foreseen that the
    work the contractor was instructed to perform might cause
    a nuisance: *Matania v. National Provincial Bank Limited*[60]
    (foreseeability of dust and noise caused by building altera-
    tions).
(2) If the defendant owed the plaintiff a duty in any event to
    perform the activity delegated to the independent con-
    tractor, *e.g.* under a repairing obligation: *Sampson v.
    Wilson.*[61]

Building works are considered further below.[62]

---

[59] [1891] 2 Ch. 409.
[60] [1936] 2 All E.R. 633.
[61] *Supra.*
[62] See para. 13–02.

CHAPTER THIRTEEN

Breach of the Covenant of Quiet Enjoyment and Derogation from Grant

No new repairing obligations created

Whilst a failure to repair can amount to a breach of covenant of quiet enjoyment or a derogation from grant, those terms can not create repairing obligations where none existed before.

    13–01

It is not open to the tenant to claim that there has been a breach of the covenant for quiet enjoyment, for example, merely because the condition of the premises has materially interfered with his or her enjoyment of them. There is no breach of the covenant against derogation from grant merely because the condition of the premises has deteriorated to the point at which the tenant cannot use the premises as the parties intended: see *Hafton Properties v. Camp.*[1]

The law was summarised by Slade L.J. in *Duke of Westminster v. Guild*[2] as follows:

"This decision [*Booth v. Thomas*[3]] shows that a mere act of omission on the part of a landlord is capable of constituting a breach of the covenant for quiet enjoyment, if, but only if, there is a duty to do something.[4] In that case 'it was the duty of the owner of this culvert, which, if neglected, might cause

---

[1] [1994] 1 E.G.L.R. 67.
[2] [1985] 1 Q.B. 688.
[3] [1926] Ch. 397.
[4] See *ibid.* at p. 403, *per* Pollock M.R., and, at p. 410, *per* Sargant L.J.

damage to the adjacent property, to prevent such damage by taking reasonable precautions'.[5] In the present case, for the reasons given earlier in this judgment, we are of the opinion that no relevant duty fell on the plaintiffs. The express covenant for quiet enjoyment and implied covenant against derogation from grant cannot in our opinion be invoked so as to impose on them positive obligations to perform acts of repair which they would not otherwise be under any obligation to perform."

In *Booth v. Thomas*,[6] accordingly, the landlord was liable under the covenant of quiet enjoyment because he had failed in his duty to take reasonable care to keep an adjoining culvert, which he owned, in repair. In *Gordon v. Selico Co. Limited*[7] the landlord was liable under the covenant for quiet enjoyment for failing to comply with his duty to keep the exterior of a block of flats in repair, with the result that there was water penetration which caused an outbreak of dry rot in the tenant's flat. Where the tenant's premises were damaged by a flood from a water tank owned by the landlord, but the landlord had not failed on the facts to exercise reasonable care, there was no breach of the covenant for quiet enjoyment: *Anderson v. Oppenheimer*;[8] *Blake v. Woolf*.[9]

Building works

13–02 There can be no doubt, however, that a landlord can carry out works of repair to the premises or to adjoining premises in such a way as to make himself liable on the express or implied covenant for quiet enjoyment. In *Mira v. Aylmer Square Investments Limited*[10] His Honour Judge Newey Q.C. held that:

> "I have no doubt that the building operations authorised by Aylmer, resulting as they did in holes being made in the ceilings, vibrations causing cracks, water penetration, scaffolding restricting windows and causing loss of privacy and noise constituted breaches of the covenant for quiet enjoyment."

Sampson v. Wilson[11] was an even worse case, and resulted in the landlord being found liable under sections 27 and 28 of the Housing Act 1988:

---

[5] See pp. 403–409, *per* Pollock M.R.
[6] *Supra.*
[7] [1985] 2 E.G.L.R. 79.
[8] (1880) 5 Q.B.D. 602.
[9] [1988] 2 Q.B. 426.
[10] (1989) 21 H.L.R. 284 (affirmed at (1990) 22 H.L.R. 182).
[11] (1994) 26 H.L.R. 486.

"It has to my mind all the appearances of classic harassment. Work is started at no notice to do things that will be unpleasant and uncomfortable for the tenant; work stops when the premises are in a worse state; the excuse is lack of money, which could have been foreseen at the start—it is not a big job—and lies are told about it. In my judgment, the truth of what was going on was quite deliberate harassment . . . ."

CHAPTER FOURTEEN

The Occupiers Liability Act 1957

General principles

14–01 Under the Occupiers Liability Act 1957 the "occupier" of premises owes the "common duty of care" to all visitors except in so far as he is free to and does restrict his liability.[1]

The duty of care

14–02 The common duty of care is a duty to take such care as in all the circumstances of the case is reasonable to see that the visitor will be reasonably safe in using the premises for the purposes for which he or she is invited there.[2]

The 1957 Act contains provisions which explain the standard of care and is considered in detail in *Clerk and Lindsell on Torts*.[3]

Who is the occupier for the purposes of the Act

14–03 A person is regarded as an "occupier" for the purposes of the Occupiers Liability Act 1957 if he or she has a sufficient degree of control over premises to be able to ensure their safety and to appreciate that a failure on his or her part to use care may result in injury to a person coming on to the premises: *Wheat v. E. Lacon & Co. Limited*.[4] A landlord who lets out the whole premises is treated as parting with all control and is not an occupier for the purposes

---

[1] s.2(1).
[2] s.2(2).
[3] 17th ed., Chap. 10.
[4] [1966] A.C. 552.

of the Act even when he has undertaken the right to repair: *Wheat v. E. Lacon & Co. Limited*[5]; *Dear v. London Borough of Newham*.[6]

Such a landlord remains liable, however, under section 4 of the Defective Premises Act 1972 in respect of defects to the premises demised. He or she also remains liable, however, as the occupier, in respect of parts of the premises retained and excluded from the demise, such as a common staircase (*Miller v. Hancock*[7]; *Fairman v. Perpetual Investment Building Society*[8]), a balcony (*Sutcliffe v. Clients Investments Co.*[9]) or a forecourt (*Jacobs v. L.C.C.*[10]).

A licensor may be treated as remaining the occupier of the entirety of the premises, at least when the terms of the licence indicate that he or she retains a sufficient degree of practical control: *Greene v. Chelsea L.B.C.*[11]; *Wheat v. E. Lacon & Co. Limited*.[12]

Potential plaintiffs

The 1957 Act is most likely to be of potential use when claims for **14–04** personal injury or property damage are made by third parties: tenant's visitors, or invitees such as milkmen, postmen and the like. For example, in *Jordan v. Achara*[13] the landlord was held liable to compensate for personal injury when the meter reader employed by the Electricity Board fell down unlit stairs in the common parts. The stairs were unlit because the landlord had failed to pay for electricity and as a result the supply had been cut off: the meter reader was coming to re-instate the supply by arrangement with the local authority.

It is, however, probable that a tenant lawfully using the common parts would be treated as a visitor for the purposes of the 1957 Act and, accordingly, owed the common duty of care by his or her landlord. For example, a claim brought by the tenant who fell down unlit stairs failed on the facts in *Irving v. London County Council*.[14] The Act could potentially be of use in such circumstances, given that the duty created by section 4 of the Defective Premises Act 1972 relates only to relevant defects to the premises and not to the common parts. On the other hand, landlords can be liable in nuisance and will be subject to an implied obligation to

[5] *Supra.*
[6] (1987) 19 H.L.R. 391.
[7] [1893] 2 Q.B. 177.
[8] [1923] A.C. 74.
[9] [1924] 2 K.B. 746.
[10] [1950] A.C. 361.
[11] [1954] 2 Q.B. 127.
[12] *Supra.*
[13] (1988) 20 H.L.R. 607.
[14] (1965) 109 S.J. 157.

take reasonable care to ensure that parts of the building retained in their control do not cause personnel injury or property damage.[15]

Landowners are not liable under the Occupiers Liability Act 1957 to persons injured by the condition of land over which they are exercising a public right of way as such persons are not invitees or licensees (*cf.* the position of tenants using the path as a means of access to their dwelling-house).[16]

Exclusion

14–05   The landlord is free to exclude liability under section 2(1) of the 1957 Act. The Unfair Contract Terms Act 1977 will probably not apply to such an exclusion clause: *Electricity Supply Nomineees Limited v. I A F Group Limited.*[17]

---

[15] See para. 8–08.
[16] *McGeown v. Northern Ireland Housing Executive* [1995] 1 A.C. 233.
[17] [1993] 1 W.L.R. 1059.

CHAPTER FIFTEEN

The Environmental Protection Act 1990

Introduction

Part III of the Environmental Protection Act 1990 is directed **15–01** towards the abatement of "statutory nuisances". It provides two methods by which this can be achieved:

(1) If a local authority is satisfied that a statutory nuisance exists, or is likely to occur or recur, the local authority is under a duty to serve an abatement notice under section 80 of the Environmental Protection Act 1990. If the person served fails to successfully appeal the notice within 21 days of service and fails to comply with the abatement notice without reasonable excuse he or she is guilty of a criminal offence and can be fined on summary conviction for the offence and any continuation thereof. The magistrates can not order the wrong-doer to abate the nuisance but in addition to, or instead of prosecuting, the local authority can abate the statutory nuisance and recover the costs under section 81 of the Environmental Protection Act 1990. If the works are urgently required the local authority can serve notice under section 76(1) of the Building Act 1984 stating that it intends to remedy specified defects (and recover its reasonable expenses).

(2) A "person aggrieved" by a statutory nuisance can serve a statutory letter before action specifying the matters complained of under section 82(6) of the Environmental Protection Act 1990 and take summary proceedings against the wrong-doer in the magistrates' court. If the magistrates are

117

satisfied that the statutory nuisance exists or is likely to recur they are required to order the wrong-doer to abate the nuisance or carry out works to prevent a recurrence and may fine the wrong-doer. In addition, the magistrates can make a compensation order under section 35 of the Powers of Criminal Courts Act 1973.

The Act does not generally give rise to a civil cause of action or create a duty of care towards the tenant: *Dear v. Newham L.B.C.*[1] *London Borough of Hackney v. Issa.*[1a]

The Environmental Protection Act 1990 can however be used by tenants to obtain nuisance orders requiring landlords to repair and if necessary improve dwelling houses which have become prejudicial to health or afflicted by a nuisance. It is this aspect of the Act which this chapter examines. It is, however, worth bearing in mind the context of Part III of the Act as a whole, so as not to lose touch with the basic environmental regulatory framework within which actions by tenants under section 82 of the Environmental Protection Act 1990 exist.

The text of relevant parts of the Act

15–02   The text of the Act as set out below contains something of the general environmental context. The scheme of the relevant parts of the Act is as follows:

(1) Section 79: basic definition of statutory nuisances, section 79(1)(a) being the relevant limb for present purposes. Section 79(7) contains crucial definitions: in particular, "person responsible" and "prejudicial to health".

Statutory nuisances and inspections therefor

79.—(1) [Subject to subsections (2) to (6A) below], the following matters constitute 'statutory nuisances' for the purposes of this Part, that is to say—
  (a) any premises in such a state as to be prejudicial to health or a nuisance;
  (b) smoke emitted from premises so as to be prejudicial to health or a nuisance;
  (c) fumes or gases emitted from premises so as to be prejudicial to health or a nuisance;
  (d) any dust, steam or other effluvia arising on industrial, trade or business premises and being prejudicial to health or a nuisance;

---

[1] (1987) 19 H.L.R. 391; *The Times*, February 23, 1988.
[1a] Unreported Court of Appeal judgment of November 19, 1996 (Ref. CCRTF/ 95/1682/E).

(e) any accumulation or deposit which is prejudicial to health or a nuisance;

(f) any animal kept in such a place or manner as to be prejudicial to health or a nuisance;

(g) noise emitted from premises so as to be prejudicial to health or a nuisance;

[(ga) noise that is prejudicial to health or a nuisance and is emitted from or caused by a vehicle, machinery or equipment in a street;]

(h) any other matter declared by any enactment to be a statutory nuisance;

and it shall be the duty of every local authority to cause its area to be inspected from time to time to detect statutory nuisances which ought to be dealt with under section 80 below [or sections 80 and 80A below] and, where a complaint of statutory nuisance is made to it by a person living within its area, to take such steps as are reasonably practicable to investigate the complaint.

[. . .]

(4) Subsection (1)(c) above does not apply in relation to premises other than private dwellings;

(5) Subsection (1)(d) above does not apply to steam emitted from a railway locomotive engine;

(6) Subsection (1)(g) does not apply to noise caused by aircraft other than model aircraft;

(6A) Subsection (1)(ga) above does not apply to noise made—

(a) by traffic [. . .]

(7) In this Part—

[. . .]

'equipment' includes a musical instrument . . .

'person responsible'—

(a) in relation to a statutory nuisance, means the person to whose act, default or sufferance the nuisance is attributable . . .

'prejudicial to health' means injurious, or likely to cause injury, to health;

'premises' includes land and, subject to subsection (12) [and section 81A(9)] below, any vessel;

'private dwelling' means any building or part of a building, used or intended to be used as a dwelling; . . .

['street' means a highway and any other road, footway, square or court that is for the time being open to the public;]

and any expression used in this section and in [the Clean Air Act 1993] have the same meaning in this section as in that Act and [section 3 of the Clean Air Act 1993] shall apply for the interpretation of the expression 'dark smoke' and the operation of this Part in relation to it.

(9) In this Part "best practicable means" is to be interpreted by reference to the following provisions—

(a) 'practicable' means reasonably practicable having regard among other things to local conditions and circumstances, to the current state of technical knowledge and to the financial implications;

(b) the means to be employed include the design, installation, maintenance and manner and periods of operation of plant and machinery, and the design, construction and maintenance of buildings and structures;

(c) the test is to apply only in so far as compatible with any duty imposed by the law;

(d) the test is to apply only so far as compatible with safety and safe working conditions, and with the exigencies of any emergency or unforeseeable circumstances;

and, in circumstances where a code of practice under section 71 of the Control of Pollution Act 1974 (noise minimisation) is applicable, regard shall be had to guidance given in it.

15–03   (2) Sections 80 and 81 relate to the powers exercisable by local authorities and are included only for completeness and for the purposes of cross-reference.

Summary proceedings for statutory nuisances

80—(1) Where a local authority is satisfied that a statutory nuisance exists, or is likely to occur or recur, in the area of the authority, the local authority shall serve a notice ('an abatement notice') imposing all or any of the following requirements—

(a) requiring the abatement of the nuisance or prohibiting or restricting its occurrence or recurrence;

(b) requiring the execution of such works, and the taking of such other steps, as may be necessary for any of those purposes, and the notice shall specify the time or times within which the requirements of the notice are to be complied with.

(2) [Subject to section 80 A(1) below, the abatement notice] shall be served—

(a) except in a case falling within paragraph (b) or (c) below, on the person responsible for the nuisance;

(b) where the nuisance arises from any defect of a structural character, on the owner of the premises;

(c) where the person responsible for the nuisance cannot be found or the nuisance has not yet occurred, on the owner or occupier of the premises.

(3) [A person served with an abatement notice] may appeal against the notice to a magistrates' court within the period of twenty-one days beginning with the date on which he was served with the notice.

(4) If a person on whom an abatement notice is served, without reasonable excuse, contravenes or fails to comply with any requirement or prohibition imposed by the notice, he shall be guilty of an offence.

(5) Except in a case falling within subsection (6) below, a person who commits an offence under subsection (4) above shall be liable on summary conviction to a fine not exceeding level 5 on the standard scale together with a further fine of an amount equal to one-tenth of that level for each day on which the offence continues after the conviction.

(6) A person who commits an offence under subsection (4) above on industrial, trade or business premises shall be liable on summary conviction to a fine not exceeding £20,000.

(7) Subject to subsection (8) below, in any proceedings for an offence under subsection (4) above in respect of a statutory nuisance it shall be a defence to prove that the best practicable means were used to prevent, or to counteract the effects of, the nuisance.

(8) The defence under subsection (7) above is not available—

(a) in the case of a nuisance falling within paragraph (a), (d), (e), (f) or (g) of section 79(1) above except where the nuisance arises on industrial, trade or business premises;

(aa) in the case of a nuisance falling within paragraph (ga) of section 79(1) above except where the noise is emitted from or caused by a vehicle, machinery or equipment being used for industrial, trade or business purposes;

(b) in the case of a nuisance falling within paragraph (b) of section 79(1) above except where the smoke is emitted from a chimney; and

(c) in the case of a nuisance falling within paragraph (c) or (h) of section 79(1) above.

(9) In proceedings for an offence under subsection (4) above in respect of a statutory nuisance falling within paragraph (g) of section 79(1) above where the offence consists in contravening requirements imposed by virtue of subsection (1)(a) above it shall be a defence to prove—

(a) that the alleged offence was covered by a notice served under section 60 or a consent given under section 61 or 65 of the Control of Pollution Act 1974 (construction sites etc); or

(b) where the alleged offence was committed at a time when the premises were subject to a notice under section 66 of that Act (noise reduction notice), that the level of noise emitted from the premises at that time was not such as to constitute a contravention of the notice under that section; or

(c) where the alleged offence was committed at a time when the premises were not subject to notice under section 66 of that Act, and when a level fixed under section 67 of that Act (new buildings liable to abatement order) applied to the premises, that the level of noise emitted from the premises at that time did not exceed that level.

(10) Paragraphs (b) and (c) of subsection (9) above shall apply whether or not the relevant notice was subject to appeal at the time when the offence was alleged to have been committed.

Abatement notice in respect of noise in street

[80A.—(1) In the case of a statutory nuisance within section 79(1)(ga) above that—

(a) has not yet occurred, or

(b) arises from noise emitted from or caused by an unattended vehicle or unattended machinery or equipment, the abatement notice shall be served in accordance with subsection (2) below.

(2) The notice shall be served—

(a) where the person responsible for the vehicle, machinery or equipment can be found, on that person;

(b) where that person cannot be found or where the local authority determines that this paragraph should

apply, by fixing the notice to the vehicle, machinery or
equipment . . .]

Supplementary provisions

81.—(1)[Subject to subsection (1A) below, where] more
than one person is responsible for a statutory nuisance
section 80 above shall apply to each of those persons
whether or not what any one of them is responsible for
would by itself amount to a nuisance.
[(1A) In relation to a statutory nuisance within section
79(1)(ga) above for which more than one person is responsible (whether or not what any one of those persons is
responsible for would by itself amount to such a nuisance),
section 80(2)(a) above shall apply with the substitution of
'any one of the persons' for 'any person';
(1B) In relation to a statutory nuisance within section
79(1)(ga) above caused by noise emitted from or caused by
an unattended vehicle or unattended machinery or equipment for which more than one person is responsible,
section 80A above shall apply with the substitution—
(a) in substitution 2(a), 'any of the persons' for 'the
    person' and of 'one such person' for 'that person'
    . . .]
(2) Where a statutory nuisance which exists or has
occurred within the area of a local authority, or which has
affected any part of that area, appears to the local authority to be wholly or partly caused by some act or default
committed or taking place outside the area, the local
authority may act under section 80 above as if the act or
default were wholly within that area, except that any
appeal shall be heard by a magistrates' court having
jurisdiction where the act or default is alleged to have
taken place.
(3) Where an abatement notice has not been complied
with the local authority may, whether or not they take
proceedings for an offence under section 80(4) above,
abate the nuisance and do whatever may be necessary in
execution of the notice.
(4) Any expenses reasonably incurred by a local authority
in abating, or preventing the recurrence of, a statutory
nuisance under subsection (3) above may be recovered by
them from the person by whose act or default the nuisance
was caused and, if that person is the owner of the premises, from any person who is for the time being the owner
thereof; and the court may apportion the expenses
between persons by whose acts or defaults the nuisance is

caused in such manner as the court considers fair and reasonable.

(5) If a local authority is of opinion that proceedings for an offence under section 80(4) above would afford an inadequate remedy in the case of any statutory nuisance, they may, subject to subsection (6) below, take proceedings in the High Court for the purpose of securing the abatement, prohibition or restriction of the nuisance, and the proceedings shall be maintainable notwithstanding the local authority have suffered no damage from the nuisance.

(6) In any proceedings under subsection (5) above in respect of a nuisance falling within paragraph (g) [or (ga)] of section 79(1) above, it shall be a defence to prove that the noise was authorised by a notice under section 60 or a consent under section 61 (construction sites) of the Control of Pollution Act 1974.

(7) The further supplementary provisions in Schedule 3 to this Act shall have effect.

Expenses recoverable from owner to be a charge on premises

[81A.—(1) Where any expenses are recoverable under section 81(4) above a person who is the owner of the premises there mentioned and the local authority serves a notice on him under this section—

(a) the expenses shall carry interest, at such reasonable rate as the local authority may determine, from the date of service of the notice until the whole amount is paid, and
(b) subject to the following provisions of this section, the expenses and accrued interest shall be a charge on the premises . . .]

Payment of expenses by instalments

[81B.—(1) Where any expenses are a charge on premises under section 81A above, the local authority may by order declare the expenses to be payable with interest by instalments within the specified period, until the whole amount is paid . . .]

15–04   (3) Section 82 contains the code for actions by persons aggrieved.

Summary proceedings by persons aggrieved by statutory nuisances

82.—(1) A magistrates' court may act under this section on a complaint made by any person on the ground that he is aggrieved by the existence of a statutory nuisance.

(2) If the magistrates' court is satisfied that the alleged nuisance exists, or that although abated is likely to recur on the same premises [or, in the case of a nuisance within section 79(1)(ga) above in the same street], the court shall make an order for either or both of the following purposes—

(a) requiring the defendant to abate the nuisance, within a time specified in the order, and to execute any works necessary for that purpose;

(b) prohibiting a recurrence of the nuisance, and requiring the defendant, within a time specified in the order, to execute any works necessary to prevent the recurrence;

and may also impose on the defendant a fine not exceeding level 5 on the standard scale.

(3) If the magistrates' court is satisfied that the alleged nuisance exists and is such as, in the opinion of the court, to render premises unfit for human habitation, an order under subsection (2) above may prohibit the use of the premises for human habitation until the premises are, to the satisfaction of the court, rendered fit for that purpose.

(4) Proceedings for an order under subsection (2) above shall be brought—

(a) except in a case falling within paragraph [(b), (c) or (d) below], against the person responsible for the nuisance;

(b) where the nuisance arises from any defect of a structural character, against the owner of the premises;

(c) where the person responsible for the nuisance cannot be found, against the owner or occupier of the premises.

(d) in the case of a statutory nuisance within section 79(1)(ga) above caused by noise emitted from or caused by an unattended vehicle or unattended machinery or equipment, against the person responsible for the vehicle, machinery or equipment.

(5) [Subject to subsection 5A below, where] more than one person is responsible for a statutory nuisance, subsection (1) to (4) above shall apply to each of those persons whether or not what any one of them is responsible for would by itself amount to a nuisance.

[(5A) In relation to a statutory nuisance within section 79(1)(ga) above for which more than one person is responsible (whether or not what any one of those persons is responsible for would by itself amount to such a nuisance), subsection (4)(a) above shall apply with the substitution of 'each person responsible for the nuisance who can be found' for 'the person responsible for the nuisance'.

(5B) In relation to a statutory nuisance within section 79(1)(ga) above caused by noise emitted from or caused by an unattended vehicle or unattended machinery or equipment of which more than one person is responsible, subsection (4)(d) above shall apply with the substitution of 'any person' for 'the person'.]

(6) Before instituting proceedings for an order under subsection (2) above against any person, the person aggrieved by the nuisance shall give to that person such notice in writing of his intention to bring the proceedings as is applicable to proceedings in respect of a nuisance of that description and the notice shall specify the matter complained of.

(7) The notice of the bringing of proceedings in respect of a statutory nuisance required by subsection (6) above which is applicable is—

(a) in the case of a nuisance falling within paragraph (g) [or (ga)] of section 79(1) above, not less than 3 days' notice; and

(b) in the case of a nuisance of any other description, not less than twenty-one days' notice;

but the Secretary of State may, by order, provide that this subsection shall have effect as if such period as is specified in the order were the minimum period of notice applicable to any description of statutory nuisance specified in the order.

(8) A person who, without reasonable excuse, contravenes any requirement or prohibition imposed by an order under subsection (2) above shall be guilty of an offence and liable on summary conviction to a fine not exceeding level 5 on the standard scale together with a further fine of an amount equal to one-tenth of that level for each day on which the offence continues after the conviction.

(9) Subject to subsection (10) below, in any proceedings for an offence under subsection (8) above in respect of a statutory nuisance it shall be a defence to prove that the best practicable means were used to prevent, or to counteract the effects of, the nuisance.

(10) The defence under subsection (9) above is not available—

(a) in the case of a nuisance falling within paragraph (a), (d), (e), (f) or (g) of section 79(1) above except where the nuisance arises on industrial, trade or business premises;

[(aa) in the case of a nuisance falling within paragraph (ga) of section 79(1) above except where the noise is emitted from or caused by a vehicle, machinery or equipment being used for industrial, trade or business purposes;]

(b) in the case of a nuisance falling within paragraph (b) of section 79(1) above except where the smoke is emitted from a chimney;

(c) in the case of a nuisance falling within paragraph (c) or (h) of section 79(1) above; and

(d) in the case of a nuisance which is such as to render the premises unfit for human habitation.

(11) If a person is convicted of an offence under subsection (8) above, a magistrates' court may, after giving the local authority in whose area the nuisance has occurred an opportunity of being heard, direct the authority to do anything which the person convicted was required to do by the order to which the conviction relates.

(12) Where on the hearing of proceedings for an order under subsection (2) above it is proved that the alleged nuisance existed at the date of the making of the complaint then, whether or not at the date of the hearing it still exists or is likely to recur, the court shall order the defendant (or defendants in such proportions as appears fair and reasonable) to pay to the person bringing the proceedings such amount as the court considers reasonably sufficient to compensate him for any expenses properly and reasonably incurred by him in the proceedings.

(13) If it appears to the magistrates' court that neither the person responsible for the nuisance nor the owner or occupier of the premises [or, (as the case may be) the person responsible for the vehicle, machinery or equipment] can be found the court may, after gibing the local authority in whose area the nuisance has occurred an opportunity of being heard, direct the authority to do anything which the court would have ordered that person to do.[2]

[2] Words in square brackets added by the Noise and Statutory Nuisance Act 1993.

Statutory nuisance

15–05   Section 79(1)(a) defines "statutory nuisances" as including "any premises in such a state as to be prejudicial to health or a nuisance".

Any premises

15–06   Section 79(7) defines "premises" as including all land "and vessels". The phrase plainly includes houses, flats, common parts, houseboats, land in its "natural" state and commercial buildings (although parts of the Act are directed only at private dwellings and parts are directed only at commercial premises.[3]

In *Birmingham District Council v. McMahon*[4] it was held that a block of flats as a whole, as well as each individual flat, was capable of being described as "premises" for the purposes of what is now section 79(1)(a). A tenant could accordingly take action in respect of the block of flats when the statutory nuisance in his or her individual flat was caused by the condition of the block as a whole, "as designed, constructed and weathered":

> "It is possible to envisage in a block of flats a prejudice to health which is not confined to any one constituent unit in the block, and which can only be related to the entire block. In that event, providing the evidence of nuisance is sufficiently compelling, the Court might well be driven to making a comprehensive order of the kind sought here."

On the facts of the case, however, although each tenant had similar complaints and sought similar remedies, there were separate statutory nuisances arising in each of the separate flats whose tenants had brought proceedings (there was direct evidence in relation to only 16 out of the 52 flats in the block). The nuisance order made by the magistrate was set aside on appeal on the ground that a tenant cannot be a "person aggrieved" for the purposes of what is now section 82 of the Act in relation to the block as a whole, when his or her complaint, on the facts, relates only to the condition of his or her individual flat.

Prejudicial to health

15–07   "Prejudicial to health" is defined in section 79(7) of the Act as "injurious, or likely to cause injury, to health". It has been

---

[3] Compare s.79(1)(d) with s.79(1)(c) read with s.79(4). The meaning of "land" is further extended by section 5 and Schedule 1 of the Interpretation Act 1980. The meaning of "premises" is further extended by section 268 of the Public Health Act 1938, as amended.

[4] (1987) 19 H.L.R. 452.

suggested that the expression means "something which produces a threat to health in the sense of a threat of disease, vermin or the like".[4a] "Health" is likely to include both physical and mental health. The definition of "personal injuries" contained in section 48 of the Limitation Act 1980 as "[including] any disease and any impairment of a person's physical or mental condition" has been applied in a variety of contexts as at least a helpful guide to the meaning of "personal injury" and is likely to be at least persuasive in this context also.[5]

Prejudice to health—a question of fact or expert evidence?

Whether premises are "prejudicial to health" is a question of fact: *Salford City Council v. McNally*.[6] It is, however, a question of fact "outside the field where a tribunal is entitled to draw on its own experience. That is a matter upon which the tribunal needs informed expert evidence": *Patel v. Mehtab*.[7]   **15–08**

A more relaxed view of the need for expert evidence was taken in *Southwark L.B.C. v. Ince*[8]:

"Before the magistrates it was argued that a court could not find that premises were in such a state as to be prejudicial to health by reason of noise unless expert evidence of injury to health was adduced. However, before us, Mr Jones made clear that he did not pursue that particular contention. The magistrates expressed themselves satisfied from the evidence of the respondents that the noise in their respective flats had adversely and materially affected their health. There was in fact some expert evidence, not relating to health but relating to noise, to the effect that the noise levels in the flats in question were indeed very high. In these circumstances, I conclude that the magistrates were justified in reaching the view which they did, that the premises were in such a state as to be prejudicial to health."

In proceedings brought under the Act evidence is invariably given on behalf of tenants by qualified Environmental Health Officers, qualified to give expert evidence as to both the physical condition of the premises and its effect, or likely effect, upon health. Where such evidence is not contradicted by evidence from another qualified expert then, it would appear to follow from *Patel*

[4a] *Coventry City Council v. Cartwright* [1975] 1 W.L.R. 845, at 849.
[5] See further paras. 23–02, 23–03.
[6] [1976] A.C. 379.
[7] (1980) 5 H.L.R. 80.
[8] (1989) 21 H.L.R. 504.

v. Mehtab,[9] that the magistrates are bound to convict unless they did not believe the expert evidence.

Cases in which there is no prejudice to health

15–09   Premises are not "prejudicial to health" merely because their condition interferes with the personal comfort of the occupiers: *Salford City Council v. McNally.*[10] There is accordingly no statutory nuisance if the premises are an eyesore or in decorative disrepair: *Springett v. Harold*[11]; *Coventry City Council v. Cartwright.*[12] There is no prejudice to health merely because of inert matter, for example a pile of building materials, which might cause cuts or bruises if trodden upon: *Coventry City Council v. Cartwright.*[13]

It follows that neither disrepair in breach of the terms of the agreement nor even the fact that premises are unfit for human habitation (*Salford City Council v. McNally*[14]) *necessarily* prove that premises are "prejudicial to health". The disrepair or unfitness has to injure or be likely to injure health.

Prejudice to health when the landlord is not in breach of contract

15–10   Conversely, the fact that the landlord has complied with all of his or her repairing obligations is *nihil ad rem* if the premises are nonetheless in such a condition as to be injurious or likely to injure health: *Birmingham District Council v. Kelly,*[15] *Clayton v. Sale Urban District Council.*[15a]

For example, condensation causing damp and mould growth arising out of the inherently defective construction of the dwelling very frequently does not involve the landlord in any breach of his or her express or implied repairing obligations: *Quick v. Taff-Ely Borough Council.*[16] If it results, however, in the premises becoming injurious or likely to cause injury to health, the landlord can be liable under the Act: *Birmingham District Council v. Kelly.*[17]

Premises from which noise emanates

15–11   Noise caused by animals falls within section 79(1)(g) and not section 79(1)(f) which is directed at the condition of the premises

[9] (1980) 5 H.L.R. 78.
[10] *Supra.*
[11] [1954] 1 All E.R. 568.
[12] [1975] 1 W.L.R. 845.
[13] *Supra.*
[14] *Supra.*
[15] *Supra.*
[15a] [1926] 1 K.B. 415.
[16] [1985] 3 All E.R. 321.
[17] *Supra.*

in which animals are kept (*e.g.* smells): *Galer v. Morrisey*.[18] Section 79(1)(g) of the Act now specifically provides that noise (defined to include vibrations) emitted from premises so as to be prejudicial to health or a nuisance can constitute a statutory nuisance. Accordingly, in *Network Housing Association v. Westminster City Council*[19] the freeholder was found liable under section 79(1)(g) in respect of noise nuisance occurring as a result of the combination of reasonable everyday activities by the flat-owners and the lack of adequate sound insulation in the voids between the flats, retained in the possession of the freeholder. The noise, although originating from the flat-owners nonetheless was "emitted" from premises (the void between the flats) in the sense that smoke is "emitted" from chimneys. The Act now deals with noise caused by vehicles, machinery or equipment in the street.[20]

Premises affected by noise

Premises which do not have adequate sound insulation with the result that the occupiers suffer unusually high noise levels (from other parts of a block of flats or from outside) can be premises in such a state as to be prejudicial to health.[21] In *A Lambert Flat Management Limited v. Lomas*[22] noise and vibration from lifts was held to be a "nuisance" within the meaning of the second limb of the statutory nuisance definition. **15–12**

Or a nuisance

"Nuisance" in the Act has the same meaning as public or private nuisance at common law.[23] *National Coal Board v. Thorne*[24]: **15–13**

> "A public nuisance at common law has been expressed to be an act or omission which materially affects the material comfort and quality of a class of Her Majesty's subjects. A private nuisance has often been defined in this way: private nuisances, at least in the vast majority of cases, are interferences for a substantial length of time by owners or occupiers of property with the use or enjoyment of neighbouring property."

---

[18] [1955] 1 W.L.R. 110 (doubted in *Coventry City Council v. Cartwright, supra*).
[19] (1994) 27 H.L.R. 189.
[20] s.79(1)(ga).
[21] *Southwark L.B.C. v. Ince supra* (flats prejudicial to health because not adequately sound-insulated; noise and vibration from traffic was as a matter of fact "adversely and materially" affecting tenants' health).
[22] [1981] 1 W.L.R. 898.
[23] See Chapter 12.
[24] [1976] 1 W.L.R. 543.

Accordingly, the tenant seeking redress under the Environmental Protection Act 1990 will not succeed under the "nuisance" limb unless his or her complaint arises out of the condition or use of *neighbouring* property. The tenant will not succeed if he or she can only show that the condition of the dwelling itself affects his or her reasonable enjoyment of the dwelling: *Betts v. Penge Urban District Council*.[25]

If the tenant can overcome that hurdle, however, and establish that his or her complaint does relate to the condition or use of neighbouring property, then the tenant does not have to go so far as to prove "prejudice to health". He or she merely has to show undue interference with his or her use or enjoyment of the dwelling.[26]

In *A Lambert Flat Management Limited v. Lomas*[27] noise and vibrations from lifts in the common parts were held to be premises which were a "nuisance".

The "person aggrieved" in section 82

15–14   A "person aggrieved" can be the tenant of the affected premises: *Birmingham District Council v. McMahon*.[28] There seems no reason in principle why a person aggrieved could not be a licensee or family member, providing there was a substantial link between that person and the dwelling in question.[29]

The correct defendant

15–15   As section 82(4) makes clear, the general rule is that proceedings are to be brought against the "person responsible for the nuisance" unless he or she "cannot be found" in which case proceedings have to brought against the owner or occupier. The exception to the general rule arises when the statutory nuisance "arises from any defect of a structural character" in which case proceedings have to be brought against the "owner".

The person responsible

15–16   "Person responsible" is defined in section 79(7) as "the person to whose act, default or sufferance the nuisance is attributable".

To put it bluntly, the issue in most proceedings under the Act is whether (as the tenant contends) the landlord is responsible for the

---

[25] [1942] 2 K.B. 154.
[26] *Salford City Council v. McNally* [1976] A.C. 379, at 389E. See further Chapter 12.
[27] *Supra.*
[28] *Supra.*
[29] See, by analogy, *Hunter v. Canary Wharf Limited* [1996] 1 All E.R. 482.

statutory nuisance or whether (as the landlord contends) the tenant is responsible for it. Such arguments will turn upon the facts of each case, but it may be helpful to bear in mind the dicta of Dillon L.J. in *Quick v. Taff-Ely Borough Council*[30]:

> "the judge appreciated that some people for financial reasons have to be sparing in their use of central heating, and he found that there was no evidence at all to suggest that the life-style of the tenant and his family was likely to give rise to condensation problems because it was outside the spectrum of life-styles which a local authority could reasonably expect its tenants to follow."

How can a tenant or occupier be the person responsible?

It is not necessary for the landlord to show that the tenant has acted in an abusive or irresponsible manner. **15–17**

In *Dover District Council v. Farrar*[31] it was held that if condensation causing a prejudice to health was not caused by any disrepair, design or construction defect, but by the tenant's failure to use the heating system, and the tenant's use, instead, of other forms of heating which on the facts increased the condensation risk, then the tenant and not the landlord was the "person to whose act, default or sufferance the nuisance is attributable".

The tenants had alleged that the form of heating supplied by the landlord was too expensive: such a view was not unreasonable. What was crucial, however, was the finding that:

> "the construction of the houses, and the method of heating supplied by the appellant council, were perfectly proper and perfectly adequate and would have maintained these houses in a state in which there was no question of their being prejudicial to health, provided that the system supplied was used by the tenant."

This was explained in *Greater London Council v. London Borough of Tower Hamlets*[32] by Griffiths L.J. who said:

> "I do not read Ormrod L.J. as saying that if a landlord provides a property which, because of the peculiar aspects of its construction, renders it wholly exceptionally vulnerable to condensation, he can escape any liability for danger to the health of those living within by asserting that the occupants should have used wholly abnormal quantities of fuel."

[30] *Supra.*
[31] (1980) 2 H.L.R. 32.
[32] (1984) 15 H.L.R. 54.

In short, if the heating system is defective, unsuitable or abnor-
mally expensive, and as a result a statutory nuisance arises, it is
probable that, on the facts, the magistrates will decide that the
landlord and not the tenant is the "person responsible".

In *Warner v. Lambeth L.B.C.*[33] it was found on the facts that at
all times since the statutory nuisance had been drawn to the
attention of the landlord it had been "willing and anxious" to carry
out the necessary work to abate it but had been refused access by
the tenants, who had also refused "three genuine efforts to provide
alternative accommodation". Although the result might have been
different had the prosecution been brought on the "owner" basis,
in respect of structural defects, on those facts, although the
landlord "may have been responsible for the original arising of the
nuisance" the landlord "[was] not responsible for its continued
existence . . . [and was] not the person by whose act, default or
sufferance the statutory nuisance continued".

The landlord as the person responsible

15–18   Public sector as well as private sector landlords can be defendants to action under section 82 of the Act: *R. v. Epping (Waltham
Abbey) Justices, ex p. Birlinson.*[34] A local authority (*e.g.* the environmental health department) cannot, however, serve an abatement
notice on itself: *R. v. Cardiff City Council, ex p. Cross.*[35]

In *Greater London Council v. Tower Hamlets L.B.C.*[36] the Court of
Appeal held that, in order to avoid being the "person responsible"
for a statutory nuisance arising as a result of condensation,
dampness and mould, the landlord is obliged to take positive steps
to ensure that the dwelling-house he or she rents out is properly
designed and constructed from the point of view of preventing such
defects:

> "If the construction of a building is so unusual that there has
> to be some special form of heating to combat condensation, it
> is reasonable that the landlord should be expected to install
> items such as storage heaters to provide that warmth. Of
> course, if the tenant does not choose to use the facilities
> provided, he will have no cause for complaint if the result is
> that condensation makes the place uninhabitable.
>
> A landlord is required to apply his mind to the necessity of
> ventilation and, if need be, to insulation and heating. The
> landlord must provide a combination of these factors to make

[33] (1984) 15 H.L.R. 42.
[34] [1948] 1 K.B. 79.
[35] (1983) 6 H.L.R. 1.
[36] *Supra.*

a house habitable for the tenant. However, once the landlord has provided the facilities, the tenant must use them . . . ."

If there was some step which the landlord could have taken and which would have prevented the statutory nuisance arising then he or she is the "person responsible" even though:

(1) The premises were built in accordance with the current building regulations.
(2) The landlord has complied with all his or her repairing obligations.

Birmingham District Council v. Kelly.[37]

The owner

A person is treated as being the "owner" for the purposes of **15–19** section 82(4)(b) if he or she owns the flat which has become prejudicial to health, even though he or she does not own the wall subject to the structural defect causing the prejudice to health (*e.g.* because he or she owns the flat under a long lease and the main walls were retained in the ownership of the freeholder): *Pollway Nominees v. Havering L.B.C.*[38]

As he or she will not be able to remedy the defect, he or she also becomes a "person aggrieved" and can proceed under section 82 against the freeholder and seek a contribution order. Alternatively, the intermediate landlord can exercise his or her civil rights against the freeholder.

It would not appear necessary to demonstrate any kind of fault on the part of the owner when the statutory nuisance arises out of defects of a structural character.

The nuisance order under section 82

If the magistrates find that the alleged statutory nuisance exists **15–20** at the time they make their determination, or is likely to recur, they "shall" make a nuisance order, requiring the defendant to carry out works sufficient to abate the nuisance, or prevent its recurrence.[39] This is so even when the premises are in a clearance area and will be demolished in seven years' time: *Salford City Council v. McNally.*[40] Having said that:

"In making the order the magistrate should take into account the circumstances in which the property is being occupied

[37] *Supra.*
[38] (1989) 21 H.L.R. 462.
[39] s.82(2) of the Environmental Protection Act 1990.
[40] *Supra.*

including, of course, the likely duration of the occupation. The shorter the period before probable demolition, the more severe must be the injury or likely injury to health or, as the case may be, the nuisance, to justify action by way of abatement. This aspect of the matter was well explained by the Divisional Court in *Nottingham City District Council v. Newton*,[41] the keynote of which is the need, in making abatement notices, to use discretion and common sense."

If the premises are to be demolished imminently then the magistrates will take that into account and not insist that the landlord carries out works which will prove a waste of money, either by requiring works to be carried out after the scheduled date of demolition, by restricting the works required to only the essential works or by taking into account imminent demolition as relevant to the "reasonable excuse" defence to a subsequent prosecution for failing to comply with the terms of a nuisance order: *Nottingham District Council v. Newton*[42]; *Salford County Council v McNally*[43]; *Lambeth L.B.C. v. Stubbs*[44]; *Coventry City Council v. Doyle*.[45]

One thing is clear: the terms of the order must be expressed with certainty, otherwise it will be successfully appealed: *R. v. Secretary of State for the Environment, ex p. Watney Mann (Midlands)*[46] (not sufficient to order that noise nuisance should be abated so that noise in the premises does not exceed 70 decibels); *Network Housing Association v. Westminster City Council*[47] (not sufficient to require sound insulation to be installed between flats "so as to provide a level of airborne sound insulation . . . of not less than 52 decibels"); *R. v. Wheatley*[48] (not sufficient to require the defendant to "do such things as may be necessary" to abate a nuisance).

It is inherently likely in condensation cases that magistrates will be asked to consider requiring the landlord to install or upgrade some or all of the heating, installation and ventilation elements in the premises. It is not uncommon for landlords to be ordered to install background or central heating, insulation to some or all of the walls and mechanical extract ventilation. The extent to which such works will be ordered depends on the magistrates' view,

---

[41] [1974] 1 W.L.R. 923.
[42] *Supra.*
[43] *Supra.*
[44] [1980] 2 E.G.L.R. 135.
[45] *Supra.*
[46] [1976] J.P.L. 368.
[47] *Supra.*
[48] (1885) 16 Q.B.D. 34.

having heard expert evidence, as to what is "necessary" for abating the nuisance or preventing its recurrence.

All the cases agree that the magistrates have a "wide discretion" as to the content of a nuisance order: *R. v. Fenny Stratford Justices, ex p. Watney Mann (Midlands) Limited*[49]; *McGilivray v. Stephenson*.[50]

The use of the word "necessary", means "reasonably necessary"; but the magistrates should bear in mind the other "very heavy housing responsibilities" of the local authority and exercise what Lord Wilberforce described in *Salford City Council v. McNally*[51] as "discretion and common sense".[52] One should not, however, attempt to take *Birmingham District Council v. Kelly*[53] too far. It is certainly no authority for the proposition that magistrates should not make wide-ranging nuisance orders in appropriate circumstances: Watkins L.J.'s complaint was that the nuisance order contained terms "which are wholly unrelated to the abatement of the nuisance complained of", while Woolf J. said "[the magistrate] had placed before him an agreed schedule of works, so certainly he cannot be criticised if he included such items as those to which I have referred, in particular full central heating". The case is, however, clear authority for the proposition that the content of the nuisance order is the public responsibility of the magistrate, who must not merely rubber stamp what the parties have agreed.

When the premises have been vacated

A statutory nuisance is not abated merely because the tenants **15–21** vacate before the magistrates' court hearing. The landlord remains liable to conviction and a nuisance order if the premises remain prejudicial to health: *Lambeth L.B.C. v. Stubbs*,[54] in which Waller L.J. said "if the tenants are removed nothing has been done to alter the state of the premises. They remain prejudicial to health . . .".

There are similar dicta in *Coventry City Council v. Doyle*.[55]

Compensation and fines

Proceedings under section 82 of the Environmental Protection **15–22** Act 1990 remain criminal, not civil, even though brought by way of

---

[49] [1976] 2 All E.R. 888.
[50] [1950] 1 All E.R. 942.
[51] *Supra.*
[52] See generally *Birmingham District Council v. Kelly supra*, in which a number of criticisms were voiced of a very wide nuisance order (made by the magistrates in terms agreed by the parties).
[53] *Supra.*
[54] *Supra.*
[55] *Supra.*

complaint and not information: *R. v. Inner London Crown Court, ex p. Bentham*[56]; *Botross v. London Borough of Hammersmith & Fulham.*[57] Accordingly, the magistrates have power to make a compensation order pursuant to section 35 of the Powers of Criminal Courts Act 1973: *Herbert v. London Borough of Lambeth*[58]; *Botross v. London Borough of Hammersmith & Fulham.*[59]

Section 35 of the 1973 Power of Criminal Courts Act 1973 provides as follows:

> **35.—(1) Subject to the provisions of this Part of this Act and to section 40 of the Magistrates' Courts Act 1980 (which imposes a monetary limit on the powers of a magistrates' court under this section), a court by or before which a person is convicted of an offence, instead of or in addition to dealing with him in any other way, may, on application or otherwise, make an order (in this Act referred to as a 'compensation order' requiring him to pay compensation for any personal injury, loss or damage resulting from that offence or any other offence which is taken into consideration by the court in determining sentence . . . and a court shall give reasons, on passing sentence, if it does not make such an order in a case where this section empowers it to do so.**
>
> **(2) Compensation under subsection (1) above shall be of such amount as the court considers appropriate, having regard to any evidence and to any representations that are made by or on behalf of the accused or the prosecutor.**

The maximum amount of compensation is £5,000.[60] There is Home Office guidance on the level of compensation orders, in Circulars 85/88 and 53/1993.

The rest of sections 35 to 38 contains further provisions in relation to the assessment of compensation orders and their enforcement. Section 38 provides that:

> **38.—(1) This section shall have effect where a compensation order . . . has been made in favour of any person in respect of any injury, loss or damage and a claim by him in civil proceedings for damages in respect of the injury, loss or damage subsequently falls to be determined.**
>
> **(2) The damages in the civil proceedings shall be assessed without regard to the order or award; but the plaintiff may**

[56] [1989] 1 W.L.R. 408.
[57] (1994) 27 H.L.R. 179.
[58] (1991) 24 H.L.R. 299.
[59] *Supra.*
[60] S.40(1) Magistrates' Courts Act 1980.

only recover an amount equal to the aggregate of the following:

(a) any amount by which they exceed the compensation; and

(b) a sum equal to any portion of the compensation which he fails to recover,

and may not enforce the judgment, so far as it relates to a sum such as is mentioned in paragraphs (b) above, without the leave of the court.

Compensation orders are not really an appropriate method of obtaining compensation for tenants if what is sought is an award of damages equivalent to an award in civil proceedings. In *Herbert v. Lambeth L.B.C.*,[61] whilst allowing an appeal against the refusal of the magistrates to make a compensation order, on the basis that section 35 of the Powers of Criminal Courts Act 1973, did apply to proceedings under Environmental Protection Act 1990 which resulted in a compensation order Woolf L.J. said:

"Before I leave this appeal, I feel it right to underline what should be the approach of the magistrates with regard to compensation. Mr Geldart has indicated that in some situations magistrates in other divisions are awarding substantial damages. With regard to that, it seems to me that it is important to bear in mind the approach which has been indicated by previous decisions of the courts dealing with compensation in other circumstances, where it has been stressed, and here I quote from paragraph 3/785 at p.843 of *Stone's Justices' Manual*:

'The machinery of a compensation order under this Act is intended for clear and simple cases. It must always be remembered that the civil rights of the victim remain, although the power to make a compensation order is not confined to cases where there is a civil liability. A compensation order made by the court of trial can be extremely beneficial as long as it is confined to simple, straightforward cases and generally cases where no great amount is at stake.'

There is a reference to *Miller*[62] for a summary of the principles to be followed when making a compensation order.

As Mr Geldart pointed out in the course of argument, it is possible in consequence of a finding of guilt under section 94(2) of the Public Health Act 1936 for the courts to make a compensation order where there may not be any civil remedy.

---

[61] *Supra.*
[62] (1976) Crim.L.R.

So be it, so long as it is remembered that the sort of compensation order which should be made is the sort reflected in the paragraph from Stones, to which I have just made reference. It seems to me that it would not be an appropriate use of the powers under section 35 of the Act for a magistrates' court to award substantial compensation for matters which can loosely be described as personal injury. If compensation for that sort of injury is to be awarded, it is preferable it should be dealt with in the course of civil proceedings rather than criminal proceedings, and if there is no power in civil proceedings to make such an award, that is a factor which should be taken into account by magistrates when exercising their powers under section 35 of the 1973 Act."

15–23   In practice, magistrates have, for some time, made compensation orders in proceedings under the Environmental Protection Act 1990 which make full use of the permitted limit of £5,000. Notwithstanding the dicta of Woolf L.J. in *Herbert v. Lambeth L.B.C.*,[63] there are good reasons for treating such awards as *sui generis* and not directly subject to the law as it has developed by reference to the general run of criminal cases. First, all matters relevant to the assessment of the quantum of the award will normally have been canvassed during the trial, as the prosecution seeks to establish the condition of the premises historically and its actual as well as potential effect on the occupiers. If a dispute arises in relation to the making of the award, there should not normally be any need to hear extensive further evidence. Secondly, where the complaint relates to condensation, while the injuries suffered by the occupiers of the premises may have been severe, and the damage to their belongings substantial, there may well be no civil remedy: *Quick v. Taff-Ely Borough Council.*[64] Thirdly, proceedings under section 82 of the Environmental Protection Act 1990 actually are *sui generis* in the sense that no criminal offence is committed until the last day of the hearing when the magistrate decides whether or not there is, on that day, a statutory nuisance on the relevant premises. A literal approach to the Powers of the Criminal Courts Act 1973 would result in no compensation being payable except in respect of any personal injury, loss or damage suffered on that day: but that has never been the practice of magistrates, who have adopted a broad and sensible view of the effect of the 1973 Act, in order that occupiers of dwellings can receive some compensation for serious injury which might not be compensated in any other forum.

[63] *Supra.*
[64] *Supra.*

In *R v. Liverpool Crown Court, ex p. Cooke,*[65] however, the crown court reduced a compensation order from £3,000 to £250 and was upheld by the Court of Appeal. Leggatt L.J. held that:

"The power to make a compensation order under section 35 of the 1973 Act is of course not peculiar to statutory nuisance. So the power, and the monetary limit to which it is subject, were not themselves tailored to the requirements of statutory nuisance. It also seems unlikely that the legislature paid regard specifically to the period in respect of which compensation would be payable. By section 35 the court may make a compensation order 'for any personal injury, loss or damage resulting from' the offence. The offence is of allowing a statutory nuisance to exist at the complainant's premises at the date of the hearing.

I see no warrant for construing section 82 (or section 35) so as to entitle the court to take account of the whole period for which the nuisance is alleged to have existed . . .

In my judgment 'the offence', from which may have resulted personal injury, loss or damage capable of being the subject of a compensation order, is the statutory nuisance complained of, in so far as it exists at the date of the hearing and has existed since the date specified in the complaint, provided that that date is not before whichever is the later of (a) the date when the statutory notice expired and (b) a date not more than six months before the complaint was made . . .

It seems to me obvious, and this court has often reiterated, that the magistrates court is not a suitable court in which to entertain any but simple, straightforward claims for compensation. On the time scale I have indicated many, if not most, claims for statutory nuisance may be expected to fall within that description. Otherwise claimants must be left to bring proceedings in the county court which is more accustomed to assessing general damages. The mere fact that magistrates have power to award compensation up to a sum of £5,000 does not mean that it is always sensible for them to involve themselves in what are essentially civil claims."

Unless successfully appealed, this decision is likely to spell the end to a period of years in which compensation orders have become a means of providing at least some compensation, albeit not on a civil scale, to occupiers of dwellings in such a poor condition that they have suffered personal injury and property damage. It will in practice be difficult to establish that losses, in particular property damage, occurred within the six months'

---

[65] [1996] *The Times*, April 22.

period referred to by Leggatt L.J.; while the significant overall
reduction in the likely compensation payable, together with the
absence of legal aid for such proceedings, will markedly affect any
costs-benefit analysis of continuing with proceedings in order to
obtain compensation when the statutory nuisance has been
abated.

Costs

15–24   Even if the statutory nuisance is abated before the hearing, the
occupier is entitled to his or her reasonable costs "properly
incurred" in bringing the proceedings, if the magistrates are
satisfied that the statutory nuisance did exist at the date the
complaint was made.[66] Costs are only "properly incurred" if the
prosecuting tenant is actually liable to pay those costs to his or her
solicitors: they are not "properly incurred" if he or she has entered
into an unlawful contingency fee arrangement with his or her
solicitors: *British Waterways Board v. Norman.*[67] In practice, costs
are awarded when there is a letter of retainer, setting out the
client's liability for costs and disbursements, win or lose, together
with the applicable rates, which is not a sham, although the
solicitor may reserve the right to waive his or her fees. A short, clear
breakdown of costs is provided to the magistrates together with a
letter signed by the client authorising the magistrates to pay
compensation and costs to the solicitors (otherwise both compensation and costs are sent direct to the client).

[66] S.82(12), *Sandwell Metropolitan Borough Council v. Bujok* (1990) 22 H.L.R.
48.
[67] (1993) 26 H.L.R. 232.

PART SIX

WHAT THE LANDLORD OR TENANT HAS AGREED TO CARRY OUT WORK TO

Introduction

Subject to the implication of terms and subject to statute, a party to a tenancy agreement is only liable to repair an element of the building which he or she has contracted to repair. A landlord who contracts only to repair the roof, for example, is not liable if the windows deteriorate, or the floor collapses. A party who contracts to repair the structure is not liable if the decorations and furnishings deteriorate as a result of condensation dampness, not caused by structural disrepair.

Essentially, what elements of the building are covered by an obligation to repair is a question of construction of the agreement, which if well drafted will specify what is to be repaired.

CHAPTER SIXTEEN

Obligations Relating to the Whole of the Premises

Introduction: words and plans

An obligation to repair "the demised premises" or "the prem-   **16–01**
ises" is the widest formulation of an obligation to repair (save of
course for obligations which relate to land not demised).

The extent of the premises leased or rented is primarily a
question of construction of the words of the agreement. Plans can
be used as an aid if referred to as part of the description, or, if
physically incorporated in the agreement, if the verbal description
is unclear: *Leachman v. L. & K. Richardson Limited.*[1] A plan said to
be used for identification purposes only can be looked at to
elucidate but not contradict the verbal description: *Hopgood v.
Brown*[2]; *Wigginton & Milner Limited v. Winster Engineering Limited*[3]; *Hatfield v. Moss.*[4]

General presumptions

In the absence of indications to the contrary there is a presump-   **16–02**
tion that a letting extends to all the land below the building (such
as cellars: *Grigsby v. Melville*[5]) and the airspace above: (neighbour's
sign projecting above demised premises was a trespass: *Kelsen v.*

---

[1] [1969] 1 W.L.R. 1129.
[2] [1955] 1 W.L.R. 213.
[3] [1978] 3 All E.R. 436.
[4] [1988] 2 E.G.L.R. 58.
[5] [1974] 1 W.L.R. 80.

Imperial Tobacco Co. (of Great Britain and Ireland) Ltd[6]). Where the letting is of the entire building there is a strong presumption that the roof is included: *Straudley Investments Limited v. Barpress.*[7]

Presumption on letting of part

16–03   There is a presumption that a letting of a part of a building, for example a flat:

(1) Includes the air space above the roof, when the roof is expressly included in the letting: *Davies v. Yadegar.*[8]

(2) Does not include the common roof: *Cockburn v. Smith*[9] (a case in which there were at least two flats on the top floor).

(3) Does include all of the external walls enclosing the demised part: *Hope Brothers Limited v. Cowan*[10]; and also projections from such walls such as eaves, footings and cornices: *Sturge v. Hackett.*[11]

(4) Does include half of internal boundary walls: *Phelps v. City of London Corporation.*[12]

(5) Ought to include half of the thickness of the joists to which the floors and ceilings of flats above and below are also attached, it being difficult to distinguish rationally between internal boundary walls which on authority are presumed to be owned half each and floors/ceilings which are similar party structures: *Phelps v. City of London Corporation*[13] (see also *Sturge v. Hackett*[14]; *Graystone Property Investments Limited v. Margulies*[15] and *Cresswell v. Duke of Westminster*[16]).

(6) Does generally extend to alterations, additions and new buildings erected during the term: *Ponsford v. HMS Aerosols Limited.*[17]

(7) Does extend to fixtures present at the date of the agreement and does extend to fixtures installed by landlord or tenant after the date of the agreement: *Crossley Bros v. Lee.*[18] Whether fixtures installed after the date of the agreement

---

[6] [1957] 2 Q.B. 334.
[7] [1987] 1 E.G.L.R. 69.
[8] [1990] 1 E.G.L.R. 71.
[9] [1924] 2 K.B. 119.
[10] [1913] 2 Ch. 312.
[11] (1983) 269 E.G. 538.
[12] [1916] 2 Ch. 254.
[13] *Supra.*
[14] *Supra.*
[15] (1983) 269 E.G. 538.
[16] [1985] 2 E.G.L.R. 151.
[17] [1979] A.C. 63.
[18] [1908] 1 K.B. 86.

are covered by any repairing obligation will depend on the wording of the obligation. Section 11 of the Landlord and Tenant Act 1985 does not extend to fixtures which the tenant is entitled to remove.[19]

(8) Does extend to the internal walls and, subject to any other stipulation in the agreement, the interior decorations. In *Proudfoot v. Hart*[20] the tenant's obligation was to keep and yield up "the said premises in good tenantable repair". Lopes L.J. said:

"As to papering and painting, generally speaking the tenant would not be bound to repaper or repaint. Most clearly he is not bound to repaper with similar paper to that which was on the walls when the tenancy began, or to repaint with similar paint. Most clearly, also, he is not bound to do repairs which are merely decorative. But if at the end of the lease the paper and paint are in such a condition as to cause portions of the premises to go into decay, he is bound to repaper and repaint to such an extent as will satisfy the terms of the definition which I have stated. Again, if the paint through the lapse of time has worn off, or the paper has become worn out, so that their condition has become such as not to satisfy a reasonably-minded tenant of the class who would be likely to take the house, then he must repaper and repaint so as to make the premises reasonably fit, within the definition, for the occupation of such a tenant . . . "

Inclusion in letting compared with obligation to repair

An obligation to keep the demised premises as a whole in repair   **16–04** may require repairs to be carried out to building elements which are not, or may not, be strictly part of the premises demised. For example, when the demised premises are in disrepair because of deteriorating joists or internal boundary walls, whether or not the joists or internal walls are demised in their entirety, they ought to be repaired if that is the practical and necessary course.

See paragraph 22–03 for consideration of the legal issues raised by repairs to property owned by someone else.

[19] See s.11(2)(c) of the Landlord and Tenant Act 1985.
[20] (1890) 25 Q.B.D. 42.

CHAPTER SEVENTEEN

Obligations Relating to the Structure of the Premises

General principles

17–01   As a general proposition, the word "structure" in the context of a repairing obligation refers to less than the entirety of the premises, but more than the load bearing elements of a building. It is usually taken to refer to: "the basic fabric and parts of the house as distinguished from its decorations and fittings": *Pearlman v. Keepers and Governors of Harrow School*[1]; or to—

> " . . . those elements of the overall dwelling house which give it its essential appearance, stability and shape. The expression does not extend to the many and various ways in which the dwelling house will be fitted out, equipped, decorated and generally made to be habitable . . . in order to be part of the structure of the dwelling house a particular element must be a material or significant element in the overall construction. To some extent, in every case there will be a degree of fact to be gone into to decide whether something is or is not part of the structure of the dwelling house."[2]

---

[1] [1979] Q.B. 56.

[2] *Irvine v. Moran* [1991] 1 E.G.L.R. 261 (see also *Campden Hill Towers Limited v. Gardner* [1977] Q.B. 823; *Blundell v. Obsdale Limited* (1958) 171 E.G. 491; *Granada Theatres Limited v. Freehold Investments (Leytonstone) Limited* [1959] Ch. 592; *Samuels v. Abbints Investments Limited* (1963) 188 E.G. 689; *Bickmore v. Dimmer* [1903] 1 Ch. 158; *Bushell v. Hammond* [1986] 2 K.B. 563; *Monk v. Murphy and Brock* (1949) 113 J.P. 247; *Toff v. McDowell* (1993) 69 P. & C.R. 535; *Howe v. Botwood* [1913] 2 K.B. 387.

It can not be emphasised too strongly that whether a particular building element forms part of the "structure" will depend in each case on a careful reading of the tenancy agreement in the context, in particular, of the construction as a matter of fact of the particular building in question.

Specific examples

It is not intended to set out all reported cases in which, in varying **17–02** contexts, different building elements have been held to be, or not to be, part of the structure of the building in question. Comprehensive analysis can be found in *Woodfall* and in *Dowding and Reynolds*. Generally speaking, however, building elements likely to be treated as part of the "structure" are:

(1) Load bearing walls, foundations, roof (these are self-evidently structural although they may or may not form part of the structure of the part actually demised).[2a]

(2) Windows (including frames, sash cords and essential window furniture): *Irvine v. Moran*.[3]

(3) External doors but not internal doors: *Irvine v. Moran*.

(4) Walls and ceilings of flats including the entirety of the structural framework and beams directly supporting floors, ceilings and walls, whether or not included in the demise: *Campden Hill Towers v. Gardner*.[4]

Special problems with plaster

Some consideration has to be given as to whether internal plaster **17–03** is likely to be treated as part of the structure with the result that damage to such plaster *per se* is damage to the structure. The decided cases point in both directions.

In *Granada Theatres v. Freehold Investment (Leytonstone) Limited*[5] the Court of Appeal treated the repair of cement rendering 3/8–7/8 inches thick as a structural repair in the context of commercial premises: but the rendering had come away from the wall and the bricks behind (plainly part of the structure) had started to deteriorate.

In *Newham L.B.C. v. Patel*,[6] Templeman L.J. remarked that:

"In the pleadings there were various particulars of disrepair, including a large number of damp wall plasters. Some of these

---

[2a] *Campden Hill Towers v. Gardner, supra*; *Douglas-Scott v. Scorgie* [1984] 1 W.L.R. 716.

[3] *Supra.*

[4] *Supra.*

[5] *Supra.*

[6] (1978) 13 H.L.R. 79.

particulars I do not think come within the description of structural disrepair required by s.32, but undoubtedly there are some, such as damp wall plasters and other items, which do come within that section."

Similar assumptions were made in *Palmer v. Metropolitan Borough of Sandwell*[7] ("the judge found that there was subsisting some disrepair of the structure, namely crumbling plaster . . . "), and in *Quick v. Taff-Ely Borough Council*[8] and *Staves v. Leeds City Council*[9] in which concessions by eminent Counsel that plaster was part of the structure for the purposes of the tenancy agreements in question were accepted. Those concessions were described as being correct by Mr Stephen Sedley Q.C. whilst sitting as an Assistant Recorder in *Hussein v. Mehlman*.[10]

It must be right that plaster may not be part of the structure in the context of certain leases or buildings: in the context of a building contract, for example, Lord Bridge observed that "it would seem to me entirely artificial to treat the plaster as distinct from the decorative surface placed upon it"—*D & F Estates Limited v. Church Commissioners for England*.[11] On balance, however, it is probable that in the context of periodic tenancies of dwelling-houses subject to section 11 of the Landlord and Tenant Act 1985, if in no other context, the correct answer is that plaster is regarded by the parties as part of the structure. In just such a context, however, there is one clear authority that plaster is *not* part of the structure. In *Irvine v. Moran*,[12] Mr Recorder Thayne Forbes Q.C. sitting as a deputy High Court Judge held that: "It seems to me that internal wall plaster is more in the nature of a decorative finish and is not part of the essential material elements which go to make up the structure of the dwellinghouse."

It is the opinion of the Law Commission that it is "more consistent with the policy of the Act" that plaster is to be regarded as part of the structure for the purposes or section 11 of the Landlord and Tenant Act 1985.[13]

---

[7] (1978) 20 H.L.R. 74.
[8] [1986] Q.B. 809.
[9] (1991) 23 H.L.R. 107.
[10] [1992] 2 E.G.L.R. 87.
[11] [1988] 2 E.G.L.R. 26.
[12] *Supra.*
[13] Law Com. 238 at p. 69.

CHAPTER EIGHTEEN

Obligations Relating to the Exterior of the Premises

General principles

As with "structure", "exterior" has a meaning which depends upon **18–01** the context of the whole of the letting agreement and the physical nature of the subject building.

There is a presumption that, without qualification, "exterior" refers to the exterior of the building itself rather than the entirety of the land demised: *McAuliffe v. Moloney*[1] (exterior did not include gate). It will normally include only parts of the building directly external to the demised premises: *Rapid Results College v. Angell*[2] (exterior of second floor offices did not include the roof above, which had been excluded from the demise): but see paragraph 18–03 below.

Specific examples

The expression generally includes: **18–02**

(1) External walls whether or not exposed to the air: *Green v. Eales*,[3] *Campden Hill Towers Limited v. Gardner*[4] (the outer side of inner party walls); *Pembery v. Lamdin*[5] (basement walls).

---

[1] [1971] I.R. 200.
[2] [1986] 1 E.G.L.R. 53.
[3] (1841) 2 Q.B. 225.
[4] [1977] 1 Q.B. 823.
[5] [1940] 2 All E.R. 434.

Windows and their frames: *Ball v. Plummer*[6]; other types of external woodwork: *Crawford v. Newton*.[7]

(3) The outer sides of horizontal divisions between the premises and other premises above and below: *Campden Hill Towers v. Gardner*.[8]

(4) Steps and a path which form the only means of access: *Brown v. Liverpool Corporation*,[9] but probably not a gate: *McAuliffe v. Moloney*.[10]

It will generally not include:

(1) A rear access path when normal access is from the front: *Hopwood v. Cannock Chase D.C.*[11]

(2) A path running along the rear of the house: *King v. South Northamptonshire D.C.*[12]

(3) A garden or yard attached to the house: *Hopwood v. Cannock Chase D.C.*[13]; *McAuley v. Bristol City Council*.[14]

(4) A separate garage and gate: *Irvine v. Moran*.[15]

Special problems with roofs

18–03   As with internal plaster in "structure" cases, roofs raise difficult questions of fact and law in "exterior" cases.

In *Rapid Results College v. Angell*[16] the Court of Appeal held that the exterior of second floor offices did not include the roof above, which had been excluded from the demise.

In the context of section 11 of the Landlord and Tenant Act 1985, however, the Court of Appeal held in *Douglas-Scott v. Scorgie*[17] that a roof might be part of the exterior of a top floor dwelling house. It was pointed out by Slade L.J. that whether a roof is part of the exterior of a top floor flat (or indeed part of the structure of a top floor flat) will be a question of fact in every case. It will depend on whether the roof and the flat or offices form an inseparable structural unit or, for example, whether there was an uninhabited attic or roof void between the two: see also *Straudley Investments v. Barpress Limited*[18] and *Hatfield v. Moss*.[19]

---

[6] (1879) 23 S.J. 656.
[7] (1886) 2 T.L.R. 877.
[8] *Supra.*
[9] [1969] 3 All E.R. 1345.
[10] *Supra.*
[11] [1975] 1 W.L.R. 373.
[12] [1992] 1 E.G.L.R. 53.
[13] *Supra.*
[14] [1991] 3 W.L.R. 968.
[15] [1991] E.G.L.R. 261.
[16] [1986] 1 E.G.L.R. 53.
[17] [1984] 1 W.L.R. 716.
[18] (1987) 282 E.G. 1124.
[19] (1988) 40 E.G. 112.

PART SEVEN

DAMAGES

CHAPTER NINETEEN

Basic Principles of Contract and Tort

First principles

For a detailed analysis of the basic principles of compensation for **19–01** breach of contract or tort the reader is referred to *McGregor on Damages*,[1] *Chitty on Contracts*[2] and *Clerk and Lindsell on Torts*.[3]

The basic principle in both contract and tort is *restitutio in integrum*: making good the whole loss. In *Livingstone v. Raywards Coal Co.*[4] Lord Blackburn defined the measure of damages in both contract and tort as: "that sum of money which will put the party who has been injured, or who has suffered, in the same position as he would have been in if he had not sustained the wrong for which he is now getting his compensation or reparation".

In *Liesbosch, Dredger v. Edison S.S.*[5] Lord Wright said that: "the dominant rule of law is the principle of *restitutio in integrum*, and subsidiary rules can only be justified if they give effect to that rule".

In *The Albazero*[6] Lord Diplock said that:

"The general rule in English law today as to the measure of damages recoverable for the invasion of a legal right, whether by breach of a contract or by commission of a tort, is that damages

[1] 15th ed., 1988.
[2] 27th ed., 1994.
[3] 17th ed., 1995.
[4] (1880) 5 App.Cas. 25.
[5] [1933] A.C. 449.
[6] [1977] A.C. 774.

155

are compensatory. Their function is to put the person whose right has been invaded in the same position as if it had been respected so far as the award of a sum of money can do so."

Damages for breach of contract

Basic principles

19–02 A claim for damages is a claim for compensation in the language of money for the fact that the plaintiff has not received the performance for which he or she bargained. The purpose of damages is not to expropriate any profit made by the contract-breaker out of his or her breach of contract, or to punish, but to make good loss suffered by the plaintiff. Loss includes:

(1) Loss of bargain (otherwise known as loss of expectation);
(2) Reliance loss (wasted expenses);
(3) Consequential loss (*e.g.* personal injury or property damage flowing from the breach of contract).

Special provision in the contract

19–03 Subject to the Unfair Contract Terms Act 1977 and common law rules as to penalty clauses, the parties to a contract are free to specify the nature and extent of remedies available upon breach. The contract may, accordingly, contain its own rules as to the circumstances giving rise to a valid claim for damages and as to how such damages are to be assessed. If and to the extent that the contract so provides, the assessment of damages depends on the meaning of the particular contract which has been breached.

Ascertaining the true and reasonable loss

19–04 Otherwise, the law on damages fills the gap with standard provisions on the assessment of money compensation. The general principles applicable were famously re-stated by Parke B. in *Robinson v. Harman*[7]:

"The next question is: what damages is the plaintiff entitled to recover? The rule of the common law is that where a party sustains a loss by reason of a breach of contract, he is, so far as money can do it, to be placed in the same situation, with respect to damages, as if the contract had been properly performed."

In *British Westinghouse Electric and Manufacturing Company Limited v. Underground Electric Railway Company of London*[8] Viscount Haldane added:

[7] (1848) 1 Ex. 850.
[8] [1912] A.C. 673.

"The quantum of damage is a question of fact, and the only guidance the law can give is to lay down general principles which afford at times but scanty assistance in dealing with particular cases . . . . Subject to these observations I think that there are certain broad principles which are quite well settled. The first is that, as far as possible, he who has proved a breach of a bargain to supply what he has contracted to get is to be placed, as far as money can do it, in as good a situation as if the contract had been performed. The fundamental basis is thus compensation for pecuniary loss naturally flowing from the breach; but this first principle is qualified by a second, which imposes on a plaintiff the duty of taking all reasonable steps to mitigate the loss consequent on the breach . . . "

When a builder, for example, fails to build in accordance with the contract, the employer's damages are prima facie the cost of re-instatement (the replacement of defective work with work which complies with the contract). The assessment of compensation is, however, always based upon fact and reasonableness. Lord Lloyd, in *Ruxley Electronics and Construction Limited v. Forsyth*[9] explained (after citing Parke B. in *Robinson v. Harman*[10]):

"This does not mean that in every case of breach of contract the plaintiff can obtain the monetary equivalent of specific performance. It is first necessary to ascertain the loss the plaintiff has in fact suffered by reason of the breach . . . the cost of re-instatement is the ordinary measure of damages for defective performance under a building contract . . . But it is not the only measure of damages . . . [after referring to *Bellgrove v. Eldridge*[11]]. Once again one finds the court emphasising the central importance of reasonableness in selecting the appropriate measure of damages. If re-instatement is not the reasonable way of dealing with the situation, then diminution in value, if any, is the true measure of the plaintiff's loss. If there is no diminution in value, the plaintiff has suffered no loss . . . [But] suppose there is no measurable difference in value, and the cost of re-instatement would be prohibitive. Is there any reason why the court should not award by way of damages for breach of contract some modest sum, not based on difference in value, but solely to compensate the buyer for his disappointed expectations?"

In that case, the builder had constructed a swimming pool in the grounds of a private house so that it was 6 feet deep instead of 7

[9] [1996] A.C. 344.
[10] [1843–1860] All E.R. 383.
[11] (1954) 90 C.L.R. 613.

feet 6 inches deep, as the contract specified. It is important to emphasise that it remained perfectly safe to dive into the pool. It was impossible to award damages based upon diminution in value because neither the house nor the pool were worth any less than they would have been worth had the pool been constructed accordingly to specification. Their Lordships were understandably reluctant to award the cost of re-instating the pool according to specification: some £21,500. They accordingly affirmed the decision of the county court judge to award £2,500 for loss of amenity and £750 for general inconvenience and disturbance: a highly unusual form of award in the context of building litigation.

Causation and remoteness

19–05   The plaintiff is prima facie entitled to recover compensation for losses which:

    (1) were caused by the defendant's breach of contract;
    (2) are not too remote.

Whether the breach of contract caused the loss

19–06   It is not sufficient for the plaintiff to prove that "but for" the breach of contract the loss would not have occurred. He or she has to prove on the balance of probabilities that the breach of contract was the effective or dominant "cause" of the loss. Ultimately, that is a question of fact and judicial common sense: *Gallo Limited v. Bright Grahame Murray.*[12] Another way of expressing the same limitation is that a defendant is only liable for losses of a kind his contractual duty obliges him to prevent: *South Australia Asset Management Corporation v. York Montague Limited.*[12a]

Multiple causes

19–07   The breach of contract need not be the sole cause of the loss: "If a breach of contract is one of two causes, both co-operating and both of equal efficacy . . . it is sufficient to carry a judgment for damages."[13]

    It was put even more broadly in *Iron and Steel Holding and Realisation Agency v. Compensation Appeal Tribunal*[14] by Winn L.J., who said:

> "It is not, however, in my opinion necessary that A should be the sole cause of B, provided that the causative effect of A

[12] [1994] 1 W.L.R. 1360.
[12a] [1996] 27 E.G. 125.
[13] *Heskell v. Continental Express Limited* [1950] 1 All E.R. 1033.
[14] [1966] 1 W.L.R. 480.

continued to operate until B occurred, as an efficient cause of B, and provided that causative factor A had not before B happened been relegated to the status of a mere historical antecedent or background feature by the intervention of an independent, unconnected and extraneous causative factor or event."

Intervening physical events

Where the defendant's breach starts off a chain of events, the defendant is treated as causing damage which was actually inflicted by an intervening event, providing the intervening event was "not unlikely": *The Heron II.*[15] The classic example is *The Monarch Steamship Company Limited v. Karlshamns Oljefabriker (A/B)*,[16] a case in which a breach of contract caused delay in shipment: the delay was greatly exacerbated by war breaking out; but the defendants were liable for the whole delay because the possibility of war and further delays caused by war was well known. An example in the disrepair field can be found in *Loria v. Hammer.*[17] In that case the tenant sought to recover the cost of repairs carried out in default of action by her landlord. The cost of the works and the tenant's consequential losses (alternative accommodation) had been increased because a violent storm caused delay. The landlord argued that: "the storm on June 6 and 7 was *novus actus*, which caused works to be prolonged beyond the date by which they would and should otherwise have been concluded and that the landlord could not be responsible for that extended period".

19–08

The judge held that:

"It is in the nature of our weather that building works even, or as some might say, especially, in June may, despite all reasonable precautions, be affected by storms and thereby be prolonged. There are stages when buildings are unusually vulnerable in the course of their repair. I cannot regard the storm as a *novus actus* in any relevant sense so as to exonerate the landlord."

Intervening acts of third parties

The voluntary, intervening act of a third party generally breaks the chain of causation. The defendant remains liable, even for the torts or crimes of third parties, however, if it was part of the defendant's contractual duty to protect the plaintiff from such acts:

19–09

---

[15] [1969] 1 A.C. 350.
[16] [1949] A.C. 196.
[17] [1989] 2 E.G.L.R. 249.

De la Bere v. Pearsons Limited[18] (a person who in breach of contract recommended a dishonest stockbroker was liable for loss caused by that broker's dishonesty); *Stansbie v. Troman*[19] (a decorator who in breach of contract left the front door unlocked was liable for the value of goods stolen by thieves: see the explanation of this case by Goff L.J. in *P Perl (Exporters) Limited v. Camden London Borough*[20]; *Morris v. Liverpool City Council*[21] (in which Slade L.J. held that if the landlord had failed in breach of contract to repair the tenant's front door timeously "I would, for my part, have held that the loss suffered by the plaintiff through the burglary was not too remote to be recoverable.").

Whether loss is "too remote"

19–10 The plaintiff can not recover loss which is too remote. The rules of remoteness were formulated in *Hadley v. Baxendale*[22] by Alderson B. as follows:

> "The damages . . . should be such as may fairly and reasonably be considered *either* arising naturally, *i.e.* according to the usual course of things, from such breach of contract itself, or such as may reasonably be supposed to have been in the contemplation of both parties at the time they made the contract as the probable result of the breach of it. Now, if the special circumstances under which the contract was actually made were communicated by the plaintiffs to the defendants, and thus known to both parties, the damages resulting from the breach of such a contract, which they would reasonably contemplate, would be the amount of injury which would ordinarily follow from a breach of contract under these special circumstances so known and communicated. On the other hand, if these special circumstances were wholly unknown to the party breaking the contract, he, at the most, could only be supposed to have had in his contemplation the amount of injury which would arise generally, and in the great multitude of cases not affected by any special circumstances, from such a breach of contract."

The defendant *was not* liable, accordingly, for loss of profits caused by delay in repairing a mill shaft, when mill-owners were known to normally keep spares but these particular mill-owners had not told the defendant that they did not have a spare.

[18] [1908] 1 K.B. 280.
[19] [1948] 2 K.B. 48.
[20] [1984] Q.B. 342.
[21] (1987) 20 H.L.R. 498.
[22] (1854) 9 Exch. 347.

The defendant accordingly *was* liable for ordinary loss of profits caused by delay in repairing a boiler needed for the plaintiff's laundry business when it knew that the plaintiff needed the boiler for immediate use in its business; but was not liable for the loss of exceptionally lucrative government contracts of which it knew nothing: *Victoria Laundry (Windsor) Limited v. Newman Industries Limited.*[23]

Had the defendants in these last two cases been informed of the special risk of loss, they would have had the opportunity to limit their liability by contract with the plaintiff, might have bargained for increased consideration; or might have sub-contracted the work to mitigate loss.

A particular item of loss or damage is not too remote if its occurrence is " 'not unlikely' as denoting a degree of probability considerably less than an even chance but nevertheless not very unusual and easily foreseeable" (Lord Reid and Lord Morris), a "serious possibility" or a "real danger" (Lord Pearce and Lord Upjohn), or "liable to result" (Lord Morris and Lord Hodson): *The Heron II,*[24] *i.e.* the test is slightly more onerous in contract than in tort, although differences can be difficult to sustain: *H Parsons (Livestock) Limited v. Uttley Ingham & Co. Limited.*[25]

It is the type of loss, rather than its extent or quantum, which has to be "not unlikely": *Christopher Hill Limited v. Ashington Piggeries Limited*[26]; *Wroth v. Tyler.*[27]

When reliance is placed on the second limb of *Hadley v. Baxendale,*[28] the plaintiff has to show more than merely casual knowledge of special circumstances on the part of the defendant, but not as much as an express or even an implied agreement to be responsible for a certain type of loss. Liability depends on "some knowledge and acceptance by one party of the purpose and intention of the other in entering the contract": *Weld-Blundell v. Stephens.*[29] Lord Reid in *The Heron II,* said that:

"The crucial question is whether, on the information available to the defendant when the contract was made, he should, or the reasonable man in his position would, have realised that such loss was sufficiently likely to result from the breach of contract to make it proper to hold that the loss flowed

---

[23] [1949] 2 K.B. 528.
[24] *Supra.*
[25] [1978] Q.B. 791.
[26] [1969] 3 All E.R. 1496.
[27] [1974] Ch. 30.
[28] *Supra.*
[29] [1920] A.C. 956.

naturally from the breach or that loss of that kind should have been within his contemplation."

The freeholder whose breaches of the lease caused the tenant to lose profit from sub-letting was liable under the first limb of *Hadley v. Baxendale: Mira v. Aylmer Square Investments Limited.*[30] The length of the lease, its provisions relating to sub-letting and the common practice of sub-letting in that part of London brought this case within the first limb of the rule.

A valuer is only liable for the difference between a correct valuation and his or her incorrect valuation and is not liable for exacerbation of loss caused by a downturn in the market because this downturn was not caused by the valuer's negligence: *South Australia Asset Management Corporation v. York Montague Limited.* [30a]

Mitigation and other control mechanisms

19–11   There are further control mechanisms developed to extend or restrict damages and which apply to claims in both contract and tort.[31]

Damages in tort

Basic principles

19–12   The basic principle of awards of damages in tort, as well as in contract, was defined by Lord Blackburn in *Livingstone v. Rawyards Coal Company*[32] in this way:

"Where any injury is to be compensated by damages, in settling the sum of money to be given for the reparation of damages you should as nearly as possible get at that sum of money which will put the party who has been injured, or who has suffered, in the same position as he would have been in if he had not sustained the wrong for which he is now getting his compensation or reparation."

In tort, as in contract, however, if the cost of re-instatement greatly exceeds the value of land or a chattel which has been damaged as a result of a tort, the courts may award the plaintiff only an amount reflecting the diminution in value caused by the tort. Lord Donaldson expressed the position in *Dodd Properties v. Canterbury City Council*[33] (a case in which negligent building operations damaged the plaintiffs' adjoining garage):

[30] (1989) 21 H.L.R. 284, affirmed (1990) 22 H.L.R. 182.
[30a] [1996] 27 E.G. 125.
[31] See paras. 19–19 to 19–24.
[32] (1880) 5 App.Cas. 25.
[33] [1980] 1 W.L.R. 433.

"The general object underlying the rules for the assessment of damages is, so far as is possible by means of a monetary award, to place the plaintiff in the position which he would have occupied if he had not suffered the wrong complained of, be that wrong a tort or a breach of contract. In the case of a tort causing damage to real property, this object is achieved by the application of one or other of two quite different measures of damage, or occasionally, a combination of the two. The first is to take the capital value of the property in an undamaged state and to compare it with its value in a damaged state. The second is to take the cost of repair or reinstatement. Which is appropriate will depend upon a number of factors, such as the plaintiff's future intentions as to the use of the property and the reasonableness of those intentions. If he reasonably intends to sell the property in its damaged state, clearly the diminution in capital value is the true measure of damage. If he reasonably intends to occupy it and to repair the damage, clearly the cost of repairs is the true measure. And there may be in-between situations."

Causation and remoteness

As in contract, the plaintiff is prima facie entitled to recover **19–13** compensation for losses which:

(1) were caused by the defendant's tort;
(2) are not too remote.

Causation on the balance of probabilities

The basic principle is that the plaintiff has to prove that on the **19–14** balance of probabilities the defendant's tort caused the damage. It is not sufficient if the tort was merely the occasion of the loss, *e.g.* for the plaintiff to say that "but for" the defendant's actions the loss would not have occurred. The plaintiff has to prove on the balance of probabilities that the tort was the effective or dominant cause of the damage. In the end the court decides the question by the application of its common sense: *Gallo Limited v. Bright Grahame Murray.*[34]

In *Hotson v. East Berkshire Health Authority*[35] the plaintiff's hip was damaged in an accident. The hospital treated him negligently and his hip developed avascular necrosis. Medical evidence established that it was 75 per cent likely that necrosis would have developed in any event; the lack of proper medical treatment deprived the plaintiff of a

---

[34] *Supra.* See also *South Australia Asset Management Corporation v. York Montague Limited* [1996] 27 E.G. 125.
[35] [1987] A.C. 750.

25 per cent chance of avoiding necrosis. The plaintiff's claim failed because the medical evidence failed to establish that on the balance of probabilities it was the negligence of the hospital that caused the necrosis to develop. Had the plaintiff been able to prove that it was 51 per cent likely that competent treatment would have prevented necrosis, he would have recovered in full.

The plaintiff may, however, succeed if he or she is able to prove on the balance of probabilities that the tort was "a cause" if not "the sole cause" of the damage, or made "a substantial contribution to the injury", in cases where causation is impossible to establish precisely: *McGhee v. National Coal Board*[36] (negligent failure of employer to provide washing facilities materially increased risk of dermatitis caused by brick dust: medical science could not say whether the employees would have contracted dermatitis in any event). In *Wilsher v. Essex Area Health Authority*,[37] however, such a claim failed as it was not established on the balance of probabilities that the administration of excess oxygen to a premature baby did actually cause blindness or materially increase the risk of blindness as a result of other "innocent" potential causes.

In disrepair cases, causation of personal injury is dealt with fairly robustly. In *McCoy & Co. v. Clark*[38] the tenant alleged that water penetration through the roof of the premises had caused him to contract pneumonia. The County Court judge heard evidence from the parties and from the tenant's G.P. who appears, at least in his report, to have gone no further than saying that the damp "may well have contributed to the onset of the pneumonia".[39] He concluded that the water penetration had caused the pneumonia, but that the tenant had also failed to look after himself properly: he awarded damages on the basis that the landlord was 50 per cent liable for the pneumonia and made an award of damages accordingly. It can therefore be said that the judge was equally robust as to both causation of damage and failure to mitigate damage. In this respect he was robustly upheld in the Court of Appeal.

Intervening physical events

19–15   Subsequent physical events will be treated as simply triggering the loss, which continues to be caused by the tort, when the intervening event was reasonably foreseeable:

[36] [1973] 1 W.L.R. 1.
[37] [1988] 1 All E.R. 888.
[38] (1982) 13 H.L.R. 87.
[39] at p. 95.

"To break the chain of causation it must be shown that there is something which I will call ultroneous, something unwarrantable, a new cause which disturbs the sequence of events, something which can be described as either unreasonable or extraneous or extrinsic."[40]

Intervening acts of third parties

When damage is proximately inflicted as a result of the torts or **19–16** crimes of independent third parties, the defendant is not normally liable, even though the injury caused by the third parties' actions may have been made possible or more likely by the defendant's torts. The damage is normally treated as the result of a new, independent cause: *Weld-Blundell v. Stephens.*[41] In *Smith v. Littlewoods Organisation Limited*[42] the owners of an empty cinema were held not liable to neighbours when young vandals broke in and caused a fire which damaged neighbouring property either because:

(1) a duty of care was owed but the owners had not known of vandalism in the area or the previous attempts to start fires so that the damage was not reasonably foreseeable(Lord Brandon);

(2) it would require an exceptional case for an owner to be liable to neighbours for damage caused by vandals (Lord Griffiths);

(3) there would have to be a high likelihood of such damage occurring for it to be reasonably foreseeable (Lord Mackay) and;

(4) there is no duty to prevent damage by third parties except:

   (i) where there is a special relationship between plaintiff and defendant in which the plaintiff assumes responsibility towards the defendant in respect of third party action;

   (ii) where the defendant negligently created a special risk which the third party exploited; or

   (iii) when the defendant knew or ought to have known that the third party was creating a danger on his or her property but failed to take steps to prevent it (Lord Goff).

---

[40] *per* Lord Wright, *The Oropesa* [1943] P. 32. There was a collision between two ships caused by negligence; the chain of causation was not broken when Master of one ship crossed to the other ship in a ship's boat to discuss salvage arrangements, and the ship's boat overturned with the result that nine men drowned.

[41] *Supra.*

[42] [1987] A.C. 241.

It is conceivable that a "special relationship" of the type referred to by Lord Goff at (a) above can exist by virtue of the tenancy agreement: *Morris v. Liverpool City Council.*[43] In such circumstances, however, the tenant would be much better off suing in contract.[44]

Whether loss is too remote

19–17 The general principle is that the defendant is not liable for all damage directly caused by his tort, only for damage which is not "too remote". The exception to the general principle is where, although highly un-foreseeable, the defendant intended the damage actually suffered to occur. Intended consequences are never too remote: *Quinn v. Leatham.*[45]

When the defendant breaches a duty to take care, he or she is generally only liable for "damage . . . of such a kind as the reasonable man should have foreseen". So long as the "kind" of damage is foreseeable and occurs, its extent need not have been foreseen, nor the precise manner of its incidence: *The Wagon Mound (No. 1).*[46]

In *The Wagon Mound (No. 2),*[47] the House of Lords held that "the foresight of the reasonable man" limited the extent of liability for damage in cases of nuisance, as well as cases of negligence.

The House of Lords re-iterated that position in *Cambridge Water Company Limited v. Eastern Counties Leather plc*[48] and also held that reasonable foreseeability of damage of the kind suffered was a prerequisite to liability for that damage in an action under the doctrine of *Rylands v. Fletcher.*[49] The defendants in that case succeeded on the basis that it was not reasonably foreseeable, prior to 1976, that spillage of small quantities of solvent would enter underground strata and corrupt water taken down-catchment.

The result is that the defendant remains strictly liable for damage caused by the escape from his or her land of things likely to do mischief if they escaped (*e.g.* he or she could not escape liability by demonstrating that reasonable or even painstaking care had been exercised): but only if damage of the kind suffered was in fact a reasonably foreseeable consequence of the escape.

The same principle applies in cases for breach of statutory duty: *Galashiels Car Company Limited v. Millar*[50] (defendant was liable

[43] *Supra.*
[44] See para. 19–09.
[45] [1901] A.C. 495.
[46] [1961] A.C. 388.
[47] [1967] A.C. 617.
[48] [1994] 1 All E.R. 53.
[49] (1868) L.R. 3 H.L. 330.
[50] [1949] A.C. 275.

for the fatal crash of a lift previously in perfect working order). It can be assumed that reasonable foreseeability of damage of the kind suffered is now the standard prerequisite of liability for the damage complained of in all torts. The House of Lords recently illustrated this principle in the case of *South Australia Asset Management Corporation v. York Montague Limited*[50a]: a valuer is only liable for the difference between a correct valuation and his or her negligent valuation, not for additional loss caused by a downturn in the property market.

Pure economic loss

In tort, the plaintiff can not normally recover financial loss unless the loss is consequential upon personal injury or property damage, *e.g.* loss of earnings consequential upon a personal injury: *Murphy v. Brentwood District Council.*[51]

19–18

Plaintiffs can only recover pure financial loss if there is some additional element: either an assumption of responsibility by the defendant to the plaintiff and reliance by the plaintiff; or clear foreseeability of economic loss, an obvious proximity of relationship and a view by the court that it would be fair, just and reasonable to impose a duty in respect of pure financial loss: *Spring v. Guardian Assurance plc*[52]; *Henderson v. Merrett Syndicates Limited*[53]; *White v. Jones.*[54]

Control mechanisms common to contract and tort

The unusually vulnerable plaintiff

Providing some damage, however slight, was foreseeable, the defendant is liable for the full extent of damage actually sustained, even when the special vulnerability of the plaintiff or his or her property results in damage which is unforeseeable in extent or in kind. In *Owens v. Liverpool Corporation*[55] Mackinnon L.J. said that:

19–19

> "one who is guilty of negligence to another must put up with idiosyncrasies of his victim that increase the likelihood or extent of damage to him: it is no answer to a claim for a fractured skull that its owner had an unusually fragile one."

In *Smith v. Leech Brain & Co Limited*[56] the plaintiff was burnt by molten metal as a result of the defendant's negligence in not

[50a] *Supra.*
[51] [1991] 1 A.C. 398.
[52] [1994] 3 All E.R. 129.
[53] [1994] 3 All E.R. 506.
[54] [1995] 2 W.L.R. 187.
[55] [1939] 1 K.B. 395.
[56] [1962] 2 Q.B. 405.

supplying protective clothing. He developed cancer and died. The defendant was liable because, even though the plaintiff was constitutionally pre-disposed to cancer, he might never have caught it but for the accident.

The impecunious plaintiff

19–20   A distinction has been drawn between special vulnerability arising out of the plaintiff's physical and mental characteristics, and special vulnerability arising out of the plaintiff's economic circumstances. In *Liesbosch Dredger v. Edison S.S.*,[57] the plaintiff recovered the cost of replacing its dredger, damaged beyond repair by the negligent defendant and loss of profits between the date of the accident and the date by which a substitute dredger could have been obtained. The plaintiff did not recover loss of profits beyond that date. Those lost profits arose because the plaintiff could not afford to buy a replacement. Lord Wright said:

> "Nor is the appellant's financial disability to be compared with that physical delicacy or weakness which may aggravate the damage in the case of personal injuries, or with the possibility that the injured man in such a case may be either a poor labourer or a highly paid professional man. The former class of circumstances goes to the extent of actual physical damage and the latter goes to interference with profit-earning capacity; whereas the appellants want of means was, as already stated, extrinsic."

The *Liesbosch* principle is difficult to reconcile logically with both cases on unusually vulnerable plaintiffs and mitigation principles.[58] A plaintiff is only required to do what is reasonable to mitigate his or her loss and, if he or she is impecunious, it may not be reasonable to expect him or her to mitigate by spending money he or she can not afford to spend. In *Clippens Oil Co. v. Edinburgh and District Water Trustees*,[59] for example, Lord Collins said: " . . . in my opinion the wrongdoer must take his victim *talem qualem*, and if the position of the latter is aggravated because he is without the means of mitigating it, so much the worse for the wrongdoer".

There is a very fine conceptual line between, on the one hand, financial loss which is too remote (and is not recovered) because it is caused by the plaintiff's impecuniosity rather than the defendant's tort, and, on the other hand, financial loss which is increased (but recovered) because the plaintiff was unable financially to mitigate.

[57] *Supra.*
[58] See para. 19–21.
[59] [1907] A.C. 291.

There is nowadays a strong tendency to distinguish the *Liesbosch* principle. In *Dodd Properties v. Canterbury City Council*[60] the plaintiffs recovered their losses as substantially increased by their decision not to carry out repairs until after trial and an award of damages. Donaldson L.J. distinguished *Liesbosch* on the following basis:

"They were not impecunious in the *Liesbosch* sense of one who could not go out into the market. On the contrary, they were financially able to carry out the work of reinstatement in 1970. However . . . they were commercially prudent in not incurring the cash flow deficiency which would have resulted from their undertaking the work in the autumn of 1970 and waiting for reimbursement until after the hearing, particularly when the defendants were denying liability and there was a dispute as to what works could and should be done by way of reinstatement."

A differently constituted Court of Appeal adopted similar reasoning in *Perry v. Sidney Phillips & Son*.[61]

It is strongly arguable, however, that the *Liesbosch* principle does not require distinguishing. All that is required is to check, before it is applied, that its application is consistent with fundamental principles. As Lord Wright himself observed, in *Monarch Steamship Co. Limited v. Karlshamns OljeFabriker*[62]:

"In *Liesbosch (Owners) v. Edison (Owners)* . . . earlier in the judgment it was said: 'The dominant rule of law is *restitutio in integrum*, and subsidiary rules can only be justified if they give effect to that rule'. In *Liesbosch (Owners) v. Edison (Owners)* it was held that loss due to the party's impecuniosity was too remote and therefore to be neglected in the calculation of damages: it was special loss due to his financial position. A different conclusion was arrived at in *Muhamad Issa el Sheikh Ahwad v. Ali*,[63] where damages consequent on impecuniosity were held not too remote, because, as I understand, the loss was such as might reasonably be expected to be in the contemplation of the parties as likely to flow from the breach of the obligation undertaken . . . These general statements could be multiplied but the question in a case like the present must always be what reasonable business men must be taken to have contemplated as the natural or probable result if the contract was broken . . . "

---

[60] *Supra*.
[61] [1982] 1 W.L.R. 1297.
[62] *Supra*.
[63] [1947] A.C. 414.

Accordingly, in *Mattocks v. Mann*[64] the Court of Appeal allowed the plaintiff the cost of hiring a car for an additional period of time during which repairs to her accident-damaged car had been completed, but the repairers would not deliver the car to the plaintiff because she could not afford to pay the repairs cost pending settlement of her claim by the defendant. Beldam L.J. held that:

"... the law has not stood still since 1933 [the year of the *Liesbosch* decision] and does not simply apply principles, whatever the circumstances in which the question arises. It has to take account of the particular circumstances of each case: and, as the law has developed, as Kerr L.J. said in the case of *Perry v. Sydney Phillips & Son*[65] the principle of *The Liesbosch* has been subjected to what he termed 'considerable attenuation' ... at the present day it is generally accepted that, in what Lord Wright termed 'the varied web of affairs' that follows a sequence of events after an accident of this kind, it is only in an exceptional case that it is possible or correct to isolate impecuniosity, as it is sometimes called, or the plaintiff's inability to pay for the cost of repairs from his own resources as a separate cause and as terminating the consequences of a defendant's wrong. It seems to me necessary today to consider whether, having regard to all the circumstances of the case and the resources available to the plaintiff, resources known by the defendant or her representatives to be of a kind that will not be able to provide for repairs themselves, in all the circumstances the plaintiff has acted reasonably and with commercial prudence ... "

Stocker and Nourse L.JJ. agreed, stressing that the guiding principle was reasonableness: compare *Ruxley Electronics and Construction Limited v. Forsyth*.[66]

Mitigation

19–21   *Basic principle.* The principle is that the plaintiff who fails to act reasonably to minimise his or her loss, or who acts unreasonably to increase his or her loss, can not recover the additional loss from the defendant. If the plaintiff's reasonable actions in fact unfortunately increase his or her loss, then the plaintiff can recover that additional loss. If the plaintiff's reasonable actions fortunately reduce his or her loss then the defendant is liable only for the loss as so reduced:

[64] [1993] R.T.R. 13.
[65] [1982] 1 W.L.R. 1297.
[66] *Supra.* See para. 19–04.

British Westinghouse Company v. Underground Railway[67]; *Hussey v. Eels.*[68]

Although lawyers often refer to "the duty to mitigate" the plaintiff is under no legal duty, as such, and is entitled to be as extravagant as he or she pleases in putting right the defendant's breaches of contract. The principle of mitigation simply means that the plaintiff can not recover the excess over reasonable expense from the defendant: *The Solholt.*[69]

Whether or not the principle applies to reduce damages in any given case is a question of fact, not law: *Payzu v. Saunders.*[70] The burden of proof is on the defendant: *Garnac Grain Company v. Faure and Fairclough*[71]; *London and South of England Building Society v. Stone.*[72]

The plaintiff's conduct is not to be "weighed in nice scales at the instance of the party whose breach of contract has occasioned the difficulty", nor is there a failure to mitigate "because the party in breach can suggest that other measures less burdensome to him might have been taken": *Banco de Portugal v. Waterlow.*[73]

In particular, the plaintiff is not to be prejudiced if he or she is financially unable to mitigate. This principle has been recently re-affirmed in *Dodd Properties v. Canterbury City Council*[74] and derives from dicta of Lord Collins in *Clippens Oil Co v. Edinburgh and District Water Trustees*[75]:

> "In my opinion the wrongdoer must take his victim *talem qualem*, and if the position of the latter is aggravated because he is without means of mitigating it, so much the worse for the wrongdoer, who has got to be answerable for the consequences flowing from his tortious act."

Collateral benefits. If the plaintiff fortuitously receives a benefit **19–22** arising directly out of the defendant's breach, or out of the actions taken by the plaintiff to remedy that breach, then the defendant is liable only for the loss as so reduced: *British Westinghouse Company v. Underground Railway.*[76] In that case the plaintiff replaced machines which were defective as a result of the defendant's breach of contract with up-to-date machines which created greater profits

[67] *Supra.*
[68] [1990] 2 Q.B. 227.
[69] [1983] 1 Lloyd's Rep. 605.
[70] [1919] 2 K.B. 581.
[71] [1968] A.C. 1130.
[72] [1983] 1 W.L.R. 1242.
[73] [1932] A.C. 452.
[74] *Supra.*
[75] *Supra.*
[76] *Supra.*

than the old machines would have created even if they had worked properly. The plaintiff was held to have suffered no net loss once additional profit had been taken into account.

If, however, the benefit received by the plaintiff is merely collateral, or *res inter alios acta*, then no account is taken of it: *Joyner v. Weeks*[77]; *Haviland v. Long*[78] (the landlord's damages payable by the tenant who failed in breach of his lease to yield up premises in repair were not to be reduced by the fact that the landlord had managed to let the premises to a new tenant on a fully repairing lease: that transaction was *res inter alios acta*); *Hussey v. Eels*[79] (the plaintiffs had been induced to purchase their home as result of a misrepresentation that there had been no subsidence. Their damages were not to be reduced by the fact that they demolished the house and managed to obtain planning permission for the construction of two dwellings on the site, which they then sold for 1 1/2 times the purchase price). The receipt by a plaintiff of sums which diminish his or her loss are treated as collateral, or *res inter alios acta*, when they derive from an insurance policy (*Bradburn v. Great Western Railway*[80]); a pension policy (*Parry v. Cleaver*[81]); gratuitous assistance from relatives (*Donnelly v. Joyce*[82]); employers (*Dennis v. L.P.T.B.*[83]) or a charity (*Redpath v. Belfast and County Down Railway*[84]).

19–23 *Betterment.* The line between loss which was avoided and benefits which were obtained collaterally can be a fine one. Mere betterment is usually treated as a collateral benefit and no account is therefore taken of it, at least when it is not possible to remedy the damage without betterment. In rejecting an analogy with the marine insurance rule of deducting one-third new for old, Dr Lushington said, in *The Gazelle*[85]:

> "[If the plaintiff] derives incidentally a greater benefit than mere indemnification, it arises only from the impossibility of otherwise effecting such indemnification without exposing him to some loss or burden, which the law will not place on him."

In *Harbutt's Plasticine Ltd v. Wayne Tank and Pump Co. Limited*[86] the plaintiff rebuilt its factory, which had been burnt down as a

[77] [1891] 2 Q.B. 31.
[78] [1952] 2 Q.B. 80.
[79] *Supra.*
[80] (1874) L.R. 10 Ex. 1.
[81] [1970] A.C. 1.
[82] [1974] Q.B. 454.
[83] [1948] 1 All E.R. 799.
[84] [1947] N.I. 167.
[85] (1844) 2 W. Rob. (Adm.) 279.
[86] [1970] 1 Q.B. 447.

result of the defendant's tort. In so doing, the plaintiff mitigated the loss of profits it would have suffered without any factory at all. Its damages were not reduced merely because it ended up with a modern (and more valuable factory). Lord Denning said:

"The destruction of a building is different from the destruction of a chattel. If a second-hand car is destroyed, the owner only gets its value; because he can go into the market and get another second-hand car to replace it. He cannot charge the other party with the cost of replacing it with a new car. But, when this mill was destroyed, the plaintiffs had no choice. They were bound to replace it as soon as they could, not only to keep their business going, but also to mitigate the loss of profit (for which they would be able to charge the defendants). They replaced it in the only possible way, without adding any extras. I think they should be allowed the cost of replacement. True it is they got new for old, but I do not think the wrongdoer can diminish the claim on that account. If they had added extra accommodation or made extra improvements, they would have to give credit. But that is not the case."

Harbutt's Plasticine was followed in *Bacon v. Cooper Metals Limited*.[87] This was a case involving a chattel and not land: the plaintiff had to replace the rotor in a metal fragmentiser damaged beyond repair by the defendant's negligence. The plaintiff replaced the old rotor which had been damaged with a new rotor. The old rotor had a further life expectancy of three and three-quarter years out of a total of seven years at the time of its destruction. The plaintiff was, nonetheless held to be entitled to the full cost of the new replacement rotor and was not restricted to the proportion of the total cost of the new rotor equivalent to the proportion the old rotor's remaining life bore to its total life (*i.e.* about 50 per cent). The reasons were that the plaintiff had acted reasonably, he had had no choice of action and the future life of the replacement rotor was too uncertain to take into account. *Harbutt's Plasticine* was also followed in *Dominion Mosaics and Tile Company Limited v. Trafalgar Trucking Company Limited*[88] (another factory destroyed by fire).

Where the tenant replaces decorations damaged as a result of the landlord's actions *Harbutt's Plasticine* has been applied so that there is no deduction on account of betterment: *McGreal v. Wake*[89]; *Bradley v. Chorley Borough Council*[90]; *Calabar Properties Limited v. Stitcher*.[91]

[87] [1982] 1 All E.R. 397.
[88] [1990] 2 All E.R. 246.
[89] (1984) 13 H.L.R. 107.
[90] (1985) 17 H.L.R. 305.
[91] [1984] 1 W.L.R. 287.

Contributory negligence

19–24   When the plaintiff's action arises in tort, his or her damages will
be reduced if the court finds that he or she was in part responsible
for his or her losses.[92]

Where there is a breach of contract, but the contractual liability
duplicates an independent tort liability, the courts will still apply
the Law Reform (Contributory Negligence) Act 1945 to reduce the
plaintiff's damages proportionately to the plaintiff's own responsibility for his or her loss.

Where, however, the defendant is liable simply because he or she
is in breach of a contractual obligation, damages can not be
reduced by reference to the principle of contributory negligence:
Forsikirings Vesta v. Butcher[93] (this issue was not considered at
House of Lords level); *Barclays Bank plc v. Fairclough Building
Limited*.[94] In the latter case, the defendant failed to clean asbestos
roofs in accordance with the provisions of the contract; damages
were not reduced because the plaintiff's safety officer had failed to
supervise properly.

The defendant who is unable to rely on contributory negligence
may, however, achieve the same result by pleading failure to
mitigate or absence of causation. In *Tennant Radiant Heat Limited
v. Warrington Development Corporation*,[95] for example, the tenant's
damages were reduced by 10 per cent because the tenant's own
breaches of contract had been a 10 per cent cause of the damage.
The tenant's damages were reduced, not on the basis of contributory negligence, but on the basis that the tenant, rather than the
landlord, had been 10 per cent to blame for the losses.

---

[92] Law Reform (Contributory Negligence) Act 1945.
[93] [1989] A.C. 852.
[94] [1995] 1 All E.R. 289.
[95] [1988] 1 E.G.L.R. 41.

CHAPTER TWENTY

The Basic Measures of Damages for Disrepair

Introduction: The two competing measures

The tenant who occupies dilapidated premises can be reasonably **20–01** perceived to suffer basic loss in two different ways:

(1) On the one hand, the tenant has not been getting what he or she has paid for. The tenant has, for example, paid rent of £100 per week for the use of premises which, in their dilapidated state, are only worth £50 per week ("diminution in value" or "loss of rental value").

(2) On the other hand, the tenant has suffered physical discomfort and inconvenience as a result of the disrepair ("damages for discomfort and inconvenience").

The predominant current practice, at county court level, is to employ either or both ways of measuring loss in order to achieve fair and reasonable *restitutio in integrum*, as the circumstances of the case suggest. It is, however, right to say that the practice of awarding damages for diminution of value is controversial in principle, not fully defined and on the face of it inconsistent with precedent.

Arguments against damages based upon loss of rental value when the tenant remains in occupation

The opponents of damages assessed on the basis of rental value **20–02** obtain powerful support from *Calabar Properties Limited v. Stitcher.*[1]

---

[1] [1984] 1 W.L.R. 287.

In that case the Court of Appeal determined that when a tenant sues his or her landlord for failing to repair in accordance with the contract, the basic measure of damages is: "what the plaintiff might have to spend on performing the landlord's covenant (assuming the landlord would not perform it himself) and substantial general damages for inconvenience and discomfort . . . "

The Court of Appeal explicitly rejected loss of rental value as an appropriate measure of the tenant's damage: "The other head of damage which counsel for the tenant says the judge was wrong to disallow was another aspect of the diminution in value of the flat to the tenant, based on some loss of capital or rental value." The Court of Appeal dismissed that part of the tenant's appeal.

The tenant had relied on a famous passage in the judgment of Bankes L.J. in *Hewitt v. Rowlands*[2]:

> "Prima facie the measure of damage for breach of the obligation to repair is the difference in value to the tenant during that period between the house in the condition in which it now is and the house in the condition in which it would be if the landlord on receipt of the notice had fulfilled his obligation to repair."

Stephenson L.J. pointed out that the Court of Appeal in *Hewitt v. Rowlands*

> "in laying down the measure of damage . . . cannot have had the capital or rental value of the cottage as a marketable asset in mind, because a statutory tenancy is not marketable.
>
> The other head of damage which counsel for the tenant says the judge was wrong to disallow was another aspect of the diminution in value of the flat to the tenant, based on some loss of capital or rental value. For this item he claims to have the support of a decision of this court in *Hewitt v. Rowlands*. He put it in the alternative: diminution in the capital value of the flat, stated, according to the report and evidence of the expert, Mr Lewis, to be £90,000 in the condition in which it was in November 1982, as against £100,000 at the same date with the defects repaired and the redecoration completed; or diminution in the rack rental value which he gave as £170 per week exclusive of rates if let furnished, and £100 per week exclusive of rates if let unfurnished, in December 1982. Before us counsel for the tenant argued only for the difference between the nil letting value which the unrepaired flat would have in the open market and the £100 a week for which it would let unfurnished when repaired . . .

---

[2] (1924) 93 L.J.K.B. 1080.

. . . to submit that what the tenant has lost by the landlord's
breach of covenant is the consequent diminution in the value
of the flat as a marketable asset is to ask the court to take a
wholly unreal view of the facts, The reality of the tenant's loss
is the temporary loss of the home where she would have lived
with her husband permanently if the landlords had performed
their covenant . . . . If she had bought the lease as a specula-
tion intending to assign it, to the knowledge of the landlords,
the alleged diminution in rental (or capital) value might be the
true measure of her damage. But she did not: she bought it for
a home, not a saleable asset, and it would be deplorable if the
court were bound to leave the real world for the complicated
underworld of expert evidence on comparable properties and
values, on the fictitious assumption that what the flat would
have fetched had anything to do with its value to her or her
husband. I do not think we are bound by the authority of
Hewitt v. Rowlands or any other decision to do something so
absurd, and the second objection of counsel for the landlords
must, in my opinion rule out any damages for difference in
rental value . . . . What is plain is that, in laying down the
measure of damage [in *Hewitt v. Rowlands*], the court cannot
have had the capital or rental value of the cottage as a
marketable asset in mind, because a statutory tenancy is not
marketable . . . . What the difference in value to the plaintiff of
the statutory tenancy of the cottage repaired and unrepaired
may have been was not an easy matter for the registrar to
assess, but I suspect he would not have gone far wrong had he
equated it with what the plaintiff might have to spend on
performing the landlord's covenant (assuming the landlord
would not perform it himself) and substantial general damages
for inconvenience and discomfort for the period from notice to
the landlord till assessment or performance of the covenant by
the plaintiff."

The reasoning of *Calabar Properties Limited v. Stitcher* was
considered and applied by the Court of Appeal in *Personal Representatives of Chiodi v. de Marney*,[3] as part of the Court of Appeals
reasoning for the conclusion that the judge "was not in error in
failing to take account of the rent as a prima facie indication of the
level of any proper award".

Similarly, in *Credit Suisse v. Beegas Nominees Limited*,[4] Lindsay J.
held:

[3] (1988) 21 H.L.R. 6.
[4] [1994] 1 E.G.L.R. 76.

"I am thus asked to make an award in respect of nearly two years' inconvenience. Mr Gaunt seeks to use the landlord's own expert's view as a guide, that expert, Mr Ian Hayward FRICS having suggested that the premises were halved in rental value by reason of their state or, upon some assumptions little related to reality, that the premises were reduced by some 20 per cent in rental value . . . . I am unconvinced that one can evaluate inconvenience to a tenant in occupation by reference simply to the diminution in prospective letting value to some hypothetical other tenant . . ."

Mr Stephen Sedley Q.C., sitting as an assistant recorder, held in *Hussein v. Mehlman*,[5] that:

"Are the plaintiffs entitled, in relation to the time before they put an end to the lease, to extinguish or diminish the rent due because of the various failures of consideration? It seems to me that there are two problems. First, the doctrine that the covenant for the payment of rent is independent of the performance of the other covenants is still, as I understand it, the law. Second, there is a potential element of double-counting in awarding damages for breach and then denying the lessor some or all of the payment due for the occupancy of the premises. On balance, although the contrary is certainly arguable, I do not think that the law permits me to award what is in effect a rebate on the rent in the circumstances of a case like this. The proper approach is laid down in the Court of Appeal in *Calabar Properties v. Stitcher*.[6] Its effect is to limit damages in a case like the present to the inconvenience of occupying a house in a condition in which it would not have been but for the breach of covenant. The rent is paid for the occupancy, the damages for the inconvenience."

Holiday cases are not directly comparable, but even they do not support a diminution of rental value approach. In *Jarvis v. Swans Tours Limited*[6a] the holiday cost £63.45 and the County Court judge had awarded damages of £37.72 because "He thought that Mr. Jarvis had got half of what he paid for". Lord Denning M.R. said that:

"I think the judge was in error in taking the sum paid for the holiday £63.45 and halving it. The right measure of damages is to compensate him for the loss of entertainment and

[5] [1992] 2 E.G.L.R. 87.
[6] [1983] 3 All E.R. 759, especially at pp. 768, 769j–770b.
[6a] [1973] 1 Q.B. 233.

enjoyment which he was promised, and which he did not get."

In addition, prima facie, the only relevant evidence admissible in the assessment of hypothetical loss of rental value is the opinion of an expert. Expert evidence on loss of rental value in the county court is the exception rather than the rule. The rent for the relevant period is ascertained, more or less exactly, following which, after hearing submissions from counsel, the judge determines what in his opinion the appropriate deduction should be. The decision would appear to be a matter of opinion if the exercise is supposed to reflect the reality of the market place (*sed quaere*).

Arguments for damages based upon loss of rental value when the tenant remains in occupation

As plain and definite as the statements of general principle are of the full Court of Appeal in *Calabar Properties Limited v. Stitcher*,[6b] the case has to be seen in its context: **20–03**

(1) The court was not able in any event to award damages for loss of rental value because that part of the claim had not been properly pleaded.

(2) The plaintiff had a long lease. Assessment of damages by reference to diminution in weekly rental was accordingly one clear stage more hypothetical than in the case of a dwelling-house which was actually being rented on a periodic tenancy.

(3) There was no citatation of cases in which damages had been awarded on a loss of rental basis: for example, *McCoy & Co. v. Clark*.[7]

(4) It was acknowledged, naturally, that fundamental contract principles were paramount. It follows from that, that "one set of rules" can never be applied to all cases. Stephenson L.J.:

"In measuring and assessing any tenant's damages for breach of a landlord's repairing covenant the court must, I think, always start with the fundamental principle that they are 'so far as possible by means of a monetary award, to place the plaintiff in the position which he would have occupied if he had not suffered the wrong complained of, be that wrong a tort or breach of contract'. I take that statement from the judgment of Donaldson L.J. in *Dodd Properties (Kent) Limited*

[6b] *Supra.*
[7] (1992) 13 H.L.R. 89, C.A.

v. Canterbury City Council[8] . . . . So the true measure of damages for persons owning or occupying land, whether in tort or contract, depends on the position of the plaintiffs and all the circumstances in which they have suffered loss and damage, in the light of the fundamental principle to which I have referred."

Griffiths L.J. held that:

" . . . it appears to me, both from the arguments at the bar and the way in which the judge expressed himself, that there may be a widely held belief by those practising in this field that when damages are claimed by a tenant for breach of a landlord's repairing covenant they must always be assessed by reference to the diminution in the open market value of the premises . . .

The object of awarding damages against a landlord for breach of his covenant to repair is not to punish the landlord but, so far as money can, to restore the tenant to the position he would have been in had there been no breach. This object will not be achieved by applying one set of rules to all cases regardless of the particular circumstances of the case. The facts of each case must be looked at carefully to see what damage the tenant has suffered and how he may be fairly compensated by a monetary award."

While there is no clear authority which repudiates or distinguishes *Calabar Properties Limited v. Stitcher*,[9] there is a large and growing body of case-law in which loss of rental value is tacitly accepted as a measure of damages which is capable of being appropriate in the case of periodic tenancies.

In *Sturolson & Co. v. Mauroux*[10] the county court judge assessed damages on a loss of rental value basis: the landlord did not object to the county court judge's approach, either in the county court or the Court of Appeal and there was accordingly no need for the Court of Appeal to consider whether the county court judge's approach was appropriate. Neither is *Calabar Properties Limited v. Stitcher*[11] referred to in any of the judgments. Nonetheless, the Court of Appeal found nothing in the county court judge's approach that called for adverse remark.

The County Court judge in *Brent L.B.C. v. Carmel*,[12] His Honour Judge Charles Q.C., considered the judgments in *Calabar*

---

[8] [1980] 1 W.L.R. 433 at p. 456.
[9] *Supra.*
[10] (1988) 20 H.L.R. 332.
[11] *Supra.*
[12] (1995) 28 H.L.R. 203.

Properties Limited v. Stitcher and held that the overriding effect of the case was that damages were to bring about *restitutio in integrum*. He found as a fact that Brent's failure to repair in accordance with its obligations resulted in one out of the three bedrooms being unusable for eight months of the year and two out of the three bedrooms being unusable for four months of the year, between 1987 and 1988. From 1988 he found that the premises were as a whole unfit for human habitation and prejudicial to health. The county court judge accordingly awarded the tenant special damages equivalent to 30 per cent of the contractual rent for 1987 and 1988 and 50 per cent of the contractual rent for six years between 1988 and the date of completion of the necessary repairs. In addition, he awarded general damages for discomfort and inconvenience of £1,000 per annum from 1981 to 1986 and of £1,500 per annum from 1987.[13] The judge said:

"In *Calabar Properties Limited v. Stitcher* it was held that the fundamental principle to be applied in measuring a tenant's damages for breach of the plaintiff's repairing covenants was to restore her, so far as money could, to the position in which she would have been in had there been no breach of covenant and that an appropriate method is to assess the difference between the value of the premises to the tenant in the condition in which it was and the value the premises would have had to the defendant if the plaintiffs had fulfilled their obligations under the repairing covenants."[13a]

The landlord appealed, *inter alia*, on the ground that the damages awarded were "wholly and manifestly excessive and wrong in principle". The full Court of Appeal refused leave to appeal. It held as follows:

"Mr Gallivan has put in a supplementary skeleton in which he raises various points, only one of which in my view requires any comment, and that is as to the quantum of damages. Mr Gallivan points out that the award in this case was, in effect, at a rate of approximately £2,750 per annum. He refers us to a decision of this court in 1988 in the case of *Chiodi v. de Marney*[14] where, at that time, this court indicated that £1,500 per annum for damages in cases of disrepair, was the top of the bracket at that time. That was a 1988 decision. The facts in that case may have been different from the facts in the present case. In my view, there can be no real prospect of this court

---

[13] See *Legal Action* (June 1995, p. 22) and the Transcript of the judgment at pp. 48 to 52.
[13a] Transcript, p. 48E.
[14] (1988) 21 H.L.R. 6.

being persuaded that the assessment of damages made by His Honour Judge Charles in the circumstances of this case was wrong in principle or manifestly excessive."

Counsel for the landlords had argued forcefully that the award was wrong in principle because it included loss of rental value, in breach of the *Calabar Properties Limited v. Stitcher* guidelines. Such arguments were plainly rejected in this case, although not in terms which seek to distinguish *Calabar Properties Limited* or which seek to consider in any way, let alone set down any principles on which damages are to be assessed.

20–04   A slightly different approach was taken by His Honour Judge Diamond at the Central London County Court in the case of *Lambeth L.B.C. v. Alicia de Freitas.*[15] Having considered all the relevant authorities, including *Calabar Properties Limited*, he held that damages for loss of rental could be awarded, but only where the disrepair had caused the premises to fall into a different rental category, *e.g.* when one or more rooms became unusable:

"In the light of these authorities (and of a number of other awards in the county court) I see no reason why in an appropriate case a tenant should not be awarded compensation separately (i) for the loss suffered through having been forced to live in a flat which, by reason of the disrepair, had a lower rental value than if the landlord had performed his repairing covenant and (ii) for the loss suffered due to the inconvenience and discomfort caused by the same state of affairs. If the two aspects of the breach can sensibly be approached separately, as is sometimes the case, then it may be desirable to itemise the award by breaking down the general damages into two separate heads of loss. An example which is sometimes given is where the tenant occupies a two bedroom flat, where due to the disrepair one bedroom is unfit for habitation and where accordingly the tenant may be said to have suffered a loss through being liable to pay rent appropriate to a two bedroom flat when he has only had the benefit of occupying a one bedroom flat. Even in this example, however, there is an obvious overlap between loss incurred through diminution in value and loss incurred through inconvenience and discomfort. To some extent two separate labels are being attached to precisely the same facts. But so long as this is borne in mind in making the assessment, the breakdown of the award into two separate heads of loss can be justified on the basis that the tenant could reasonably perceive that he has

---

[15] Case No. 12942, judgment of November 8, 1994.

suffered loss in two different ways and that he should be compensated accordingly . . .

. . . Where a statutory or protected tenancy is concerned, it can seldom be appropriate to call valuation evidence. The loss is often suffered over a long period and it is not uncommon to find that the agreed or assessed rent has changed considerably over the relevant period. There has in fact been no actual pecuniary loss suffered by the plaintiff where he has continued to occupy the flat for months or years in its unrepaired state and where the landlord has eventually done the repairs but has done them late. In some cases the Court can take a mean figure for the rental value which would be too high for the early period of the tenancy if assessed separately and too low for the later period if assessed separately and apply to this figure a percentage representing the extent to which, on average, the beneficial use of the flat has been reduced by the landlord's breach. This is however necessarily a field in which no exact instrument exists by which to measure the tenant's loss. In some cases a broad approach can be adopted; in others it may be more realistic to award a single sum to cover inconvenience discomfort and diminution in the rental value of the dwelling . . .

Third, where the court awards a sum for diminution in the rental value of the dwelling, what it is doing is to break down an award of general damages so as to itemise different aspects of the tenant's loss. Except in cases where damages are being awarded for an actual pecuniary loss suffered by the tenant, up to the period of the trial, due to the wrongful act of the landlord, the case should in my judgment be regarded as one of general damages and the award should carry interest at the rate appropriate to general damages.

In the present case there are a number of reasons why it would be wholly inappropriate to award the tenant separate sums for diminution in value and inconvenience and discomfort. First, while the effect of the landlord's breach of his repairing covenant was to impair living conditions in the flat, it did not cause the flat to fall into a different rental category from that to which it would have belonged if the landlord's repairing covenant had been performed. The flat was at all times a one bedroom Council flat for which no market value existed but for which the same rental would have been charged irrespective of the defects. It would not have occurred to the tenant that she was suffering a loss through diminution in the rental value of the flat. She perceived the loss as being one due to the inconvenience, hardship and discomfort suffered by her and the other occupants of the flat due to the appalling living conditions resulting from the landlord's failure to do the repairs. Not only is it unrealistic in these circumstances to assess the tenant's loss separately for diminution in value and inconvenience but there is in this case such an overlap between the two concepts that it is hard to see how this can be done."

If one reads through the Housing Updates in the *Legal Action* magazine, one can find a number of other cases in which damages for loss of rental value have been awarded in addition to general damages for discomfort and inconvenience. Of particular interest is the recent report of *Bell v. Mazehead Limited.*[16] In that case Recorder Rayner James awarded diminution in value at 50 per cent of the contractual rent (rising at 5 per cent per annum over a five year period) in addition to general damages for discomfort and inconvenience of £1,000 per annum. He expressly refused to discount the damages for diminution in value on account of the fact that the rent had been met by way of housing benefit.

An as yet not resolved question is whether, if loss of rental value is awarded, the damages should be treated as special or general damages. H.H.J. Diamond in *Lambeth L.B.C. v. Alicia de Freitas*[17] expressed the view that such damages were general damages. H.H.J. Charles in *Brent L.B.C. v. Carmel*[18] awarded them as special damages. The distinction is of importance because special damages attract significantly higher awards of interest.[19] Although the Court of Appeal refused leave to appeal in the case of *Brent London Borough v. Carmel*,[20] it seems that damages for loss of rental value are more likely to be general damages. The test is in *British Transport Commission v. Gourley*[21]:

"In an action for personal injuries the damages are always divided into two main parts. First, there is what is referred to as special damage, which has to be specially pleaded and proved. This consists of out-of-pocket expenses and loss of earnings incurred down to the date of trial, and is generally capable of exact calculation. Secondly, there is general damage which the law implies and is not specially pleaded. This includes compensation for pain and suffering and the like, and, if the injuries suffered are such as to lead to continuing or permanent disability, compensation for loss of earning power in the future."

[16] *Legal Action*, March 1996, p. 14.
[17] *Supra.*
[18] Legal Action, June 1995, p. 22.
[19] See Chapter 25.
[20] *Supra.*
[21] [1956] A.C. 185.

The relevance of the rent payable when assessing general damages conventionally

Whether or not the stage has been reached at which loss of rental value, at least in the case of periodic tenancies, has become an acceptable measure of damage, it is fairly clear that comparison between the amount of rent payable, or the amount of premium paid, and the condition of the premises, is of *relevance* to the assessment of damages and always has been.   **20–05**

The rent as a useful cross-check

In *Elmcroft Developments Limited v. Tankersley-Sawyer*[22] the Court   **20–06**
of Appeal refused to interfere with an award of general damages of £1,300 [£2,340] per annum in a case in which severe rising damp had caused the plaintiff substantial discomfort and inconvenience. Ackner L.J. found it useful to compare the general damages award with the rental value:

> "I think there is force in Mr Dowding's observation that the figure of £2,600, which is £1,300 a year, which in turn is £26 a week, is unlikely to represent the rental value of Miss Tankersley-Sawyer's flat if it had been in a proper state of repair. She herself gave evidence that she expected to be able to dispose of the flat for approximately £40,000 when it had been put into a proper state; and, if that is its value, £26 a week does not represent what one would expect to be a fair return on the net capital."

Rent as more than a guide when there is insufficient evidence of discomfort

Toff v. McDowell[23] was a case in which damages were awarded for   **20–07**
noise nuisance. Evans-Lombe J. held that:

> "I have really no evidence upon which I can base any measurement of damage save that I know that the plaintiff, when he took his assignment of the flat, paid the sum of rather more than £60,000 for the unexpired portion of the lease. It is submitted that a flat purchased with such a purchase price would be likely to command an annual rental of approximately £3,000 a year. It seems to me that, as I have been told in many other similar cases, the court must simply do the best it can and to some extent that must result in plucking a figure out of the air. I find that the diminution in the flat's enjoyment

[22] (1984) 15 H.L.R. 63.
[23] (1993) 25 H.L.R. 650.

during the six-month period of the occupation by the three tenants between July 1990 and January 1991 diminished the enjoyment of the plaintiff of his flat at the rate of £2,000 per annum but that otherwise the diminution of his enjoyment can be valued at approximately £1,000 [per annum]."

In *McCoy & Co. v. Clark*[24] decided before *Calabar Properties Limited v. Stitcher*,[25] the County Court judge had said: "The flat is not particularly important to him, it is just a place to put his head down" and awarded general damages at 10 per cent for one period, then 20 per cent for another period, of the rent of £9 per week. The Court of Appeal doubled the percentages. Sir David Cairns said:

"It is all very well to say that the defendant was not spending a great deal of the day in the flat and that he was using it mainly as a sleeping place. If he had the flat as a sleeping place and was willing to pay £9 a week for the flat for that purpose, then he is entitled to a flat which is comfortable for that purpose, and if it is substantially reduced in the degree of comfort, then I think what he ought to recover is something proportional to that reduction."

In *Sella House Limited v. Mears*[26] the Court of Appeal declined to interfere with the County Court judge's award of £1,250 when the landlord had kept the common parts basically clean, but had let them get dingy and failed to keep them "up to the condition that would be expected of a block of residential flats in that very good part of London". There was no evidence of physical discomfort: the only basis on which damages could have been awarded was to infer diminution in value.

In *Sampson v. Wilson*[27] H.H.J. Roger Cooke, sitting as a deputy High Court judge, had to deal with a case in which the premises were in substantial disrepair. The landlord was an absentee and his agents carried out works of repair in such a manner as to deliberately make matters worse and drive out the tenants. Because works were carried out without permission or exceeding any permission there was a trespass (in addition to a breach of contract) thereby permitting an award of exemplary damages to be made. H.H.J. Cooke held as follows:

"(1) For the relevant period each plaintiff should be taken as having suffered damage equivalent to the whole of his rent;

---

[24] (1982) 13 H.L.R. 89.
[25] *Supra*.
[26] [1989] 12 E.G. 67.
[27] (1994) 26 H.L.R. 486.

that is, having an uninhabitable home and losing the whole value of it.

(2) But I have also to consider exemplary damages. As to (1) the number of weeks for Mr Sampson—April 17 to November 26—is 32 weeks; for Mr Kohlbacher they were from April 17 to January 4, which is 37 weeks. Mr Sampson's rent was £25 per week, Mr Kohlbacher's £40. Mr Sampson comes out at £800.00 and Mr Kohlbacher at £1,480 . . . it is a proper case for exemplary damages . . . I am, of course, limiting myself to the period before the tenants go . . . I award against Mitchell at this point £2,000 in respect of each tenant."

These decisions are of interest because they indicate how loss of rental value is relevant evidence in the assessment of damages where there is no evidence of physical discomfort. Any inconsistency with *Calabar Properties Limited v. Stitcher*[28] is resolved by reference to the fundamental principles of the assessment of damages. As Viscount Haldane put it in *British Westinghouse Electric and Manufacturing Company Limited v. Underground Electric Railway Company of London*[29]: "The quantum of damage is a question of fact, and the only guidance the law can give is to lay down general principles which afford at times but scanty assistance in dealing with particular cases . . .

Amount of rent increasing or decreasing the size of the award

In an extreme case, *Newham L.B.C. v. Patel*[30] the rent had been very low: £2.83 per week (as against the norm for that time and for a house of that type in reasonable repair of £7.53 per week). Templeman L.J. went so far as to hold that "Mr Patel cannot have both the benefit of a low rent and an award of damages for the same reason—that is why the rent was so low". That dicta has to be seen, however, in the context of the case as a whole. The ratio of the decision was that the prospective life of the dwelling was so short that, despite its poor condition, the landlord had not in fact been in breach of the implied repairing covenants in section 11 of the Landlord and Tenant Act 1985.

Notwithstanding *Newham L.B.C. v. Patel*,[31] the prevailing view is that, where the landlord is in breach of covenant, although a low rent is a factor, it can not artificially restrict the award of damages, for example, by placing a ceiling on the award equal to the

20–08

---

[28] *Supra.*
[29] [1912] A.C. 673.
[30] (1978) 13 H.L.R. 77.
[31] *Supra.*

maximum annual rent. In that sense, the cases are at one with holiday cases such as *Jarvis v. Swans Tours Limited*[32] in which Lord Denning M.R. said:

> "I think the judge was in error in taking the sum paid for the holiday £63.45 and halving it. The right measure of damages is to compensate him for the loss of entertainment and enjoyment which he was promised, and which he did not get.
>
> Looking at the matter quite broadly, I think the damages in this case should be the sum of £125."

In *Personal Representatives of Chiodi v. de Marney*[33] Ralph Gibson L.J., having referred in detail to both *Hewitt v. Rowlands*[34] and *Calabar Properties Limited v. Stitcher*,[35] held that the level of rent payable was not even a prima facie indication of the level of general damages:

> "The Notice of Appeal takes two points only; first it is said that the learned Recorder failed to give sufficient weight to the fact that the recoverable rent was only £8 per week . . . [counsel for the landlords] referred to *Hewitt v. Rowlands* . . . [and] a passage from the judgment of Bankes L.J. at p. 761 where he said:
>
> Now, prima facie the measure of damages for breach of the obligation to repair is the difference in value to the tenant during that period between the house in its then condition, and its value if the landlord on receipt of the tenant's notice, had fulfilled the obligation to repair . . .
>
> Mr Van Hee invited the court to say that the value to the tenant in the sense contended for in the judgment of Bankes L.J. could not exceed the recoverable rent, and that that amount should provide at least some guide or test to the maximum award for inconvenience, discomfort and distress in circumstances of this nature . . .
>
> In my judgment the approach of the learned Recorder, in seeking to assess a sum to compensate fairly for discomfort and loss of enjoyment or, as he put it, for 'inconvenience and distress' was right, and he was not in error in failing to take account of the rent as a prima facie indication of the level of any proper award."

---

[32] [1973] Q.B. 233.
[33] *Supra.*
[34] *Supra.*
[35] *Supra.*

Accordingly, the Court of Appeal refused to interfere with an award of damages for discomfort and inconvenience at £30 per week, whilst the rent had been only £8 per week. Ralph Gibson L.J.'s judgement does not, however, necessarily mean that the level of rent should never be taken into account.

In *Sturolson & Co. v. Mauroux*[36] the landlord argued that the tenant had already been compensated for the disrepair because the Rent Officer had registered a fair rent for the flat and, in so doing, had had regard to its condition, as he or she was bound to do. The Court of Appeal rejected that argument, but only on the narrow basis that:

"Obviously the rent of a property in disrepair is less than that of a property in repair, even with a repairing covenant in the lease. But the rent for a property in disrepair but with a landlord's repairing covenant will be greater than such a property where there is no repairing covenant. Therefore . . . the Rent Officer has not wholly taken disrepair into account because he must have valued the value of the repairing covenant and the failure thereafter to carry out that covenant sounds in damages."

It is explicit in the parts of the county court judgment set out in the case, and implicit in what Glidewell L.J. has just said, that the damages awarded to the tenant *were* reduced in part because the statutory rent registration machinery had already required a rent reduction on account of disrepair. The reduction was, however, only partial on the basis that the Rent Officer would have taken into account the existence of the landlord's repairing covenant.

Where there is a relatively high rent, conversely general damages are often increased. In *Credit Suisse v. Beegas Nominees Limited*[37] Lindsay J. assessed damages in this way:

"General damages are notoriously large, but doing the best I can to have regard to the inconvenience suffered by staff and customers in these expensive and prestige premises over the period I have described I fix general damages at £40,000."

In *Sella House Limited v. Mears*[38] the Court of Appeal declined to interfere with the County Court judge's award of £1,250 when the landlord had kept the common parts basically clean, but had let them get dingy and failed to keep them "up to the condition that would be expected of a block of residential flats in that very good

[36] (1988) 20 H.L.R. 332.
[37] *Supra.*
[38] *Supra.*

part of London". It is clear however that the value and location of
the flat led to a relatively high award of damages.

*Diminution in value: interference with the tenant's attempts to
sell or sub-let*

20–09   If the tenant:

(1) sells the premises for less than he or she would have received
had the landlord performed his or her repairing covenants;
or

(2) rents out the premises for less than he or she would have
received (or is prevented from making any rental income at
all because of the landlord's failure to repair)

then the appropriate measure of damages is the difference in value
between what sums the tenant actually received and the sums the
tenant would have received on the open market had the landlord
complied with his or her repairing obligations:

> "If the tenant has rented the property to let it and the landlord
> is aware of this, then the 'difference in value to the tenant' may
> be measured by his loss of rent if he cannot let it because of the
> landlord's breach. If the tenant is driven out of occupation by
> the breach and forced to sell the property 'the difference in
> value to the tenant' may be measured by the difference
> between the selling price and the price he would have obtained
> if the landlord had observed his repairing covenant.[39]

> The damages recoverable must either be such as would fairly
> and reasonably be considered to have arisen naturally, accord-
> ing to the usual course of things (the first rule in *Hadley v.
> Baxendale*), or be such as the parties concerned may reason-
> ably be supposed to have had in contemplation at the time
> when the contract was made (the second rule in *Hadley v.
> Baxendale*) . . . . The lease of flat 18 which Aylmer granted to
> Mrs Villiers was for 125 years, a period so long that it was
> inevitable that there would be changes in ownership and
> occupation during the term. The flat was in terms of size, type
> and location similar to many thousands in London which are
> continually changing hands by assignment and subletting. The
> lease made express reference to subletting in covenant 3(7)(6),
> which prohibited it for more than 12 months unless certain
> requirements were fulfilled . . . . In my judgment for Mrs
> Villiers, or her assignees, Mr and Mrs Mira, to sublet was
> something which was likely to arise naturally and the ordinary

---

[39] *Calabar Properties Limited v. Stitcher, supra, per* Lord Griffiths.

course of events; in other words within the first rule of *Hadley v. Baxendale* . . . but for the building works, Mr and Mrs Mira would have been able to sublet their flat for the whole period during which they were abroad . . . as to probable rent . . . it would I think be reasonable to take as figure the £210 . . . Mr and Mrs Mira may recover the loss of rent of £210 per week . . . less a deduction in respect of letting agents' fees and other liabilities . . . . Dr Bush allowed Mr and Mrs Maxwell to remain in possession of the flat, paying £200 per week, when, but for the Aylmers' breach of covenant, he could no doubt have obtained £250. He is, I think, entitled to recover the difference."[40]

If the landlord's failure to repair results in the tenant being unable to sell, then in principle the tenant may recover: (a) the costs of an abortive sale by auction; and (b) running losses, where interest on the loan to acquire the premises, rates and other running costs exceeds the rental income; but not (c) the value of wasted executive time spent endeavouring to get the landlord or local authority to deal with the repairs; or (d) loss of opportunity to make profits on the profit the tenant should have been able to make on the sale of the flat: *City and Metropolitan Properties Limited v. Greycroft*[41] (but note that *Tate & Lyle Food and Distribution Limited v. Greater London Council*[42] does not appear to have been cited. In this case, Forbes J. held that expenditure of managerial time in remedying an actionable wrong could be awarded as special damages; but that no award would be made on the facts of the case because the plaintiff had failed to properly record the amount of managerial time spent).

In *Credit Suisse v. Beegas Nominees Limited*[43] the landlord's failure to repair commercial premises resulted, *inter alia*, in the tenant not being able to assign them. Because of a subsequent collapse in the market, it was unlikely, at the date of trial, that the tenant would be able to assign and would accordingly have to remain tenant until expiry of the lease. The tenant was awarded, in addition to general damages for the discomfort caused to its employees and clients whilst in occupation, £85,000 being the likely sale price the tenant would have achieved for the lease; legal and other costs associated with abortive attempts to sell; rent, service charges and other outgoings in respect of the premises up until trial; rent, service charges and other outgoings up until the effluxion of the lease, less what the tenant could obtain by sub-letting.

[40] *Mira v. Aylmer Square Investments, supra.*
[41] [1987] 3 All E.R. 839.
[42] [1981] 3 All E.R. 716.
[43] *Supra.*

CHAPTER TWENTY ONE

Some Defences to the Basic Award of Damages

Failure to Mitigate

Failure to complain

21–01 Where the landlord is only liable to repair after notice[1] failure to put the landlord on notice is fatal to the cause of action itself. Where the landlord is liable irrespective of notice,[2] failure to complain can be treated as a failure to mitigate.

In *Minchburn Limited v. Peck*[3] the landlord's covenant to repair was not subject to the implied pre-condition of notice. The question arose whether, despite that, the tenant's damages should be reduced because he failed to notify his landlord of the disrepair and therefore was, to an extent, the author of his own misfortune. Dillon L.J. said:

" . . . it does not turn the landlord's responsibility into a responsibility to repair on notice. He remains liable to do the repairs whether or not he has been given notice. It is only a question not of liability but of how far some sorts of damage can be claimed and, in particular, damage for discomfort and inconvenience when the person claiming to have suffered the discomfort and inconvenience could have improved his position by giving notice to the landlord.

[1] See Chapter 5.
[2] See Chapter 5.
[3] [1988] 1 E.G.L.R. 53.

It is, however, implicit in that that the landlord would have done something if given notice. The history of the state of repair of this property is not very encouraging in that field-. . . . There is, however, a possibility that if the defendant had badgered at a yet earlier date, the final result might have been achieved a bit sooner. On the whole, I am of the view that some small allowance ought to be made by way of mitigation and, accordingly, I would for my part reduce the sum of £800, which the judge awarded as compensation for discomfort and dampness and so forth, to a sum of £700."

Failure to allow access

If the tenant unreasonably refuses to allow the landlord access to   **21–02**
repair, the landlord's liability to repair or pay damages on account of his failure to repair is suspended. The principle was stated by Jenkins L.J. in *Granada Theatres Limited v. Freehold Investment (Leytonstone) Limited*[4]:

"If the landlord attempts within a reasonable time to do the work but is prevented from so doing by the tenant refusing him entry on the premises in accordance with the implied licence, the tenant cannot, I apprehend, maintain his action for damages so long as he persists in his refusal, because, in such circumstances, the landlord is not in breach of his covenant, or, at all events, has only been put in breach of it by the tenant's own conduct . . . . On the other hand, [the landlord] must be reasonable in the exercise of his licence to enter and (as I think) give the tenant sufficient notice of his intention to enter, and information as to the nature and extent of the work he proposed to carry out. On his part, the tenant must not unreasonably obstruct the landlord in the exercise of his right of entry for the purpose of doing the work, or take the matter out of the landlord's hands by doing the work himself before the landlord has had a reasonable opportunity of doing so."

Reasonableness is the touchstone, but whether the landlord or tenant has acted reasonably can be a difficult question and, in fact, divided the Court of Appeal in *Granada Theatres Limited v. Freehold Investment (Leytonstone) Limited.*[5] The majority, Jenkins L.J. dissenting, held that in that case the landlord had acted reasonably when the repairs they proposed to carry out would in fact have complied with their repairing obligations even though they gave the

[4] [1959] 1 W.L.R. 570.
[5] *Supra.*

tenants only the barest indication of what works they required access to carry out. Ormerod L.J. said:

"The tenants are, I think, entitled to know the general nature and purpose of the work to be performed. They have to put up with the inconvenience of having workmen on the premises, and it is reasonable that they should have such information as would enable them to judge whether the proposed repairs would be likely to fulfil their purpose . . . The tenants and their architect were demanding a specification of the proposed work, and the landlords were failing, for some reason, to make any attempt to comply with the demand . . . it appears sufficiently from the correspondence between the parties that the landlords were prepared to do such work in the repair of the roof as would have complied with the tenants' original notice of want of repair . . . [the tenants] however, continued to insist on a written specification, which, as I have said, they were not entitled to demand."

It may well be, however, that in other circumstances, a court might be prepared to hold that a reasonable landlord could only properly exercise his rights to enter to repair if he provided the tenant and his or her advisors with full details of the works. The answer will depend on the precise facts of every case: "there may be cases in which it is possible to infer a refusal because of continual prevarication, but in each case it is a question of fact and degree whether in the circumstances there has been a refusal by the tenant to allow access".[6]

An extreme example of a refusal of access by the tenant which could not possibly suspend the landlord's liability arose in *Barrett v. Lounova (1982) Limited*[7]:

"When the time for the hearing of this appeal approached, a few days after the expiry of the six month period on the 10 June, it appears that a builder was sent to the premises, but without any prior notice, and not surprisingly he was not admitted by the tenant in those circumstances."

It may be putting the case too high to submit that no account should be taken of any refusal of access by a tenant unless the landlord's request to have access was a perfectly lawful, proper exercise of his rights under the terms of the contract: but express or implied conditions relating to access will be an indicator as to the reasonableness of the tenant's conduct.

---

[6] *per* Beldam J. in *Empson v. Forde* [1990] 1 E.G.L.R. 131.
[7] [1990] 1 Q.B. 348.

It should further be realised by those acting for landlords and tenants equally that when a dispute of this nature arises, the first and sometimes last impulse of the court is to knock the parties heads together, or, at least, the heads of their legal advisors. In *Empson v. Forde*[8] Woolf L.J. terminated his judgment with these words:

> "I return to what I said in opening this judgment about the regrettable situation which has arisen in this case. It is clear beyond a peradventure that these repair works must be carried out. It is clear that the learned judge took the view that it would be necessary for the defendants to move out of the premises while the repair work was being carried out . . . bearing in mind that both parties have the benefit of legal advisers, I would very much hope that one result of this appeal will be that the parties, before they leave this court, will sort out their differences and work out a sensible and practical arrangement to enable the work which is necessary to be carried out by agreement and without involving the courts further. It is in the interests of the parties that this should happen and it is about time that they showed sufficient maturity to achieve the agreement which is necessary."

Failure to carry out running repairs

In *Sturolson & Co. v. Mauroux*[9] Glidewell L.J., with whom Taylor L.J. agreed, said this: **21–03**

> "The second argument for the [landlords] is that the Mauroux', on ordinary principles, were only entitled to claim damages under any head if they had taken reasonable steps to mitigate their loss. They could, it is argued, have done this by carrying out some of the repairs themselves, or Mr Mauroux carrying them out and then by withholding the cost of doing that from their rent—to which it is suggested there would have been no answer . . . Mr Ferris argues that, on the evidence, the Mauroux did almost nothing. They could at least, he says, have cleaned out the drains, or replaced the lights in the corridors, or replaced window panes from time to time. And, as I have said, they could, if necessary, if that involved them in cost, have withheld their rent. Their failure to do so was so unreasonable that no judge could properly find that they had behaved reasonably.

[8] See n. 6.
[9] (1988) 20 H.L.R. 332.

With this I also disagree. The parts of the works of repair which it is alleged the Mauroux could have done were, of course, all relatively minor and it may be that they could have done them. It may be that some other persons differently situated, without a wife who had gone blind and the worry that that entailed, and without the financial stringency that the judge found the Mauroux were under certainly for most of the relevant period, would have carried out such works . . . . My view does not depend upon a finding of any fact by this court, I regard it as being a matter singularly within the province of the learned judge. He heard the evidence. He was able to decide . . . what his view was of the relative conduct of the parties . . . . The conclusion that he reached that it was not reasonable to expect Mr and Mrs Mauroux to have done anything more than they did is one which, in my view, we cannot and should not interfere."

In *Personal Representatives of Chiodi v. de Marney*[10] Ralph Gibson L.J. appears to have been surprised that the landlord failed to run a mitigation argument:

"It has not been suggested that the defendant was, in any regard, in breach of her duty to mitigate the consequences of the landlord's breach; even, for example, by making crude but effective repairs to keep out the rain and the cold wind from the defective window by fixing some plastic sheet to it, with or without the assistance of the gentleman with whom she shared the flat . . . "

Issues of mitigation in such cases need to take into account what the tenant's obligations are: see for example para. 10–04 *ante*.

Failure to wrap up against the cold

21–04 In *McCoy & Co. v. Clark*[11]:

"The judge concluded that the pneumonia was in part due to the dampness of the premises resulting from the fault of the plaintiffs, but that it was in part due to the defendant's failure to look after himself properly, and he assessed the amount of damages . . . treating the situation as one in which the defendant was to the extent of 50 per cent responsible for his own suffering . . .

There is no appeal on either side as to that proportion. It is accepted that the defendant had not behaved sensibly in

---

[10] (1988) 21 H.L.R. 6.
[11] (1982) 13 H.L.R. 87.

regard to keeping himself warm, and perhaps in other ways, and to that extent he rightly had his damages reduced."

Use of Calor gas fires

In *Brent L.B.C. v. Carmel*[12] the Court of Appeal does not appear **21–05** to have considered that a tenant had failed to mitigate her losses as a result of using Calor gas fires, which on the facts of the case substantially added to a condensation problem in her flat. This was a case, however, in which the landlord's central heating system had been "wholly inadequate" and in which the landlord had not warned the tenant of the dangers of Calor gas for some time.

Refusal of alternative accommodation

In *Lubren v. Lambeth L.B.C.*[13] the Court of Appeal dismissed the **21–06** landlord's contention that the County Court judge should have reduced the damages because the tenant failed to mitigate by accepting one of two offers of alternative accommodation. Parker L.J. said that:

"When one examines such evidence as there is of the offers, the fact that they were made but not taken up cannot in my view affect the question of damages; they were offers which, so far as we are aware, were not refused capriciously in any way . . . "

General lifestyle

When the landlord alleges that loss is too remote because the **21–07** tenant has failed to mitigate or, indeed, has actually caused the damage, the issue is essentially one of fact. It may, however, be helpful to bear in mind the dicta of Dillon L.J. in *Quick v. Taff-Ely Borough Council*[14] and, in particular, his concept of a "spectrum of lifestyles" within which reasonable behaviour can be found:

"the judge appreciated that some people for financial reasons have to be sparing in their use of central heating, and he found that there was no evidence at all to suggest that the lifestyle of the tenant and his family was likely to give rise to condensation problems because it was outside the spectrum of lifestyles which a local authority could reasonably expect its tenants to follow."

---

[12] (1995) 28 H.L.R. 203.
[13] (1987) 20 H.L.R. 165.
[14] [1985] 3 All E.R. 321.

Failure to pay rent

21–08   The tenant's failure to pay rent is normally no defence to an action for specific performance of a landlord's repairing obligation: *Yorkbrook Investments v. Batten*[15]; *Gordon v. Selico Company Limited*.[16]

Neither should it be any reason to reduce the amount of damages payable by the landlord to the tenant on account of the landlord's failure to repair. The question was dealt with decisively by Sir John Arnold in *McMillan v. Singh*,[17] (an illegal eviction case). The County Court judge had refused to make an award of exemplary damages against the landlord because the tenant had been in arrears of rent at the time of the eviction:

> "That is a conception that is very familiar in equity cases where one is seeking the intervention of the court by the award of an equitable remedy and it is held that the plaintiff . . . fails to come to equity, as it is said, with clean hands . . . . All that this man did was to fall into arrears from time to time with his rent. It seems to me remote altogether from the conception, but apart from that this is a common law claim, and it is no defence in a common law claim that you have failed in the transaction, or any associated transaction, to behave with that propriety which enables you to be a successful plaintiff in equity; nor, so far as I know, has the conception ever been applied to the quantification of damage."

Effect of assignments on actions for disrepair

Liability of original landlord

21–09   Where a lease or fixed term agreement has been entered into the original landlord remains liable to the tenant or the tenant's assignee on the repairing covenants until the expiry of the agreed term: *Stuart v. Joy and Nantes*.[18] The tenant can sue notwithstanding that he or she may have assigned the residue of the term: *City & Metropolitan Properties v. Greycroft*.[19] In the case of dwellings, section 3 of the Landlord and Tenant Act 1987 provides that all landlords remain liable for breaches of covenant until the tenant has been notified of the assignment.

Section 6 of the Landlord and Tenant (Covenants) Act 1995 permits the original landlord to apply to be released from future

---

[15] [1985] 2 E.G.L.R. 100.
[16] [1985] 2 E.G.L.R. 79, affirmed [1986] 1 E.G.L.R. 71.
[17] (1984) 17 H.L.R. 120.
[18] [1904] 1 K.B. 362.
[19] [1987] 1 W.L.R. 1085.

liabilities under the lease on assignment of the reversion. The Act in this respect applies only to tenancies granted after January 1, 1996. It applies to covenants which are express, implied or imposed by law. If the landlord is so released by the tenant, or the court, the *quid pro quo* is that the landlord ceases to be entitled to the benefit of the tenant covenants in the lease: section 7(4) of the Landlord and Tenant (Covenants) Act 1995.

Rights of original landlord

On an assignment of the reversion the landlord loses the right to sue for pre-assignment breaches unless he or she expressly reserves that right: *Re King, Robinson v. Gray.*[20]   **21–10**

In relation to tenancies granted after January 1, 1996, however, the Landlord and Tenant (Covenants) Act 1995 applies, and although the right to enforce tenants' covenants passes to the assignee on an assignment of the reversion (see section 3) the right to sue in respect of pre-assignment breaches (to the extent that they are not continuing breaches) remains with the assignor unless expressly assigned pursuant to section 23.

Liability of assignee landlords

Assignees of the reversion can be sued by tenants for failing to comply with repairing obligations in the tenancy agreement in respect of periods post-assignment: section 142 of the Law of Property Act 1925. They are not liable for any failures to repair, pre-assignment, by the assignor of the reversion: *Duncliffe v. Caerfelin Properties,*[21] who remains liable for his or her pre-assignment breaches. In the case of dwellings, intermediate landlords remain liable for breaches post-assignment, until proper notice of the assignment is given to the tenant: section 3 of the Landlord and Tenant Act 1987.   **21–11**

In the case of tenancies granted after January 1, 1996, the Landlord and Tenant (Covenants) Act 1995 applies, and sections 79 and 142 of the Law of Property Act 1925 are replaced by section 3 of the Landlord and Tenant (Covenants) Act 1995. The effect is, however, the same for most purposes.

Rights of assignee landlords

The right to enforce repairing covenants against tenants passes to assignees of the reversion automatically by virtue of section 141 of the Law of Property Act 1925. The effect is that the assignee and   **21–12**

---

[20] [1963] Ch. 459.
[21] [1989] 2 E.G.L.R. 38.

not the assignor has the right to sue for pre-assignment breaches by the tenant, subject to any express reservation of that right by the assignor: *Re King, Robinson v. Gray.*[22]

In the case of tenancies granted after January 1, 1996, to which the Landlord and Tenant (Covenants) Act 1995 applies, the position is the same except that, subject to any express assignment of the right, the assignor and not the assignee is entitled to sue the tenant for pre-assignment breaches: section 23 of the Landlord and Tenant (Covenants) Act 1995.

Liabilities of original tenants

21-13 The original tenant remains liable on the repairing covenants in a fixed-term agreement for the rest of the term notwithstanding any assignment, unless the landlord formally releases him or her from liability: *Deanplan v. Mahmoud.*[23]

In the case of tenancies granted after January 1, 1996 the effect of the Landlord and Tenant (Covenants) Act 1995 is that on an assignment of the whole premises the original tenant (and his guarantor) cease to be liable for post-assignment breaches. The *quid pro quo* is that he or she ceases to be entitled to sue for post-assignment breaches by the landlord: section 5 of the Landlord and Tenant (Covenants) Act 1995. Tenants who are not original tenants but who enter into direct covenants are in the same position.

Liabilities of assignee tenant

21-14 Assignees of the residue of the term are liable on the tenants' repairing covenants only whilst the term is vested in them: *Taylor v. Shum*[24]; *Beardman v. Wilson.*[25] That does not prevent the landlord from forfeiting the lease on account of a pre-assignment breach, providing the breach has not been waived: *Parry v. Robinson-Wyllie.*[26] Assignees of the term have no right to sue in respect of pre-assignment breaches: *Martyn v. Williams.*[27]

The position is substantially the same in respect of tenancies granted after January 1, 1996. The rules relating to the assignment of such tenancies are contained in section 3 of the Landlord and Tenant (Covenants) Act 1995.

[22] *Supra.*
[23] [1993] Ch. 151.
[24] (1797) 1 B.&P. 21.
[25] (1868) L.R. 4 C.P. 57.
[26] [1987] 2 E.G.L.R. 133.
[27] (1857) 1 H.&N. 817.

CHAPTER TWENTY TWO

Special Damages

General principles

The distinction for pleading purposes between general and special **22–01**
damages is set out in *British Transport Commission v. Gourley*[1]:

"In an action for personal injuries the damages are always
divided into two main parts. First, there is what is referred to
as special damage, which has to be specially pleaded and
proved. This consists of out-of-pocket expenses and loss of
earnings incurred down to the date of trial, and is generally
capable of exact calculation. Secondly, there is general damage
which the law implies and is not specially pleaded. This
includes compensation for pain and suffering and the like,
and, if the injuries suffered are such as to lead to continuing or
permanent disability, compensation for loss of earning power
in the future."

The most important point is that special damage needs to be
pleaded. The relevant law was encapsulated by Stephenson L.J. in
Calabar Properties Limited v. Stitcher[2]:

"It is trite law that special damage must be pleaded so that a
defendant may know what case he has to meet and may be in
a position to meet it with evidence and perhaps with a
payment into court: see R.S.C. Ord. 18, r. 12 and the notes to
that rule in *The Supreme Court Practice* 1982 vol. I, esp p. 330,
para. 18/12/29 and the cases there cited, to some of which

[1] [1956] A.C. 185.
[2] [1984] 1 W.L.R. 287.

201

counsel for the landlords referred us. I refer only to what Lord Donovan said in giving the judgment of this court in *Perestrello e Cia Lda v. United Paint Company Limited.*[3] He there pointed out that the test whether damage should be pleaded is not whether it is general or special damage but whether fairness to the defendant requires it to be pleaded, and some general damage must be pleaded as having been suffered, as well as special damage as having been incurred which is capable of substantially exact calculation . . . "

All items of special damage, then, for which a claim is made must be set out in the pleaded case. The pleading should indicate the amount claimed in respect of each item. It should make the plaintiff's case sufficiently clear as to why the defendant is liable for the loss and how the figure claimed was arrived at. A pleading is sufficiently clear if it allows the opponent a fair opportunity of understanding the relevant claim and therefore being able to obtain evidence, whether by discovery or otherwise, to contest it.

The cost of remedial works

22–02   It is proper to include in a claim for the cost of remedial works VAT, professional fees, redecoration and cleaning up costs.[4] There should generally be no reduction of the damages claimed on account of betterment[5] or because the costs have been met by insurance.[6]

Recovery of cost of works actually carried out

22–03   The tenant can sue his or her landlord to recover the cost of works carried out by the tenant in default of the landlord discharging his or her obligations: a modern example is *Loria v. Hammer.*[7]

Where the tenant has carried out repairs to the demised premises in default of the landlord discharging his or her repairing obligations he or she has an ancient common law right to recoup the expenditure out of future rents: *Taylor v. Beal*[8]; *Waters v. Weigall*[9]; *Davies v. Stacey*[10]; *Lee-Parker v. Izzet.*[11] The tenant is "entitled to

---

[3] [1969] 1 W.L.R. 570 at p. 579; [1969] 3 All E.R. 479 at p. 485–486.
[4] See para. 22–07.
[5] See para. 19–23.
[6] See para. 19–23.
[7] [1989] 2 E.G.L.R. 249.
[8] (1591) Cro. Eliz. 222.
[9] (1795) 2 Anst. 575.
[10] (1840) 12 Ad. & El. 506.
[11] [1971] 1 W.L.R. 1688.

treat the expenditure as payment of rent": *Lee-Parker v. Izzet.* In that case, Goff J. held that:

"I do not think this is bound up with technical rules of set off. It is an ancient common law right. I therefore declare that so far as the repairs are within the express or implied covenants of the landlord, the third and fourth defendants are entitled to recoup themselves out of future rents and defend any action for payment thereof. It does not follow however that the full amount expended by the third and fourth defendants on such repairs can properly be treated as payment of rent. It is a question of fact in every case whether and to what extent the expenditure was proper.

For the sake of avoiding misunderstanding, I must add that of course the *Taylor v. Beal* right can only be exercised when and so far as the landlord is in breach and any necessary notice must have been given to him.

In so far as the repairs fall outside the landlord's covenants there can in my judgment be no set off against the plaintiffs . . . "

The point is slightly more difficult when the tenant carries out repairs to parts of the building retained in the ownership of the landlord. The act of carrying out such repairs prima facie involves a trespass to the property of the landlord. In *Sedgwick Forbes Bland Payne Group Limited v. Regional Properties Limited*[12] Oliver J. held that the tenant's *Taylor v. Beal* right to carry out repairs in default did not create an implied right of access to the building element in disrepair. The tenant was accordingly left with a right to sue for damages or specific performance only. That is not satisfactory because in some circumstances, in particular where work is urgently required to prevent serious damage, basic fairness requires that there should be such a right of entry to repair. In *Loria v. Hammer*[13] Mr John Lindsay Q.C. held that a tenant who had carried out repairs to common parts retained in the ownership of the landlord had not trespassed because she did have such an implied right of entry: *Sedgwick Forbes Bland Payne Group Limited v. Regional Properties Limited*, however, was not cited. Mr Lindsay Q.C. held, however, that in any event, even if there had been a trespass, that in itself would not affect the tenant's entitlement to recover the cost of the works.

The solution to the question of access may, it is submitted, lie in the field of nuisance. If the condition of the adjacent property owned by the landlord deteriorates to such an extent that it

[12] (1980) 257 E.G. 64.
[13] *Supra.*

interferes with the tenant's reasonable enjoyment of his or her premises, then he or she can exercise the common law right of any person affected by a common law nuisance, to enter the offending property and abate the nuisance: see *Clerk & Lindsell on Torts*[14] for a description of the right and the limitations within which the right must be exercised. The tenant can then sue for damages. If the condition of the landlord's adjoining property does not get into such a state, then it is no hardship to the tenant to be left only with a right to sue for damages or specific performance.

Recovery of the future cost of repairs: pre-judgment

22–04   Where the tenant has not carried out the works of repair he is entitled to claim the cost of works as special damages. In *Calabar Properties Ltd v. Stitcher*,[15] Stephenson L.J. held that:

> "What the difference in value to the plaintiff of the statutory tenancy of the cottage repaired and unrepaired may have been was not an easy matter for the registrar to assess, but I suspect he would not have gone far wrong if he equated it with what the plaintiff might have to spend on performing the landlord's covenant (assuming the landlord would not perform it himself) and substantial general damages for inconvenience and discomfort for the period from notice to the landlord till assessment or performance of the covenant by the plaintiff."

If the landlord fails to carry out works, in breach of his or her contractual obligations, the sum of money necessary to remedy that breach prima facie is the cost of the repairs. The tenant is entitled to claim that sum in lieu of, or in the alternative to, the discretionary remedy of specific performance.[16] In *Dodd Properties v. Canterbury City Council*[17] (a case in which negligent building operations damaged the plaintiffs' adjoining garage) Lord Donaldson held:

> "The general object underlying the rules for the assessment of damages is, so far as is possible by means of a monetary award, to place the plaintiff in the position which he would have occupied if he had not suffered the wrong complained of, be that wrong a tort or a breach of contract. In the case of a tort causing damage to real property, this object is achieved by the application of one or other of two quite different measures of damage, or occasionally, a combination of the two. The first is

---

[14] 17th Ed., 1995, at para. 29–22.
[15] [1984] 1 W.L.R. 287.
[16] See para. 27–01.
[17] [1980] 1 W.L.R. 433.

to take the capital value of the property in an undamaged state and to compare it with its value in a damaged state. The second is to take the cost of repair or reinstatement. Which is appropriate will depend upon a number of factors, such as the plaintiff's future intentions as to the use of the property and the reasonableness of those intentions. If he reasonably intends to sell the property in its damaged state, clearly the diminution in capital value is the true measure of damage. If he reasonably intends to occupy it and to repair the damage, clearly the cost of repairs is the true measure. And there may be in-between situations."

The point is not free from doubt. Slesser L.J. said in *Pembery v. Lamdin*[18] that the cost of repairs would not be the right measure of damage. That part of the judgment is however *obiter*, because the Court of Appeal held that there was no failure to repair on the part of the landlord. It seems difficult to reconcile with basic contract principles, and with the established right of tenants who have carried out repairs to sue for reimbursement of the cost or recoup themselves out of the rent. It is difficult to reconcile with cases suggestive that orders of specific performance raise serious difficulties of principle: see paragraph 27–01.

In *Marenco v. Jacramel Company Limited*[19] the landlord refused to carry out repairs until all the tenants had paid their share of the service charges. The Court of Appeal ordered the landlord to pay the plaintiff tenant the full cost of the works (less her personal service charge contribution) so that she could carry them out.

When the tenant succeeded in an action for noise nuisance she was awarded as part of her damages a sum sufficient to enable sound insulation works to be carried out: *Sampson v. Hodson-Pressinger*[20] (damages awarded against freeholder); *Toff v. McDowell*[21] (damages awarded against adjoining long leaseholder).

If the court makes an award of damages which includes the cost of repairs, it is likely to require a carefully drafted order which contains sufficient safeguards of the landlord's interests.[22]

Although the tenant is entitled to claim the cost of the works, it is implicit in the passage from *Calabar Properties Ltd v. Stitcher*[23] set out above that if the landlord submits to an order of specific performance or undertakes to carry out the necessary work, it is unlikely, although not inconceivable, that the court will award the

[18] [1940] 2 All E.R. 434.
[19] [1964] E.G.D. 319.
[20] [1981] 3 All E.R. 710.
[21] (1993) 25 H.L.R. 650.
[22] See para. 22–05.
[23] *Supra*.

tenant the cost of the works as damages. That is because within reasonable limits the performing party is entitled to decide how to repair: *Murray v. Birmingham City Council.*[24] Once a precisely drawn order of specific performance is made, however, the dispute can become a fine one and the outcome will depend on all the facts of the case.

Recovery of the future cost of repairs: post-judgment

22–05   Different considerations may apply if the landlord fails to comply with an undertaking or order of specific performance to carry out works. R.S.C. Ord. 45, r. 8 provides that:

> "If an order . . . for the specific performance of a contract is not complied with, then, without prejudice to its powers . . . the Court may direct that the act required to be done may, so far as practicable, be done by the party by whom the order or judgment was obtained or some other person appointed by the court, at the cost of the disobedient party, and upon the act being done the expenses incurred may be ascertained in such manner as the Court may direct and execution may issue against the disobedient party for the amount so ascertained and for costs."

R.S.C. Ord. 45, r. 8 can be applied by the county court judge: see section 76 of the County Courts Act 1984 and *Rose v. Laskington Limited.*[25] If the tenant does not have sufficient funds to carry out the works, there seems to be no reason why the court may not require the landlord to pay the required sum into court or provide security for it. Such an order was made by His Honour Judge Graham in *Barrett v. Lounova (1982) Limited*[26] when the case returned to the county court after the landlord's unsuccessful appeal to the Court of Appeal.[27] The judge: (a) directed the tenant to carry out the works which the landlord had failed to carry out, properly or at all; (b) required the landlord to pay into court or lodge a banker's guarantee in the sum of £27,000 (the cost of the works plus professional supervision and VAT); (c) gave directions for the ascertainment of costs upon completion of the works and the payment out to the tenant's surveyor of funds in court. A number of similar orders have been made in the County Court and have resulted in successful completion of the works. Browne-Wilkinson L.J. in *Parker v. Camden L.B.C.*[28] expressed the view

---

[24] [1987] 2 E.G.L.R. 53.
[25] [1989] 3 All E.R. 306.
[26] [1989] 2 W.L.R. 137.
[27] *Legal Action,* November 1989, p. 19.
[28] [1985] 2 All E.R. 141.

that if an order of specific performance was made and not complied with, an order under R.S.C. Ord. 45, r. 8 would be appropriate. In *Hooker-Goodman v. Cohane*[29] the plaintiff tenant was awarded general and special damages of £3,480 on account of the landlord's failure to repair. On ascertaining that the landlord was outside the jurisdiction and forming the view that enforcement of maintaining orders would be difficult, the judge ordered the landlord to pay the plaintiff's solicitor £7,400 on an interim payment to fund remedial works, with liberty to apply for further amount if required. See also *Cook v. Horford Investment Limited and Taj*.[29a]

Impact on service charges of recovery of costs of repair

When the tenant recovers the cost of works which he or she **22–06** intends to carry out the court will normally deduct from the damages a sum equivalent to the service charge contribution towards those works which the plaintiff tenant would have been obliged to pay: *Marenco v. Jacramel Company Limited*[30] *Loria v. Hammer*.[31] The landlord is unlikely to be permitted to recover through the service charge any increased repair costs attributable to the landlord's breach of his or her repairing obligations. Mr John Lindsay Q.C. said in *Loria v. Hammer*:

> "Mr Powell-Jones submits that the lessor's expense in a timely performance of his repairing covenant may properly be passed on to the lessees but that the consequences of his not punctually performing his covenant, he says, may not. It is in the nature of building defects that they get worse with the passage of time, often at an accelerating rate. A stitch in time, he reminds me, can save nine; the landlord can, as it were, recover the cost of the timely one stitch but, if he fails to make that one stitch, he cannot later pass on the cost of the nine which would have become necessary simply because the one was not made or was not made in good time . . . All but the costs of a timely repair to the asphalt under the tanks and a timely fixing of the guttering are, in my judgment, a consequence of the landlord's failure to promptly perform his covenant. To mark the fact that the landlord could have recovered the cost of those timely repairs had he done them, I propose to deduct £150 from what otherwise would have been

---

[29] Reported in *Legal Action*, September 1992 at page 22.
[29a] Reported in *Legal Action*, September 1993 at page 16.
[30] [1964] E.G.D. 319.
[31] *Supra*. See also a claim which failed on its facts in *Postel Properties Ltd v. Boots the Chemists* [1996] 41 E.G. 164.

my award . . . The [landlord's] argument, if right, would lead
to the grossly unjust conclusion I have already described in
that the longer the tenants suffered periods of disrepair
through their landlord's failure to repair, then not only the less
valuable their possession would have become by reason of his
failures but also the more likely they would be to have to pay
greater sums by way of service charge"

The cost of redecoration/cleaning up

22–07   In *McGreal v. Wake*[32] the Court of Appeal held that the tenant
was entitled to recover:

(1) The cost of re-decorating after structural repairs had dam-
    aged the decorations: "we consider that the landlord's
    obligation to effect repairs must carry with it an obligation
    to make good any consequential damage to decorations".
    There was no deduction on account of betterment.
(2) Damages for having to clear up debris and clean up after the
    conclusion of the works.

There was no need to prove that the repairs had been carried out
negligently.

In *Bradley v. Chorley Borough Council*[33] the Court of Appeal
confirmed that the landlord is liable to pay for damage to the
tenant's decorations consequential upon carrying out works of
repair whether or not the landlord was in breach of covenant at the
time he or she carried out the works, *e.g.* it applies to a landlord
who repairs within a reasonable time of notice where liability is
contingent upon notice. There was no deduction for betterment
even though the decorations were of highly doubtful quality and
the tenant had carried out no decoration since his tenancy began.
It made no difference that the tenant was responsible under the
terms of the tenancy agreement for re-decorating. Conversely, it
probably does not matter that the tenant is not obliged under the
terms of the tenancy agreement to remedy the damage, if he or she
intends to do so and it is otherwise reasonable to do so: *Green v.
Eales*.[34]

Any agreement which purports to restrict the landlord's liability
to pay for the cost of redecoration consequential upon repairs
falling within section 11 of the Landlord and Tenant Act 1985 is
probably void by virtue of section 12 of that Act: *McDougall v.
Easington District Council*.[35]

[32] (1984) 13 H.L.R. 109.
[33] (1985) 17 H.L.R. 305.
[34] (1841) 2 Q.B. 225.
[35] [1989] 1 E.G.L.R. 93.

If the landlord damages decorations as a result of carrying out improvements to the premises (rather than as a result of complying with his or her repairing obligations) the extent to which the landlord is obliged to compensate the tenant will depend upon the terms of any agreement. If there is no agreement, the position is as set out in *McDougall v. Easington District Council*[36]:

> "I would prefer to see the relationship as creating a licence, whereby the tenants allowed the council to come in and do the work.
>
> What, then, were the terms upon which the council were to exercise the liberty? If the exchanges between the parties had been completely silent on the question, I would have had no difficulty in finding an implied obligation on the council to reimburse the tenants for the cost of any uncompleted redecoration, such obligation arising in an entirely conventional manner from the request by the council to act in a certain way, and by the tenants in fact acting by that way."

Damage to the tenant's belongings

Tenants routinely recover compensation when the landlord's **22–08** failure to repair results in damage to or destruction of carpets and curtains, beds and bedding, furniture and other belongings. There is no reported case in which a landlord has challenged the tenant's right in principle to recover damages for losses of this type. The issues that arise most frequently in the county court are (a) as to causation (whether the damage was caused by the landlord's breach, or by condensation or some other cause for which the landlord was not liable, and whether the damage occurred within the relevant limitation period); (b) mitigation (whether the belonging could have been repaired or cleaned instead of being replaced); (c) betterment (whether any deduction should be made).

The judgment of the County Court judge in *Brent L.B.C. v. Carmel Murphy*[37] deals with damaged belongings as follows:

> "*Curtains*
> There are three sets of curtains charged for. That was because the water, condensation and penetration around the window frames was such that the defendant was obliged to lay towels over the sill and on the floor below the windows to mop up the extent of condensation and/or water seepage. The curtains against the windows obviously were affected. There is substantial mould, as shown in the photographs in 1990, on all

---

[36] *Ibid.*
[37] Case No. 93 W.G. 1219, March 14, 1994 at Wood Green Trial Centre.

these bedroom windows and mould, as one knows, cannot be washed out. It stains and then rots the fabric. Therefore, as the defendant claims, the curtains had to be renewed on three occasions in the bedrooms . . .

Bedding

On the evidence £2,220.00 has been spent replacing pillows, bedspreads, continental quilts, blankets, quilt covers and sheets, *etc.* They are substantial in amount. The defendant, I am perfectly satisfied, was doing her utmost to wash and to clean her soft fabrics in the house, including the bedding, but they can only stand so much and it was because of the damp that they had to be washed and cleaned so much more frequently than would otherwise be the case.

Bedroom furniture

A sum of £3,000 is claimed for a double bed, two singlebeds and bedroom units, including wardrobes, bedside tables and a chest of drawers. That I accept in full.

Clothing for the three occupiers of the flat, that is, the defendant and her family

She has worked out a sum of £2,037, averaging approximately £330 odd for the three of them per annum. By no stretch of the imagination could that be called an excessive claim and I allow it.

Carpeting

She claims £2,000 . . . I am not satisfied that an item as substantial or as easy to remember supplying is correct and I award the sum of £1323.00 for that, which is the figure that the defendant has been able to justify . . .

Household Towels

This is a claim for a hundred towels at £10 each . . . It is my view that for a period of 12 years, using towels which will rot from excessive washing necessitated by the mopping up practice that the defendant was obliged to adopt, I can well understand that these towels just rotted and disintegrated over a period of time and had to be replaced . . . . But it does seem to me that £10 a towel over the course of 12 years is probably taking today's prices and applying it over that period. Prices have gone up and I would have thought that a figure of £800 would suffice.

Carpet cleaning

There is a bill here and . . . I am satisfied that she hired carpet cleaning equipment herself and did it herself, thereby minimising the claim under that head and I am satisfied with that . . .

Finally the defendant claims £1,872 for the extra washing, use of washing powder, washing machine and tumble drier at the rate of £3 per week over a 12 year period. I think that is perfectly reasonable and I allow it."

It is not uncommon for County Court judges not to award the full cost some types of special damages on the basis that:

(1) There is a second-hand market for certain types of damaged belongings (*e.g.* furniture) and that it would be reasonable to award damages on the basis of second-hand replacement value;

(2) The tenant's loss should be calculated on the basis of the second-hand value of the article lost, because it was about to be replaced shortly in any event (*e.g.* children's clothes) or because the real loss was simply having to replace the damaged belongings somewhat earlier. The replacement cost is reduced usually by about 25 per cent, but it can be 50 per cent.

Unless a second hand substitute or reasonable alternative is available, and ought reasonably to be purchased, however, it may be difficult to distinguish the cases on betterment.[38]

Where the tenant's belongings are damaged by the landlord who is carrying out works to the premises he or she is not obliged or entitled under the terms of the tenancy agreement to carry out, *McDougall v. Easington District Council.*[39]

Cost of purchasing heating installations

Tenants can recover the cost of purchasing replacement heating **22–09** installations (usually portable electric or gas heaters) if they establish that such purchases were a reasonable response to either the landlord's failure in breach of contract to keep the heating installations in proper working order or to increased cold at the premises on account of the landlord's failure to keep them in repair.

The County Court judge in *Brent L.B.C. v. Carmel Murphy*[40] awarded the plaintiff the cost of purchasing three electric convector

---

[38] See para. 19–23.
[39] [1989] 1 E.G.L.R. 93.
[40] *Supra.*

heaters for three bedrooms and £50 per annum as an approximate running cost, a Calor gas fire (and a replacement fire when the first broke) for downstairs, together with the cost of gas cylinders (six per year) and additional gas costs of £50 per annum from using the cooker to provide extra heat in the kitchen/dining room. The judge also allowed the cost of hot water bottles (£96 over 12 years) as, "A hot water bottle, particularly for a young person, as these two children were at the time, is a great comfort both physically and mentally when you are living in a room that wreaks of damp, that is cold and is damp, and no doubt their beds were damp." In *Hussein v. Mehlman*[41] Assistant Recorder Sedley Q.C. as he then was awarded part of the cost of acquiring a Calor gas heater and two bottles when the landlord failed to keep the heating working in winter. He did not award the full cost on the basis that the equipment "will have had some residual value".

The cost of fuel

22–10   If premises become unusually damp or draughty as a result of the landlord's failure to repair, almost inevitably, the tenant will have to spend more on heating the premises. The difficulty lies in quantifying the amount.

It is highly desirable, although not essential, that the tenant is in a position to produce gas or electricity bills verifying consumption for the periods in question. Ideally, the tenant should then produce bills for periods of normal consumption before or after the period of excessive consumption: the difference, after adjusting for increases in the prices of fuel, affords a reasonable idea of the loss. The process is not accurate as it does not take into account changes in the average ambient temperature from year to year. In *Hussein v. Mehlman*[42] Assistant Recorder Sedley Q.C., as he then was, awarded the cost of running replacement Calor gas fires in this way:

> "The Calor gas heater with two gas bottles cost £139, but the equipment will have had some residual value apart from its use in the absence of working gas fires. Equally, the cost of refills at £9.99 was in substitution for mains gas, which would also have cost money. Each gas bottle was used only in the evenings for a couple of hours . . . Clearly this was a cumbersome and expensive form of gas heating by comparison with a properly fitted gas fire. Assuming, therefore, that something like £150 was spent on bottled gas in addition to the cost of the equipment, and discounting the sums spent for the reasons I have indicated, I awarded £200 for the additional trouble and

[41] [1992] 32 E.G. 59.
[42] *Ibid.*

expense caused by having to introduce a Calor gas heater into the house."

The tenant's excessive fuel charges can be contrasted with average fuel consumption patterns published by the Department of Trade and Industry and the Central Statistical Office (the Family Expenditure Survey conducted by the Office of Population Censuses and Surveys). The table below is Table 55 reproduced from the *Digest of United Kingdom Energy Statistics*[43] published by the Department of Trade and Industry. Further and more detailed statistical information can be obtained from the Department of Trade and Industry or the Central Statistical Office. The Table is based upon a survey of a representative sample of private households which consume the fuel in question. After 1993 data was produced on a financial year basis.

Table Average expenditure on fuel per consuming household: United Kingdom

| | £ per week | | | | |
	1990	1991	1992	1993	1993/4
Electricity					
All households	5.62	6.09	6.54	6.79	6.75
With electric central heating	8.65	9.32	9.76	10.19	10.11
Without electric central heating	5.26	5.70	6.18	6.43	6.40
Heating oils and other fuels	5.88	6.30	6.50	7.38	7.19
Solid fuel	11.18	13.16	12.46	12.09	12.50
Gas					
All households	5.53	6.40	6.63	6.65	6.65
With gas central heating	6.21	7.05	7.32	7.31	7.29
Without gas central heating	3.49	4.24	4.07	4.12	4.21
All fuels (excluding motor fuel)	11.07	12.31	12.92	13.27	13.27

The cost of alternative accommodation

The circumstances in which the tenant is entitled to recover the **22–11** costs associated with a move to alternative accommodation are

---

[43] 1995 edition.

considered in *Calabar Properties Limited v. Stitcher*[44] and *McGreal v. Wake*.[45]

The basic rule is that the landlord is not bound to either find or pay for alternative accommodation occupied by the tenant whilst the landlord carries out works to the premises. The basic rule applies if:

(1) the landlord is not in breach of covenant (*e.g.* he or she is repairing promptly after notice); and
(2) vacant possession is strictly necessary in order for the works to be carried out at all; or
(3) the tenant elects to move out for his or her own convenience whilst works are being carried out.

The landlord is responsible for the cost of alternative accommodation if:

(1) The landlord is in breach of his or her repairing obligations and, as a result of that breach (*e.g.* as a result of the delay) the tenant moves out because:
   (a) The premises have become so dilapidated it was reasonable for the tenant to move out; or
   (b) because of the delay in repairing it has become strictly necessary for the landlord to have vacant possession to carry out the works of repair; or
   (c) it is not strictly necessary for the landlord to have vacant possession but the works have become so much more extensive on account of the landlord's delays that moving out is reasonable in all the circumstances.
(2) The landlord desires the tenant to move out so as to facilitate works.

The tenant can only recover the cost of alternative accommodation if "she can show that her expenditure flowed from the defendant's breach of covenant".[46] If the landlord is in breach of covenant because of his or delay, but if the damage to the building was such that the tenant would have had to move out in any event, to that extent it would appear to be arguable that the expense of alternative accommodation is not recoverable on general principles: *Hotson v. East Berkshire Health Authority*.[47] On the other hand, the tenant might then argue that the rental value of his original accommodation had dropped to zero for the period of the works.

---

[44] [1984] 1 W.L.R. 287 (which explains the earlier cases of *Saner v. Bilton* (1878) 7 Ch.D. 815 and *Green v. Eales* (1841) 2 Q.B.D. 225).
[45] (1984) 13 H.L.R. 109.
[46] *per* Sir John Donaldson M.R. in *McGreal v. Wake, ibid.*
[47] [1987] A.C. 750.

The cost of alternative accommodation can include the cost of renting the accommodation itself if reasonable, the cost of moving furniture out and back, and storing it, the cost of removing and re-laying carpets and so forth: *McGreal v. Wake*.[48]

In addition, the tenant can claim general damages for the inconvenience of having to occupy alternative accommodation: In *Lubren v. Lambeth L.B.C.*[49] the Court of Appeal refused to interfere with an award of £500.00 for the inconvenience and distress of having had to occupy alternative accommodation (which was in all respects satisfactory in itself) for a period of 11 months over and above the time scheduled for the works in an interlocutory order. In *Bailey v. Bullock*[50] the plaintiff successfully sued his solicitors for negligently failing to obtain possession of the flat which he had rented out but had come to require for personal occupation. He was awarded general damages for the inconvenience of having to spend about an extra 15 months living with his wife and six year old child at his wife's parents' home in cramped and inconvenient circumstances. Barry J. awarded general damages of £300.00 [£4,995.00]. He refused to take into account in assessing damages the fact that the plaintiff and his wife had been unable to have a second child because of their cramped circumstances. In *Ezekiel v. McDade*[51] the Court of Appeal reduced an award from £6,000 to £4,000 when as the result of surveyor's negligence the plaintiff, his wife and their three young children had to spend 10 weeks in one-bedroom hostel accommodation, then 10 months in a cold and cramped two-bedroom house before obtaining reasonable accommodation.

Costs and outgoings in relation to the demised premises, including the rent, remain payable in principle: *Calabar Properties Limited v. Stitcher*.[52]

Medical expenses and similar costs

In *Allen v. Waters & Co.*[53] the tenant's wife was injured as a result **22–12** of the landlord's negligent failure to repair the premises and had to go to hospital. The Court of Appeal held that if there was a legal liability binding on the tenant or his wife to pay the hospital's charges even though that liability had not been enforced the landlord would be ordered to pay the sum involved (Lord Hanworth M.R. and Romer L.J.). Goddard J. went further and held

---

[48] *Supra.*
[49] (1987) 20 H.L.R. 169.
[50] [1950] 2 All E.R. 1167.
[51] [1995] 47 E.G. 150.
[52] *Supra.*
[53] [1935] 1 K.B. 200.

that if sending the tenant's wife to hospital was a reasonable and proper course of action then the landlord should be ordered to pay the cost, even though there was no longer any legal liability to pay the cost, although the sum awarded would be held for the hospital and would have to be paid to the hospital. *Dennis v. London Passenger Transport Board*[54] is a decision to similar effect. In *Schneider v. Eisovitch*.[55] Paull J. held that:

"Strict legal liability is not the be-all and end-all of a tortfeasor's liability. A plaintiff cannot claim a sum of money because he would like to pay a friend for his services. That would alter the character of the services given. The services must be treated as friendly services given freely by a friend. But to pay out-of-pocket expenses in respect of necessary services freely given does not alter the character of the services. I do not think the test is whether there is a moral duty to pay. Before such a sum can be recovered the plaintiff must show first that the services rendered were reasonably necessary as a consequence of the tortfeasor's tort; secondly, that the out-of-pocket expenses of the friend or friends who rendered these services are reasonable bearing in mind all the circumstances including whether expenses would have been incurred had the friend or friends not assisted, and, thirdly, that the plaintiff undertakes to pay the sum awarded to the friend or friends."

Miscellaneous types of special damages

22–13   All losses caused by the breaches of contract are recoverable unless too remote. A good example of a successful claim, which many a competent practitioner might not even have pursued, is the award of £1862.00 for air fresheners made by the county court judge in *Brent L.B.C. v. Carmel Murphy*,[56] which the Court of Appeal refused to interfere with:

"I am satisfied that air fresheners were required. Mr Walsh noticed the smell of damp in the maisonette and one does know how singularly unpleasant that smell is. It is such that you cannot avoid it. Air fresheners were applied in all the rooms in order to minimise the odour and the unpleasantness."

---

[54] [1948] 1 All E.R. 779.
[55] [1960] 1 All E.R. 169.
[56] *Supra.*

CHAPTER TWENTY THREE

General Damages For Personal Injury and Discomfort

General principles

When the landlord fails in breach of contract to repair a dwelling-house the courts will compensate the tenant for: **23–01**

(1) personal injury, consequential pain, suffering and mental distress (and consequential special damages, *e.g.* cost of medicine, loss of wages and so forth);

(2) physical discomfort and inconvenience, together with consequential feelings of pain or mental distress (and consequential special damages).

When the landlord fails in breach of contract to repair a dwelling-house the courts:

(1) may not award the tenant compensation for mental distress which is not consequential upon either personal injury or physical discomfort or inconvenience;

(2) are nonetheless, it seems, able to award the tenant compensation where there is no personal injury or physical discomfort but where as a result of the failure to repair the premises were worth less to the tenant than they would have been had the landlord fulfilled the contract: *Sella House Limited v. Mears*[1] (£1,250 awarded because the landlord had kept the common parts basically clean, but had let them get dingy and failed to keep them "up to the condition that

---

[1] [1989] 12 E.G. 67.

would be expected of a block of residential flats in that very good part of London").

General damages should be particularised sufficiently for the defendant to be informed of the case he or she will have to meet at trial so as to enable the defendant to make an informed payment into court and gather necessary evidence. In particular, any special inconvenience, hardship or injury needs to be particularised. If the claim includes a personal injury claim, then the rules of court at C.C.R. Ord. 6, r. 1 relating to personal injury claims have to be observed. Stephenson L.J. in *Calabar Properties Limited v. Stitcher*[2] expressed the principle in this way:

> "I refer only to what Lord Donovan said in giving the judgement of this court in *Perestrello e Cia Lda v. United Paint Company Limited.*[3] He there pointed out that the test whether damage should be pleaded is not whether it is general or special damage but whether fairness to the defendant requires it to be pleaded, and some general damage must be pleaded as having been suffered, as well as special damage as having been incurred which is capable of substantially exact calculation . . ."

Personal injury

23–02   Subject to the ordinary rules as to remoteness[4] if a tort or breach of contract causes personal injury the defendant is liable to pay compensation for that injury and consequential pain, suffering and mental anguish. There are many well-known tort cases establishing this principle. The following are cases in which the action for personal injury was brought on a contract: *Wren v. Holt*[5] (defective food sold for human consumption); *Grant v. Australian Knitting Mills Limited*[6] (defective clothes causing dermatitis); *Godley v. Perry*[7] (defective catapult causing injury to user). Personal injury is never likely to be too remote a consequence of a failure to keep a building in repair: *Summers v. Salford Corporation*[8] (broken sash cord caused window to fall injuring hand); *Griffin v. Pillett*[9] (tenant suffered personal injury by falling down steps which remained in

---

[2] [1984] 1 W.L.R. 287.
[3] [1969] W.L.R. 570 at p. 579; [1969] 3 All E.R. at p. 485–486.
[4] See paras. 19–05 and 19–13.
[5] [1903] 1 K.B. 610.
[6] [1936] A.C. 85.
[7] [1960] 1 W.L.R. 9.
[8] [1943] A.C. 283.
[9] [1926] 1 K.B. 17.

disrepair despite notice), *McCoy & Co. v. Clark*[10] (pneumonia caused by damp and cold).

In such cases compensation is awarded even though the pain and suffering, or, mental distress, is out of all normal proportion to the personal injury sustained, providing there is no malingering: *James v. Woodall Duckham Construction Co. Ltd*[11]; *Lucy v. Mariehamns Rederi*,[12] *Stojalowski v. Imperial Smelting Corpn.*[13]

Psychiatric injury

Subject, again, to the general principles of remoteness, where **23–03** feelings of distress caused by a breach of contract lead to depression or mental illness the defendant is liable to pay compensation, at least where the risk of physical injury was forseeable. *Page v. Smith*[14] is an interesting illustration of this principle in a tort context. The defendant drove negligently, causing an accident which caused the plaintiff no physical injury (although it could have done) but caused him to suffer the onset of myalgic encephalomyelitis (ME) from which he had suffered in the past but was then in remission. The judgments in the House of Lords contain an interesting consideration of the difficulty in drawing distinctions between physical and psychiatric injury and the ability of emotional trauma as well as physical trauma to cause psychiatric injury in "normal people". Lord Lloyd said:

"Nor in the case of a primary victim is it appropriate to ask whether he is a person of 'ordinary phlegm'. In the case of physical injury there is no such requirement. The negligent defendant, or more usually his insurer, takes his victim as he finds him. The same should apply in the case of psychiatric injury. There is no difference in principle, as Geoffrey Lane J. pointed out in *Malcolm v. Broadhurst*,[15] between an eggshell skull and an eggshell personality. Since the number of potential claimants is limited by the nature of the case, there is no need to impose any further limit by reference to a person of ordinary phlegm. Nor can I see any justification for doing so.

As for bogus claims, it is sometimes said that if the law were such as I believe it to be, the plaintiff would be able to recover damages for a fright. That is not so. Shock by itself is not the subject of compensation, any more than fear or grief or any

[10] (1992) 13 H.L.R. 89.
[11] [1969] 1 W.L.R. 903.
[12] [1971] 2 Lloyd's Rep. 314.
[13] (1976) 121 S.J. 118.
[14] [1995] 2 All E.R. 736.
[15] [1970] 3 All E.R. 508, D.C.

other human emotion occasioned by the defendant's negligent conduct. It is only when shock is followed by recognisable psychiatric illness that the defendant may be held liable.

There is another limiting factor. Before a defendant can be held liable for psychiatric injury suffered by a primary victim, he must at least have foreseen the risk of physical injury . . ."

Attia v. British Gas plc[16] is a case in which a breach of contract led to psychiatric injury. Contractors negligently installed central heating resulting in a fire which destroyed the plaintiff's home. The plaintiff witnessed the fire and suffered psychiatric injury as a result.

In disrepair cases, feelings of depression are a common result of the landlord's failure to repair. Severe clinical depression is unfortunately far from unknown as a consequence. Such consequences are unlikely to be regarded as too remote.

Physical discomfort or inconvenience

23–04   Damages can be recovered in tort where there is no personal injury but discomfort and inconvenience has been suffered: *Halsey v. Esso Petroleum Co.*[17] (nuisance caused by noise and smell), *Bone v. Seale*[18] (nuisance caused by smells), *Bunclark v. Hertfordshire County Council*[19] (nuisance caused by spreading tree roots cracking wall and causing anxiety); *Ward v. Cannock Chase District Council,*[20] (negligence resulting in discomfort of living in damaged property).

Where a breach of contract causes physical discomfort or inconvenience general damages are awarded for the discomfort and inconvenience and injury to feelings directly resulting therefrom: *Bailey v. Bullock*[21] (damages awarded when the plaintiff lost the use of his home for a period and had to live in uncomfortable, cramped alternative accommodation: damages were not awarded for loss of social prestige or general injury to feelings not arising directly out of physical inconvenience); *Watts v. Morrow*[22] (damages for the inconvenience of having repairs carried out to a weekend home whilst plaintiff's were present during weekends); *cf. Branchett v. Beaney*[23] (landlord breached covenant of quiet enjoyment by

---

[16] [1988] Q.B. 304.
[17] [1961] 1 W.L.R. 683.
[18] [1975] 1 W.L.R. 797.
[19] (1977) 234 E.G. 455.
[20] [1986] Ch. 546.
[21] [1950] 2 All E.R. 1167.
[22] [1991] 1 W.L.R. 142.
[23] [1992] 3 All E.R. 910.

starting to build a road in the garden: the tenant was not caused physical inconvenience but did suffer great distress: no damages for distress could be awarded). Damages for consequential distress are routinely awarded when the distress is directly related to physical discomfort and inconvenience caused by disrepair: *Personal Representatives of Chiodi v. de Marney*.[24] The notion of physical discomfort can be quite broad. In *Piper v. Daybell Court-Cooper & Co.*[25] the solicitor failed to inform his client of a right of way over the garden of the house he was purchasing and the client was awarded general damages for the inconvenience of having persons crossing and re-crossing the garden in front of his windows —compare *Branchett v. Beaney* above).

Mere distress

Mental distress alone does not complete a cause of action in the   **23–05** case of torts actionable only on proof of damage: "The general principle embedded in the common law [is] that mental suffering caused by grief, fear, anguish and the like is not assessable."[26] Where a tort is only actionable on proof of damage (negligence, for example), mental distress is not by itself sufficient to complete the cause of action, even if the distress results in dizziness, sweating, shortness of breath and so forth: *Reilly v. Merseyside Regional Health Authority*.[27]

Once certain torts have been established—principally libel or slander, deceit, assault, trespass or nuisance—the court will as a general principle without further enquiry award damages for injury to feelings arising out of the tort: *Owen and Smith v. Reo Motors*[28] (defendants removed car from garage (trespass) and dismantled it in the street observed by member of the public including a creditor of the plaintiffs); *Drane v. Evangelou*[29] (landlord's illegal eviction involved a trespass for which damages for injury to feelings could be awarded), *Millington v. Duffy*[30] (landlord's illegal eviction involved a trespass for which damages for injury to feelings could be awarded); *Guppys (Bridport) Limited v. Brookling*[31] (landlord causing nuisance). Distress consequential upon personal injury of physical discomfort can be included as an element of damages in all torts.

---

[24] (1988) 21 H.L.R. 6.
[25] [1969] E.G.D. 535.
[26] *Behrens v. Bertram Mills Circus* [1957] 2 Q.B. 1, at 28.
[27] *The Times*, April 29, 1994.
[28] (1934) 151 L.T. 274.
[29] [1978] 1 W.L.R. 455.
[30] (1984) 17 H.L.R. 232.
[31] (1983) 14 H.L.R. 1.

As a general principle, in an action for breach of contract the courts will not award damages for feelings of distress, unhappiness, worry, fear, embarrassment, stress, humiliation and so forth where such feelings are the only consequence of the breach of contract. Such feelings have to arise directly out of personal injury, property damage or physical inconvenience to be compensated.

The rule is really no more than an illustration of the principle that damage which is too remote is not compensatable and derives from the wrongful dismissal case of *Addis v. Gramophone Co. Ltd*,[32] in which the House of Lords denied the employee damages for the injury to his feelings caused by the "harsh and humiliating" manner of his dismissal. Accordingly, in *Groom v. Crocker*[33] solicitors retained to defend the plaintiff conceded in breach of contract that their client had been negligent but were not liable to pay as part of the damages compensation for mental distress.

There is an exception to this general rule in the case of contracts which have as their object the provision of pleasure or the avoidance of the pain suffered as a result of the breach. The basic principles were restated in *Watts v. Morrow*[34] where Bingham L.J. said:

> "A contract-breaker is not in general liable for any distress, frustration, anxiety, displeasure, vexation, tension or aggravation which his breach of contract may cause to the innocent party. This rule is not, I think, founded on the assumption that such reactions are not foreseeable, which they surely are or may be, but on considerations of policy.
>
> Where the very object of a contract is to provide pleasure, relaxation, peace of mind or freedom from molestation, damages will be awarded if the fruit of the contract is not provided or if the contrary result is procured instead. If the law did not cater for this exceptional category of case it would be defective . . .
>
> In cases not falling within this exceptional category, damages are in my view recoverable for physical inconvenience and discomfort caused by the breach and mental suffering directly related to that inconvenience and discomfort . . . ."

In *Watts* the purchasers of a house sued their surveyor who had, in breach of his contractual duty to exercise reasonable care and skill, failed to alert the purchasers to substantial defects requiring urgent repair. The purchasers were not entitled to damages on

[32] [1909] A.C. 488.
[33] [1939] 1 K.B. 194.
[34] *Supra.* at p. 1445.

account of the considerable "distress, frustration, anxiety, displeasure, vexation, tension or aggravation" caused to them thereby. They were, however, entitled to damages on account of the physical discomfort caused to them whilst repairs were being undertaken and the mental distress flowing from that discomfort.

Example of contracts falling within the exceptions to the general rule are contracts to provide a holiday: see *Jarvis v. Swans Tours Limited*.[35] Another example is a solicitor's contractual retainer to obtain a non-molestation injunction which, when bungled, resulted in an assault: *Heywood v. Wellers*.[36]

A tenancy agreement, as distinct from a license to use a hotel room whilst on holiday, is not an agreement falling within this category. In *Branchett v. Beaney*,[37] accordingly, the Court of Appeal would not award damages for injury to feelings caused by a breach of the covenant for quiet enjoyment which did not cause physical discomfort.[38]

It appears that the courts might be able to award damages for "loss of amenity" where there has been loss caused by a breach of contract but no other conventional award would be appropriate: *Ruxley Electronics and Construction Limited v. Forsyth*.[39] The extent of this power is yet to be worked out. In disrepair cases the court in any event has power to award damages for loss of rental value where the breach of contract does not cause physical discomfort and this in a sense obviates the need for a award in respect of mere distress. *Stella House Limited v. Mears*.[39a]

Aggravated and exemplary damages

Aggravated damages are awarded to compensate the plaintiff for   **23–06** distress, not caused by the defendant's wrong as such, but by the gratuitously malicious, spiteful or humiliating manner in which the defendant acted. Exemplary damages are awarded to punish the defendant and to deter similar torts in the future, in cases in which an award of compensatory damages (including aggravated damages where appropriate) is considered to be insufficiently chastening: *Rookes v. Barnard*[40]; *Broome v. Cassell & Co. Limited*.[41]

---

[35] [1973] Q.B. 233.
[36] [1976] Q.B. 446.
[37] [1992] 3 All E.R. 910.
[38] But see *Piper v. Daybell Court-Cooper & Co.* [1969] E.G.D. 535 above at para. 23–04.
[39] [1996] A.C. 344. See para. 19–04.
[39a] [1989] 12 E.G. 67, *McCoy v. Clark* [1982] 13 H.L.R. 89; and see Chapter 20 generally.
[40] [1964] A.C. 1129.
[41] [1972] A.C. 1027.

Concerning aggravated damages, Lord Devlin said in *Rookes v. Barnard*[42]:

> "the jury . . . can take into account the motives and conduct of the defendant where they aggravate the injury done to the plaintiff. There may be malevolence or spite or the manner of committing the wrong may be such as to injure the plaintiff's proper feelings of dignity and pride. These are matters which they jury can take into account in assessing the appropriate compensation."

It is often said that aggravated damages can not be awarded in contract. There, is, however every reason in principle why such damages should be awarded for breaches of contract which are capable of attracting compensation for mental distress[43]: *McCall v. Abelesz*.[44]

Exemplary damages are only awarded in tort and not for breaches of contract: *Perera v. Vandiyar*[45]; *Paris Oldham & Gustra v. Staffordshire B.C.*[46]; *Reed v. Madon*.[47] They can probably only be awarded for torts in there is precedent for an award of exemplary damages. Exemplary damages can almost certainly therefore not be awarded in the tort of deceit, or negligence: but they can clearly be awarded in actions for nuisance, trespass, false imprisonment and defamation: *Broome v. Cassell & Co. Limited*.[48]

In *Rookes v. Barnard*,[49] as explained in *Broome v. Cassell & Co. Limited*, Lord Devlin set out the criteria for an award of exemplary damages. There has to be:

(1) "oppressive, arbitrary or unconstitutional action by servants of the government" (construed broadly, *e.g.* as including the police or local government officials); or

(2) "cases in which the defendant's conduct has been calculated by him to make a profit for himself which may well exceed the compensation payable to the plaintiff . . . . This category is not confined to moneymaking in the strict sense. It extends to cases in which the defendant is seeking to gain at the expense of the plaintiff some object—perhaps some property which he covets—which either he could not obtain

---

[42] *Supra.*
[43] See para. 23–05.
[44] [1976] Q.B. 585.
[45] [1953] 1 W.L.R. 672.
[46] [1988] 2 E.G.L.R. 29.
[47] [1989] Ch. 408.
[48] *Supra.*
[49] *Supra.*

at all or not obtain except at a price greater than he wants to put down."

Cases in which landlords commit torts in order to obtain vacant possession fall into this second category: in *Cassell & Co. Limited v. Broome*[50] Lord Hailsham described the bullying tactics of Rachmanism as a near perfect example of behaviour calling for an award of exemplary damages. Exemplary damages have accordingly been awarded when the landlord has forcibly trespassed as part of a plan to force out the tenant: *Drane v. Evangelou*[51]; *Asghar v. Ahmed*[52]; *McMillan v. Singh*[53]; *Jones & Lee v. Miah*[54]; *Ramdath v. Daley*,[55] *Sampson v. Wilson*.[56] They have also been awarded when the landlord has caused a nuisance as part of his plan to force out the tenant: *Guppy (Bridport) Limited v. Brookling and James*.[57]

Whilst exemplary damages will not be awarded merely for breach of a contractual repairing obligation, they can be awarded if a tort can be proven, *e.g.* nuisance, when the state of property retained in the ownership and possession of the landlord interferes unreasonably with the tenant's enjoyment of his or her premises.[58] In *Sampson v. Wilson* exemplary damages were awarded against a landlord who, by entering without permission to carry out repairs, and by carrying out detrimental repairs exceeding his permission, was considered to have trespassed.

Exemplary damages should not be awarded unless the court is satisfied that compensatory damages, increased as may be necessary to compensate the plaintiff for any aggravating conduct on the part of the defendant, and taking into account any criminal sanctions to which the defendant has been exposed, are insufficiently punitive. In assessing the amount of exemplary damages payable the court must: (a) ensure that the plaintiff him or herself was the victim of the punishable behaviour; (b) ensure that the award is not itself oppressive of liberty (bearing in mind that the defendant is not able to avail him or herself of the safeguards which apply to criminal process); and (c) take into account the means of the defendant. If there are a number of defendants: (a) exemplary

---

[50] [1972] A.C. 1027.
[51] [1978] 1 W.L.R. 455.
[52] (1984) 17 H.L.R. 25.
[53] (1985) 17 H.L.R. 120.
[54] (1992) 24 H.L.R. 578.
[55] (1993) 25 H.L.R. 273.
[56] (1994) 26 H.L.R. 486.
[57] (1983) 14 H.L.R. 1.
[58] *Supra.*

damages should not be awarded at all if they ought not to be awarded against even one of the defendants; (b) they should be awarded at a level which takes into account the means of the poorest: *Rooks v. Barnard*[59]; *Broome v Cassell & Co. Limited.*[60]

[59] *Supra.*
[60] *Supra.*

CHAPTER TWENTY FOUR

The Mechanics of an Award of General Damages

Link between injury and money

There can be no fully logical connection between injury suffered **24–01** and the financial compensation ordered by the court. To attempt to establish such a connection: "involves an attempt to equate the incommensurable. Such an equation is insoluble and in the logical sense there is no answer which is right."[1]

Notwithstanding the difficulties involved, a dependable link between injury and money has been forged. As Lord Diplock expressed it in *Wright v. British Railways Board*[2]:

> "Such loss is not susceptible of measurement in money. Any figure at which the assessor of damages arrives cannot be other than artificial and, if the aim is that justice meted out to all litigants should be even-handed instead of depending on idiosyncrasies of the assessor . . . the figure must be 'basically a conventional figure derived from experience and from awards in comparable cases'."

As the law develops, awards in comparable cases form "brackets". It is by reference to the "bracket" of comparable awards that the court awards damages which take into account the particular features of the case before it, the effect of inflation and advances in

---

[1] *per* Diplock L.J. in *Every v. Miles* (1964) C.A. No. 261.
[2] [1983] 2 A.C. 733.

227

medical knowledge. Lord Diplock in *Wright v. British Railways Board*[3]:

"As regards assessment of damages for non-economic loss in personal injury cases, the Court of Appeal creates the guidelines as to the appropriate conventional figure by increasing or reducing awards of damages made by judges in individual cases for various common kinds of injuries. Thus, so-called 'brackets' are established, broad enough to make allowance for circumstances which make the deprivation suffered by an individual plaintiff in consequence of the particular kind of injury greater or less than in the general run of cases, yet clear enough to reduce the unpredictability of what is likely to be the most important factor in arriving at settlement of claims. 'Brackets' may call for alteration not only to take account of inflation, for which they ought automatically to be raised, but also, it may be, to take account of advances in medical science which may make particular kinds of injuries less disabling or advances in medical knowledge which may disclose hitherto unsuspected effects of some kinds of injuries or industrial diseases."

In a personal injuries case, the court assesses damages by reference to the facts at the date of trial: *Jobling v. Associated Dairies Limited*.[4] This principle applies to both past and future loss, as Lord Denning M.R. put it in *Birkett v. Hayes*[5]:

"The figure for pain, suffering and loss of amenities is always assessed as at the date of the trial. The judge then has before him the full story up to that date, and the outlook for the future. The plaintiff's condition may have deteriorated more than expected, or it may have improved. The judge has to award compensation *for the past*, and also *for the future* pain, suffering and loss of amenities."

It is submitted that the same principle applies when the personal injury, discomfort and distress and/or diminution in value occur in a disrepair context, *a fortiori* when the breach continues down to trial. In such cases, R.S.C. Ord. 37, r. 6 permits damages where there is a continuing cause of action "to be assessed down to the time of the assessment". In *Hewitt v. Rowlands*[6] the Court of Appeal agreed that the normal measure of damages is:

[3] *Ibid.*
[4] [1982] A.C. 794.
[5] [1982] 1 W.L.R. 816.
[6] (1924) 93 L.J.K.B. 1080.

"the difference in value to the tenant of the premises, *from the date of the notice to repair down to the date of the assessment of damages*, between the premises in their present condition and their value, if the landlord on receipt of the tenants' notice had fulfilled the obligation of the covenant."

Damages for personal injuries have been awarded so often and for such a long time that the bracketing of awards for different types of injury has reached a high degree of sophistication. On the one hand, it is usually possible to find closely analogous cases in *Kemp & Kemp: The Quantum of Damages, Current Law* or *Butterworths Personal Injury Litigation Service*. On the other hand, recourse may be had to the tariff or guidelines contained in *Guidelines for the Assessment of General Damages in Personal Injury Cases*.[7]

Where general damages are sought for disrepair, practitioners and judges find that the law remains in a relatively rudimentary state. In *Hussein v. Mehlman*[8] Mr Stephen Sedley Q.C. as he then was, sitting as an assistant recorder at Wood Green Trial Centre, observed that:

"There is no 'tariff' as there is in most personal injury cases, for awards of this kind, but a line of recent cases has given some indication of the proper range. In particular, I have had regard to *Lubren v. Lambeth London Borough Council*,[9] in which the Court of Appeal indicated broad approval of a median figure of £1,000 a year for a five-year deterioration of premises from habitable to 'appalling'. But there is no principle, any more than there is in false imprisonment cases, by which a single multiplier or divisor can be applied to such a figure to reflect greater or lesser periods of time."

Up-dating awards

When advising or making submissions as to quantum, the lawyer **24–02** has to convert earlier comparable awards into the money of the day. The universal method of up-dating is to use the Inflation Tables or the Retail Prices Index Tables in *Kemp & Kemp: The Quantum of Damages*.[10]

Strictly, one should ascertain the month of the earlier award and ascertain the value of that award as at the month of the current assessment, using the Retail Prices Index Tables.

Most practitioners, for most purposes, however, employ the Inflation Table, which is simple to use and which up-dates awards

[7] 2nd ed., 1994.
[8] [1992] 32 E.G. 59.
[9] (1987) 20 H.L.R. 165.
[10] See App. 2, p. 315.

from earlier to later years. It is the Inflation Table which is used in this book although Appendix One indicates both the Inflation Table and the Retail Price Index. Where an old award is cited, figures in square brackets after the award indicate the value of the award as at March 1996.

If, for example, the lawyer decides to rely upon the case of *Lubren v. Lambeth L.B.C.*,[11] he or she will ascertain that the award at the rate of £1,000 per annum was made by the County Court judge in June 1987. Applying the Inflation Table in *Kemp & Kemp*, the award was worth £1,520 in March 1996. That is the sum of damages which equivalent circumstances would merit in March 1996.

[11] *Supra.*

CHAPTER TWENTY FIVE

Interest on Damages

General principles

The award of interest and the rate at which interest is awarded is   **25–01**
discretionary, even though in personal injury cases exceeding £200
the discretion must be exercised in favour of the plaintiff unless
there is a "special reason" to the contrary.[1]

A claim for interest must be pleaded[2] and the advocate must be
ready to justify the claim for interest, the period for which it is
claimed and the appropriate rate. There may be a contractually
agreed rate of interest (which, if pleaded, the court should allow as
damages), equitable interest (where there has been a breach of a
fiduciary duty the court permits compound interest to be charged
at expropriatory rates), commercial interest (usually 1 per cent over
average base rates) or interest may be awarded at a special rate
which appears to fit the justice of the case. For consideration of
some of the different interest rates which might be applied by the
court, see the notes to R.S.C. Ord. 6, r. 2 and *McGregor on
Damages*.[3]

Interest, other than equitable interest, is always simple and not
compound. Generally it is at a rate which the court applies to
plaintiffs in general: *Miliangos (No. 2)*.[4] The court has a discretion
to award interest at a higher rate, however, if the plaintiff has had
to borrow money at a higher rate to mitigate the effect of the

---

[1] s.35A of the Supreme Court Act 1981; s.69 of the County Courts Act 1984.
[2] R.S.C. Ord. 18, r. 8; C.C.R. Ord. 6, r. 1A.
[3] 15th ed., 1988.
[4] [1977] Q.B. 489.

defendant's breaches: *Tate & Lyle Food Distribution v. Greater London Council.*[5] In that case Forbes J. held:

"I do not think the modern law is that interest is awarded against the defendant as a punitive measure for having kept the plaintiff out of his money. I think the principle now recognised is that it is all part the attempt to achieve *restitutio in integrum.* One looks, therefore, not at the profit which the defendant wrongfully made out of the money he withheld . . . but at the cost to the plaintiff of being deprived of the money which he should have had. I feel satisfied that in commercial cases the interest is intended to reflect the rate at which the plaintiff would have had to borrow money to supply the place of that which was withheld. I am also satisfied that one should not look at any special position in which the plaintiff may have been; one should disregard, for instance, the fact that a particular plaintiff, because of his personal situation, could only borrow money at a very high rate or, on the other hand, was able to borrow at specially favourable rates. The correct thing to do is to take the rate at which plaintiffs in general could borrow money. This does not, however, to my mind, mean that you exclude entirely all attributes of the plaintiff other than that he is a plaintiff. There is evidence here that large public companies of the size and prestige of these plaintiffs could expect to borrow at 1% over MLR, while for smaller and less prestigious concerns the rate might be as high as 3% over MLR. I think it would always be right to look at the rate at which plaintiffs with the general attributes of the actual plaintiff in the case (though not, of course, with any special or peculiar attribute) could borrow money as a guide to the appropriate interest rate. If commercial rates are appropriate I would take 1% over MLR as the proper figure in this case."

If the evidence established that, for example, relatively less affluent plaintiffs were only above to borrow at, say, 8 per cent over base rates then they should recover interest on their special damages at that rate and not at the Special Account Rate, which might be several per centage points cheaper. Conversely, if replacement goods were purchased by means of an interest free Social Fund loan then in principle there should be no award of interest. In *Bacon v. Cooper (Metals) Limited*[6] Cantley J. had no difficulty in ordering the defendant to pay as damages the high finance charges the plaintiff was obliged, as a result of his impecunious position, to lay out on a replacement rotor for a metal fragmentiser.

[5] [1982] 1 W.L.R. 149.
[6] [1982] 1 All E.R. 397.

Interest automatically accrues on High Court judgments at the Judgment Rate, pursuant to section 17 of the Judgments Act 1838. In the County Court, interest accrues on most judgments for £5,000 and over, again at the Judgment Rate, by virtue of section 74 of the County Courts Act 1984 and the County Courts (Interest of Judgment Debts) Order 1991: all judgments in disrepair cases are included in the scope of the Order. Since April 1, 1993 the Judgment Rate has been 8 per cent per annum. Before that, until April 16, 1985, the rate was 15 per cent per annum.

The Judgment Rate applies from the date damages are finally assessed or agreed (not from the date of an interlocutory judgment for damages to be assessed): *Thomas v. Bunn*.[7] Interest on costs, however, runs not from the date costs are taxed but from the date of judgment or order: *Hunt v. R M Douglas (Roofing) Limited*,[8] paragraph 2 of the County Courts (Interest of Judgement Debts) Order 1991.

It would seem that, under the usual form of Tomlin Order, when an action is stayed upon agreed terms, statutory interest at the Judgment Rate does not become payable until, in the event of default, judgment is entered on the Order. If interest on delayed payment is intended, the terms of the Tomlin Order would have to make express provision for it.

Interest on general damages

In addition to up-dating earlier comparable awards to reflect the   **25–02** "money of the day" of assessment, the court awards interest on general damages, generally from the date of service of the writ. In the simplest type of case where liability was never seriously in doubt interest should run from the date of the letter before action: *Jefford v. Gee*[9]; *Wright v. British Railways Board*.[10]

The reason interest is added to awards of general damages is to compensate the plaintiff for being kept out of his or her compensation since the time it should have been paid (which is taken to be the date of service of the writ, or, exceptionally, in very simple cases, the date of the letter before action). It might, at first blush, be suspected that there was an element of duplication involved in (a) up-dating awards to their value as at the date of trial; and (b) then adding interest on to that sum from the date of service of the writ to trial. There is no such duplication. The award at the date of trial is, in fact, exactly the same *in real terms* as the sum of money that would have been awarded as at the date of service of the writ.

[7] [1991] 1 A.C. 362.
[8] [1988] 3 W.L.R. 975.
[9] [1970] 2 Q.B. 130.
[10] [1983] 2 A.C. 773.

Interest is added to that sum to compensate the plaintiff, not for inflation, but for being kept out of that money from the earlier time he or she ought to have had it.[11] Lord Wilberforce expressed the distinction in *Pickett v. British Rails Engineering Limited*[12] as follows:

"As to interest on damages, I would restore the decision of the judge. This was varied by the Court of Appeal on the theory that as damages are now normally subject to increase to take account of inflation, there is no occasion to award interest as well. I find this argument, with respect, fallacious. Increase for inflation is designed to preserve the 'real' value of money, interest to compensate for being kept out of that 'real' value. The one has no relation to the other. If the damages claimed remained, nominally, the same, because there was no inflation, interest would normally be given. The same should follow if the damages remain in real terms the same."

The matter was put with equal clarity by Purchas L.J. in *Auty v. National Coal Board*[13]:

"the sum upon which [the award of interest] is based represents damages assessed at the date of trial and, therefore, includes an inflationary element related to the period between service of the writ and the date of trial . . . . The progress of inflation in these circumstances is established, and the computation is a retrospective one without imponderables. It must, therefore, be a low figure for interest."

The guideline rate of interest is 2 per cent per annum and will remain 2 per cent until the Court of Appeal otherwise directs in view of changes in inflation levels: *Wright v. British Railways Board*.[14] Special circumstances, for example delay in prosecuting the action, can persuade the court to vary the rate of interest or the period for which it is awarded: *Corbett v. Barking and Brentwood Health Authority*.[15] In *Tate & Lyle Food and Distribution Limited v. Greater London Council*,[16] however, Forbes J. indicated that: "the unreality of the other two rates [Special Account and Judgement Debt] is acceptable in personal injury cases, where there is a certain degree of unreality in the award of damages for pain and suffering . . . ".

[11] s.35A Supreme Court Act and s.69 County Courts Act 1984.
[12] [1980] A.C. 136.
[13] [1985] 1 W.L.R. 784.
[14] *Supra.*
[15] [1991] 2 Q.B. 408.
[16] *Supra.*

In *Saunders v. Edwards*[17] general damages were awarded to compensate purchasers of a flat for the disappointment and inconvenience of being deprived of a roof terrace. Bingham L.J. said:

"The intervention of statute has made general damages for pain and suffering and loss of amenity in personal injuries actions a special case. The damages awarded here for inconvenience and disappointment have no special features. The judge's award was clearly intended to compensate the plaintiffs for the inconvenience they had suffered throughout their occupation of the flat up to the date of trial and for disappointment during the same period. It was a single global award, modest in amount but intended to cover the past and the future. It is somewhat analogous to an award of general damages to a defamation plaintiff for mental distress and suffering, which have never, as I think, been augmented by interest up to the date of the trial. I consider this approach to be correct in principle, because in neither case can the damages be realistically seen as having accrued due to the plaintiff at a certain time in the past and as having thereafter been wrongly withheld from him . . . any award of interest on these damages is inappropriate. The same rule would ordinarily apply in similar or analogous cases."

It is arguable that an award of general damages for disrepair not causing personal injury should also be dealt with by the making of a global award, rather than an award plus interest. That it is not, however, current practice.

Interest on special damages

Interest on special damages is generally awarded by reference to **25–03** the court's Special Account rate (formerly known as the Short-Term Investment rate). The relevant figures are:

From November 1, 1987	11.25%
From December 1, 1987	11.00%
From May 1, 1988	9.50%
From August 1, 1988	11.00%
From November 1, 1988	12.25%
From January 1, 1989	13.00%
From January 1, 1990	14.25%
From April 1, 1991	12.00%
From October 1, 1991	10.25%
From February 1, 1993	8.00%

---

[17] [1987] 1 W.L.R. 1116.

Where there has been a continuing loss (such as loss of earnings, or excessive gas or electricity bills) or a series of smaller, one-off losses spread reasonably evenly over the relevant period of time, justice is normally done in personal injury cases by multiplying the loss by half of the average applicable Special Account rates between the accrual of the cause of action and the date of trial: *Jefford v. Gee.*[18]

In disrepair cases, albeit that there is a continuing cause of action, the same approach is often adopted: A rate of 5 or 6 per cent is applied to all such special damages from the start of the cause of action until the date of trial.

Where there have been one or more relatively major, one-off losses, however, it is potentially unfair to both defendant and plaintiff (depending on how close to trial the loss arose) not to award the full amount of interest at the relevant Special Account rates, but from the actual date of (the bulk of the) loss: *Prokop v. DHSS.*[19] When interest on particular items of special damages will be sought at the full Special Account rate, the pleading should make that clear: *Dexter v. Courtaulds Limited.*[20]

The decision of the Court of Appeal in *Prokop v. DHSS* is not consistent with the decision of the Court of Appeal in *Dexter v. Courtaulds Limited* (which applied the *Jefford v. Gee* approach to two clearly ascertained incidences of loss) but has been followed in *Duffey v. Bateman*[21] and *Braithwaite v. Latham.*[22] It is submitted that *Prokop* is to be preferred.

---

[18] *Supra.*
[19] (1983) C.A. July 5 (unreported).
[20] [1984] 1 W.L.R. 372.
[21] (1989) November 23 (unreported).
[22] (1990) May 22 (unreported).

CHAPTER TWENTY SIX

Actions by the Landlord

Restrictions on suing for damages or forfeiture in cases of tenancies granted for more than seven years where there are three years or more left

The Leasehold Property (Repairs) Act 1938, as extended by **26–01** section 51 of the Landlord and Tenant Act 1954, applies to all tenancies or leases of residential or commercial premises, except for agricultural or farm business tenancies, providing that:

(1) the tenancy was granted for a term certain of not less than seven years;

(2) at least three years of the term remain on the date proceedings are issued or a notice under section 146 of the Law of Property Act 1925 is served.[1]

The landlord may not sue for damages on account of the tenant's failure to comply with the tenant's repairing obligations unless he or she:

(1) Serves on the tenant a notice under section 146 of the Law of Property Act 1925 (which, *inter alia*, specifies the failures to repair).[2]

(2) Includes in such notice a further notice as to the tenant's right to serve a counter-notice under the Leasehold Property (Repairs) Act 1938.[3]

---

[1] s.51 Landlord and Tenant Act 1954.
[2] s.1(2) Leasehold Property (Repairs) Act 1938.
[3] s.1(4) Leasehold Property (Repairs) Act 1938.

If within 28 days the tenant serves the landlord with a counter-notice stating that he or she claims the benefit of the Leasehold Property (Repairs) Act 1938, the landlord cannot without the leave of the court take proceedings against the tenant, by action or otherwise, for damages or for forfeiture, on account of the tenant's failure to repair.[4]

The landlord has to show that despite the fact that the tenant and not the landlord is entitled to possession for the rest of the term, there is good reason for the application, of a kind set out in section 1(5) of the Leasehold Property (Repairs) Act 1938:

1.—(5) Leave for the purposes of this section shall not be given unless the lessor proves—

(a) that the immediate remedying of the breach is requisite for preventing substantial diminution in the value of his reversion, or that the value thereof has been substantially diminished by the breach;

(b) that the immediate remedying of the breach is required for giving effect in relation to the premises to the purposes of any enactment, or of any bylaw or other provision having effect under an enactment or for giving effect to any order of a court or requirement of any authority under any enactment or any such bylaw or other provision as aforesaid;

(c) in a case in which the lessor is not in occupation of the whole of the premises as respects which the covenant or agreement is proposed to be enforced, that the immediate remedying of the breach is required in the interest of the occupier of those premises or of part thereof;

(d) that the breach can be immediately remedied at an expense that is relatively small in comparison with the much greater expense that would probably be occasioned by the postponement of the necessary work; or

(e) special circumstances which in the opinion of the court, render it just and equitable that leave should be given.

(6) The court may, in granting or in refusing leave for the purposes of this section, impose such terms and conditions on the lessor or on the lessee as it may think fit.

---

[4] s.1(3) Leasehold Property (Repairs) Act 1938.

The landlord has to prove the breach and the ground relied on the ordinary standard of balance of probabilities: *Associated British Ports v. C. H. Bailey.*[5]

If the landlord proves his or her case for leave, the court retains a discretion not to grant leave, if "clearly convinced" that for some special reason leave should not be granted: *Re Metropolitan Film Studios.*[6] More likely is that, should the landlord prove his case for leave, either the tenant will know what he or she has to do to avoid a forfeiture action, or the court will adjourn the application on condition that the tenant carries out the requisite works of repair: *Associated British Ports v. C. H. Bailey.*[7]

If the tenancy agreement expressly confers on the landlord the right to enter, carry out works and recover the cost from the tenant, the landlord's claim in those circumstances is for payment of a debt and not for damages and is therefore not subject to procedural restriction: *Jervis v. Harris.*[8] So are other claims for fixed sums of money under the lease, *e.g.* expenses of preparing notices under sections 146 or 147 of the Law of Property Act 1925: *Middlegate Properties v. Gidlow-Jackson.*[9] The Leasehold Property (Repairs) Act 1938 does not apply to such claims.

Claims for damages during the term

Where the landlord sues during the term, damages are limited to **26–02** the amount of money by which the value of the reversion has been depreciated by the tenant's failure to repair in accordance with his or her obligations. That is the rule at common law. Statute also provides that damages on account of the tenant's failure to repair during the term may not exceed the amount by which the failure diminishes the value of the reversion.[10]

The amount by which the reversion has been diminished in value is obviously a matter of expert evidence. If the term is about to expire, or the landlord is liable to a superior landlord to carry out repairs, then the fall in the market value of the reversion may approximate closely to the cost of repairs. Otherwise the fall in value will depend on the period left before the term expires and may be slight or non-existent: *Conquest v. Ebbetts.*[11]

---

[5] [1990] A.C. 703.
[6] [1962] 1 W.L.R. 1315.
[7] *Supra.*
[8] [1996] 1 All E.R. 303.
[9] (1977) 34 P.&C.R. 4.
[10] s.18(1) Landlord and Tenant Act.
[11] [1896] A.C. 490.

Claims for damages after the term has expired

26–03 At common law the measure of damages where the tenant left the premises without having fulfilled his or her repairing obligations was the full cost of carrying out the relevant work plus loss of rent until completed: *Conquest v. Ebbetts*.[12] Damages were not reduced where the landlord had no intention of actually carrying out the work because he was about to demolish the premises: *Inderwick v. Leech*[13]; or had already re-let on a fully repairing lease: *Joyner v. Weeks*[14]; or where the rental value of the premises was not affected: *Morgan v. Hardy*.[15]

Parliament intervened to ameliorate repetition of such unfairness, by enacting section 18(1) of the Landlord and Tenant Act 1927:

> **18.—(1) Damages for a breach of a covenant or agreement to keep or put premises in repair during the currency of a lease, or to leave or put premises in repair during the currency of a lease, or to leave or put premises in repair at the termination of a lease, whether such covenant or agreement is express or implied, and whether general or specific, shall in no case exceed the amount (if any) by which the value of the reversion (whether immediate or not) in the premises is diminished owing to the breach of such covenant or agreement as aforesaid; and in particular no damage shall be recovered for a breach of any such covenant or agreement to leave or put premises in repair at the termination of a lease, if it is shown that the premises, in whatever state of repair they might be, would at or shortly after the termination of the tenancy have been or be pulled down, or such structural alterations made therein as would render valueless the repairs covered by the covenant or agreement.**

The cost of the repairs (plus VAT where the landlord can not recover it and professional supervision where warranted) remains prima facie evidence of the diminution in the value of the reversion; and is very strong evidence if the landlord is about to or has in fact

---

[12] *Ibid.*
[13] (1885) 1 T.L.R. 484.
[14] [1891] 2 Q.B. 31.
[15] (1886) 17 Q.B.D. 770.

carried out the works: *Jones v. Herxheimer*[16]; *Haviland v. Long*[17]; *Smiley v. Townshend*.[18]

If the diminution in value equals or exceeds the cost of repairs the statutory cap is not reached and the landlord recovers the cost of repairs: *Culworth Estates v. Society of Licensed Victuallers*.[19]

No account is to be taken of a new lease negotiated by the landlord under which the incoming tenant covenants to put and keep the premises in repair, as such a new lease is *res inter alios acta*[20]: *Haviland v. Long*.[21] But where the landlord inherits sub-tenants who are bound by similar covenants, it may well be that the value of his or her reversion is not diminished at all by the outgoing mesne tenant's failure to repair: *Crown Estate Commissioners v. Town Investments*.[22]

All questions are resolved by reference to the market place. In practice, the landlord's expert values the cost of the works necessitated by the tenant's breaches of the agreement and their effect on the value of the landlord's reversion. The loss of the reversion's value caps the award of damages, no matter how much it would cost to effect the works: *Mather v. Barclays Bank plc*,[23] is an extreme case in which the works would have cost £271,000 (in 1984) but in which expert evidence demonstrated that there was no diminution in the value of the reversion).

Section 18 (1) of the Landlord and Tenant Act 1927 applies to actions for damages. An action at the expiry of the term for a fixed sum required in the lease to be laid out on repairs each year or paid over to the landlord is an action for a debt, not for damages, and is not caught by the Act: *Moss' Empires v. Olympia (Liverpool)*.[24] If the tenancy agreement expressly confers on the landlord the right to enter, carry out works and recover the cost from the tenant, the landlord's claim in those circumstances, during the currency of the term, is for payment of a debt and not for damages: *Jervis v. Harris*.[25] It would appear difficult to argue that a *Jervis v. Harris* type action, at the end of the term, fell within the Act.

---

[16] [1950] 2 K.B. 106.
[17] [1952] 2 Q.B. 80.
[18] [1966] 2 K.B. 311. A reversion which has a negative value can be diminished in value if the disrepair results in the negative value increasing: *Shortlands Investments Ltd v. Cargill plc* (1995) 69 P.&C.R. D9.
[19] (1991) 61 P.&C.R. 211.
[20] See para. 19–22
[21] *Supra*.
[22] [1992] 1 E.G.L.R. 61.
[23] [1987] 2 E.G.L.R. 254.
[24] [1939] A.C. 544.
[25] *Supra*.

Damages for waste

26–04   Voluntary waste is a tort and remains a tort even though the lease
contains a repairing code which expressly precludes waste. Accordingly, exemplary damages can be awarded: *Whitham v. Kershaw.*[26]
Otherwise, the basic measure of damages is the diminution in the
value of the reversion: *Whitham v. Kershaw.* See further paragraph
10–04.

---

[26] (1886) 16 Q.B.D. 613) (the case is referred to in *Broom v. Cassell & Co. Limited*
[1972] A.C. 1027).

PART EIGHT

OTHER REMEDIES

CHAPTER TWENTY SEVEN

Specific Performance, Interlocutory Injunctions and the Special Rights of Secure Tenants

Specific performance of the landlord's obligations: limitations on the remedy

In *Jeune v. Queen's Cross Properties*[1] Pennycuik V.-C. said: "where **27–01** there has been a plain breach of covenant to repair and there is no doubt at all what is required to remedy the breach, I cannot see why an order for specific performance should not be made". The landlord was ordered to repair a stone balcony in the common parts. In *Francis v. Cowlcliffe Limited*[2] and *Peninsular Maritime Limited v. Padseal Limited*[3] the landlord was required to repair a lift in the common parts. See 27–03 to 27–10 for limitations on the exercise of power.

Lack of mutuality can result in the court refusing to make an order of specific performance: *Lumley v. Ravenscroft*.[3a] There is a lack of mutuality between tenants' and landlords' repairing obligations, in that tenants can obtain orders of specific performance against landlords but landlords can not obtain orders of specific performance against tenants. Section 17 of the Landlord and Tenant Act 1985 therefore expressly provides that in the case of

---

[1] [1974] Ch. 97.
[2] (1976) 33 P. & C.R. 368.
[3] (1981) 259 E.G. 860.
[3a] [1895] 1 Q.B. 683. See also *Price v. Strange* [1978] Ch. 337, at 360.

repairs to dwelling-houses the court is not to refuse to make an order of specific performance on the ground of lack of mutuality.

It remains arguable that a landlord should not be specifically ordered to carry out repairs to the demised premises when they are not a dwelling (leaving the tenant to his or her remedy in damages): *Granada Theatres Limited v. Freehold Investment (Leytonstone) Limited*,[4] *Gordon v. Selico Co. Ltd.*[4a] The Law Commission recommends that specific performance should be made clearly available to landlords and tenants alike, to enforce repairing obligations in all leases and tenancies, whether of commercial, agricultural or domestic premises.[4b]

Specific performance of the tenant's obligations: limitations on the remedy

27–02   The law, as it currently stands, is that the court will not generally order specific performance of a tenant's repairing covenant: *Hill v. Barclay*[5]; *Regional Properties Ltd v. City of London Real Property Co. Ltd.*[6] The landlord has to rely on his or her rights to forfeit, to enter and repair at the tenant's expense or to seek damages.[7] If a case arises in which there is a very good reason why these alternative remedies are plainly inadequate, it is thought that the courts may well grant injunctive relief or make an order of specific performance. Furthermore, the Law Commission has (a) strongly suggested that changes in the legal context have undermined reasoning in *Hill v. Barclay*,[8] (b) recommended that the remedy of specific performance is made available to landlords by statute.

The need for a sufficiently detailed order

27–03   The court will take into account but is unlikely to refuse to make an order of specific performance merely because the order would require constant supervision to ensure compliance: *Tito v. Waddell (No 2)*.[9]

It is, however, essential that the order of specific performance is sufficiently detailed so that the defendant knows sufficiently clearly what he or she has to do. Lord Upjohn summarised the principle in *Morris v. Redland Bricks Limited*[10] as follows:

[4] [1959] 1 Ch. 592.
[4a] [1985] 2 E.G.L.R. 79.
[4b] Law Com. 238.
[5] (1810) 16 Ves. Jun. 402.
[6] [1981] 1 E.G.L.R. 33, at 34.
[7] See Chapter 26.
[8] Law Com. 238.
[9] [1977] Ch.D. 106, 321–322.
[10] [1970] A.C. 652. See also *Wolverhampton Corporation v. Emmons* [1901] Q.B. 515, *Ford Sellar Morris Developments Limited v. Grant Seward Ltd* [1989] E.G.L.R. 40.

"If in the exercise of its discretion the court decides that it is a proper case to grant a mandatory injunction, then the court must be careful to see that the defendant knows exactly in fact what he has to do and this means not as a matter of law but as a matter of fact, so that in carrying out an order he can give his contractors the proper instructions."

In *Morris v. Redland Bricks Limited* the House of Lords rejected an order requiring the defendant to "take all necessary steps to restore the support to the [respondent's] land". In the circumstances of that case the order imposed an "unlimited and unqualified" obligation "without giving [the defendants] any indication of what was to be done".

Sufficient detail does not always require detail to be given

Although it is normal for orders to be made by reference to **27–04** detailed schedules of work prepared by surveyors, that is not always what is required. Lord Upjohn himself recognised in *Morris v. Redland Bricks Limited*[11] that great detail was not always necessary: "There may be some cases where, to revert to the simple illustration I gave earlier, the defendant can be ordered 'to restore the right of way to its former condition'. This is so simple as to require no further elucidation in the court order".

In *Jeune v. Queen's Cross Properties Limited*[12] the order was that the landlord "do forthwith reinstate the York stone balcony situate in the front of the building . . . in the form in which it existed prior to its partial collapse . . . ".

In *Peninsular Maritime Limited v. Padseal Limited*[13] an interlocutory order enjoining the landlord to use its best endeavours to put a lift into good working condition easily survived an appeal on the ground of absence of particularity. ("If the lift works, the order will be complied with; if it does not, subject to a further point, it will not have been complied with.")

On the other hand, in *Parker v. Camden L.B.C.*[14] the Court of Appeal refused to make an order requiring the landlord to restore a boiler to proper working condition, even though the situation was one of great urgency and of real danger to health, without knowing whether what was required was as simple as "throwing a switch" or

[11] *Ibid.*
[12] *Supra.*
[13] *Supra.*
[14] [1986] Ch. 162.

as complex and expensive as "rebuilding the boiler or the system".

Lack of detail when the plaintiff is not able to be specific

27–05   Irrespective of the terms of the tenancy agreement, the court has the power to order either tenant or landlord to permit the other party's expert to inspect and report so that a detailed order can be made.[15]

Notwithstanding that right, the court can make orders in fairly general terms when the building element in question is in the ownership and possession of the other party. In *Gordon v. Selico Company Limited*[16] the roof, which was in the ownership and possession of the landlord, was leaking. The court ordered the landlord to "put the building of which the premises form part into such reasonable condition as not to cause damage to the plaintiffs or to the premises demised by the incursion of water, the propagation of dry rot, or otherwise" with liberty to apply for directions or for the settling of a detailed schedule of works. It may be relevant in such circumstances that the principle is that the performing party has the right to choose between alternative methods of performing his or her covenant.

If the premises have become dangerous, then it can be more important to avert the danger than wait for precise details of the works required. Young J. said in *Greetings Oxford Koala Hotel Property Limited v. Oxford Square Investments Property Limited*[17]:

> "It has been recognised in the case of interlocutory injunctions, that it is sometimes better to take the risk that the defendant may have some problems in comprehending exactly what the injunction covers, rather than make no injunction at all."

Defences generally

27–06   Orders of specific performance are discretionary, albeit that the discretion is not freewheeling but "governed as far as possible by fixed rules and principles": *Lamare v. Dixon*.[18] Specific performance can be refused if the plaintiff has delayed inexcusably in asserting his or her rights and the delay has caused prejudice to the defendant or if the plaintiff has behaved unconscionably. Full consideration of the ambit of such defences can be found in Spry's

---

[15] R.S.C. Ord. 29, r. 2; applied in the County Court by C.C.R. Ord. 13, r. 7.
[16] [1985] 2 E.G.L.R. 79, affirmed at [1986] 1 E.G.L.R. 71.
[17] (1989) 18 N.S.W.L.R. 33.
[18] (1873) L.R. 6 H.L. 414, 423.

Equitable Remedies,[19] Fry's *Specific Performance*[20] and the Law Commission's report,[21] *Landlord and Tenant: Responsibility for State and Condition of Property.*

Damages instead of specific performance

Specific performance will be ordered when it will "do more perfect and complete justice than an award of damages": *Tito v. Waddell (No 2).*[22] The question is not whether damages are an adequate remedy, but "is it just in all the circumstances that the plaintiff should be confined to his remedy in damages?": *Evans Marshall & Co. Limited v. Bertola SA.*[23] Relevant consideration are: how easy it is to precisely calculate the amount of damages that would be required, whether an award of damages would resolve the dispute once and for all, whether damages enable satisfactory equivalent performance to be obtained: *Ford Sella Morris Developments Ltd v. Grant Seward Ltd.*[23a]

27–07

Impecuniosity or hardship as a defence

Mere financial difficulties have never been a ground for refusing specific performance: *Francis v. Cowcliffe*[24] (impecunious landlord ordered to repair lift); *Patel v. Ali*[25] (impecuniosity by itself would not have prevented the court from ordering conveyance of a dwelling-house according to the terms of the contract); *Mountford v. Scott*[26] (specific performance would not be refused to purchaser merely because vendor would find it difficult to purchase alternative accommodation in the rising market); *Howard E Perry v. British Railways Board*[27] (specific performance ordered despite risk of strike by defendant's employees). Similarly, the fact that the tenant is in breach of obligations to pay service charges will not of itself prevent the landlord being ordered to perform his or her obligations: *Yorkbrook Investments v. Batten*[28]; *Gordon v. Selico Company Limited.*[29]

27–08

The courts might, however, refuse to make an order of specific performance if the cost is out of all proportion to the benefit: *Tito*

---

[19] 4th ed.
[20] 6th ed.
[21] Law Com. 238.
[22] [1977] Ch. 106, 322.
[23] [1973] 1 W.L.R. 349, 379.
[23a] [1989] 2 E.G.L.R. 40, at 41–2.
[24] (1977) 33 P. & C.R. 368.
[25] [1984] Ch. 283.
[26] [1975] Ch. 258.
[27] [1980] 1 W.L.R. 1375.
[28] [1985] 2 E.G.L.R. 100.
[29] [1985] 2 E.G.L.R. 79; affirmed [1986] 1 E.G.L.R. 71.

v. Waddell (No 2)[30] (to replace soil to the necessary depth and to effectively re-establish coconut plantations would cost $A50million, take about 100 years and be "an absurd exercise" since coconuts could be purchased in perpetuity for a fraction of the price); *Morris v. Redland Bricks Limited*[31] (unreasonable to order defendant to carry out work costing £30,000 to plaintiff's land worth £12,000: but only because the defendant (although in the wrong) had not behaved unreasonably let alone flagrantly) and because the damage feared had (a) not yet occurred (b) could be compensated for in full by an award of damages).

The court may not grant specific performance if it would result in *severe* hardship (not merely financial difficulties) to the defendant. The circumstances have to be "extraordinary and persuasive": *Patel v. Ali*.[32]

Delay

27–09 Culpable delay by the tenant which has resulted in the landlord being put at some disadvantage may make it unconscionable for an order of specific performance to be made or an injunction granted. Such cases are likely to be rare when it comes to specifically enforcing or enjoining compliance with repairing obligations. In *Howard v. Midrome Limited*[33] Warner J. said:

> "Before I deal with Mr Denyer-Green's next point I will deal with his last point, which was that the delay which the plaintiffs have allowed to elapse should debar them from obtaining interlocutory relief. They served their notice, as I have mentioned, in August 1989; the originating summons was issued in December 1989; and this motion was launched in July 1990. I have already said that in my view it is just and convenient to make the order sought. I think that that is so notwithstanding the delay, because another winter is on its way, the deterioration in the property is continuing, and so is the lack of management of the property."

Impossibility as a defence

27–10 The court will not order the impossible and will accordingly not order the landlord to carry out works which are legally impossible. An example often given is where to perform the order the defendant has to enter upon land in respect of which he or she does not have a legal right of entry. Where the Access to Neighbouring

---

[30] *Supra.*
[31] *Supra.*
[32] [1984] Ch. 283.
[33] *Supra.*

Land Act 1992 applies, or where the relevant landowner upon enquiry appears willing to allow entry upon reasonable terms there is no reason why an order in appropriate terms should not be made.

Interlocutory injunctions

The court has the power to make an interlocutory injunction **27–11** requiring the landlord to carry out his or her repairing obligations pending trial. The leading authority is *Parker v. Camden L.B.C.*[34] There are generally two requirements:

(1) the work required must be agreed between the parties or it must be clear to the court what is required;
(2) the circumstances must be exceptional, *e.g.* posing an immediate risk to health or safety.

It is, however, a question for the discretion of the court on the facts of each case.[34a]

In the county court case of *Sheriden v. Broadbridge*[34b] the judge held that at least one defect was sufficiently serious to satisfy the *Parker v. Camden* criteria and that in the circumstances of the case, it would be invidious not to order the landlord to carry out all other work agreed to be necessary.

The special rights of secure tenants

By section 96 of the Housing Act 1985, the Secure Tenants of **27–12** Local Housing Authorities (Right to Repair) Regulations 1994[35] and the Secure Tenants of Local Housing Authorities (Right to Repair) (Amendment) Regulations 1994[36] secure tenants of local housing authorities have the right to have "qualifying repairs" carried out at their landlords' expense.

The repair has to be to one of the defects set out in the Schedule to the Regulations which will not "in the opinion of the landlord" cost more than £250 to effect. The procedure is that the tenant applies to his or her landlord for the work of repair to be carried out. The landlord then (in theory) inspects, if it wishes, and in any

---

[34] [1986] Ch. 162.
[34a] In *Hi-lift Elevator Services v. Temple* (1995) 70 P.&C.R. 620 the Court of Appeal held that the county court judge had been wrong to grant an interlocutory injunction preventing the landlord from carrying out works to the roof which the tenant considered excessive. It was the landlord's decision *now* to repair, within the bounds of reasonableness. The tenant's remedy was for a declaration that the cost was unreasonable for the purposes of their service charge, relying on sections 17 and 18 of the Landlord and Tenant Act 1985.
[34b] (1995) 16 June, reported at *Legal Action*, September 1995 issue at page 16.
[35] S.I. 1994 No. 133.
[36] S.I. 1994 No. 844.

event notifies the tenant in writing whether it is "satisfied" that the repair is a qualifying repair. If the landlord "is satisfied" that the repair is a qualifying repair it is required to issue a "repairs notice" to a contractor, with a copy to the tenant. If the repair is not carried out with the "prescribed period" (set out in relation to each repair, in the Schedule) the tenant has the right to require the landlord to issue a second repairs notice, to another contractor, requiring repairs to be carried out within the prescribed period (as defined in the Schedule). The landlord must issue such a notice "where it is reasonably practicable". If the repair is not carried out by the second contractor, there is no further provision for a repairs notice, but the landlord is obliged to pay the tenant compensation. The "specified sum" of compensation is a £10 basic award plus £2 multiplied by the number of days that elapse between the second prescribed period and completion of the repair. If there is a delay of five days, for example, the "specified sum" would be £10 plus (£2 × 5) = £20. Any dispute is to be determined by the County Court.

The regulations themselves are fairly complex and also depend, if they are to work, on public sector landlords taking a number of steps in compliance with the regulations: inspection; service of repair notices on contractors and payment of compensation in certain circumstances. The fatal flaw in the regulations is that if the local authority landlord was minded to comply with its legal duties at all, it would carry out the repair it is legally obliged to effect within a reasonable period of time after being notified that it was required. A further flaw is the complexity of the regulations and deferral of any legal obligation until after the local authority has formed a series of positive opinions: which it might or might not form. It would be interesting to learn whether and if so to what extent the regulations have been successfully employed in practice.

CHAPTER TWENTY EIGHT

Other Remedies

Self help by the tenant: works to the demised premises

The tenant has the right to carry out works to the demised **28–01** premises when the landlord is in breach of his or her obligations. The tenant is then entitled to sue his or her landlord to recover the cost of works as damages: a modern example is *Loria v. Hammer.*[1]

Instead of suing for the cost of the works as damages, the tenant is entitled to recoup his or her expenditure out of future rents: *Taylor v. Beal*[2]; *Waters v. Weigall*[3]; *Davies v. Stacey*[4]; *Lee-Parker v. Izzet.*[5] In *Lee-Parker v. Izzet* Goff J. held that:

"I do not think this is bound up with technical rules of set off. It is an ancient common law right. I therefore declare that so far as the repairs are within the express or implied covenants of the landlord, the third and fourth defendants are entitled to recoup themselves out of future rents and defend any action for payment thereof. It does not follow however that the full amount expended by the third and fourth defendants on such repairs can properly be treated as payment of rent. It is a question of fact in every case whether and to what extent the expenditure was proper.

For the sake of avoiding misunderstanding, I must add that of course the *Taylor v. Beal* right can only be exercised when

[1] [1989] 2 E.G.L.R. 249.
[2] (1591) Cro.Eliz. 222.
[3] (1795) 2 Anst. 575.
[4] (1840) 12 Ad. & El. 506.
[5] [1971] 1 W.L.R. 1688.

and so far as the landlord is in breach and any necessary notice must have been given to him.

In so far as the repairs fall outside the landlord's covenants there can in my judgment be no set off against the plaintiffs . . . "

Self help by the tenant: works to the landlord's premises

28–02   The position is more difficult when the tenant carries out repairs to parts of the building retained in the ownership of the landlord. The act of carrying out such repairs prima facie involves a trespass to the property of the landlord.

In *Sedgwick Forbes Bland Payne Group Limited v. Regional Properties Limited*[6] Oliver J. held that the tenant's *Taylor v. Beal* right to carry out repairs in default did not create an implied right of access to the building element in disrepair. The tenant was accordingly left with a right to sue for damages or specific performance only. That is not satisfactory because in some circumstances, in particular where work is urgently required to prevent serious damage, basic fairness requires that there should be such a right of entry to repair.

In *Loria v. Hammer*[7] Mr John Lindsay Q.C. held that a tenant who had carried out repairs to common parts retained in the ownership of the landlord had not trespassed because she did have such an implied right of entry: *Sedgwick Forbes Bland Payne Group Limited v. Regional Properties Limited*[8] was not cited. Mr Lindsay Q.C. held, however, that in any event, even if there had been a trespass, that in itself would not affect the tenant's entitlement to recover the cost of the works.

The solution to the question of access may, it is submitted, lie in the field of nuisance. If the condition of the adjacent property owned by the landlord deteriorates to such an extent that it interferes with the tenant's reasonable enjoyment of his or her premises, then he or she can exercise the common law right of any person affected by a common law nuisance, to enter the offending property and abate the nuisance: see *Clerk & Lindsell on Torts*[9] for a description of the right and the limitations within which the right must be exercised. The tenant can then sue for damages. If the condition of the landlord's adjoining property does not get into such a state, then it is no hardship to the tenant to be left only with a right to sue for damages or specific performance.

---

[6] (1980) 257 E.G. 64.
[7] *Supra.*
[8] *Supra.*
[9] 17th Ed., 1995 at para. 29–22.

Self help by the landlord

28–03 If the landlord has no express or implied right to enter to carry out repairs[10] he can be restrained by injunction from so doing, even though his own lease might be liable to be forfeited: *Stocker v. Planet Building Society*[11]; *Regional Properties v. City of London Real Property Co.*[12]

If the landlord does actually enter and carry out works in default, he or she will recover the costs if the claim is a debt and not for damages despite the fact that he or she technically committed a trespass: *Colley v. Streeton.*[13]

If the landlord enters and carries out works his claim against the tenant for reimbursement is prima facie a claim for damages. As such, the landlord's claim would be severely restricted by the Leasehold Property (Repairs) Act 1938 and section 18 of the Landlord and Tenant Act 1927. If, however, the tenancy agreement expressly confers on the landlord the right to enter, carry out works and recover the cost from the tenant, the landlord's claim in those circumstances is for payment of a debt and not payment of damages. The landlord is entitled to pursue that claim without statutory interference: *Jervis v. Harris.*[14]

Set off against rent

28–04 The tenant has a common law right to set off against rent sums expended on repairs.[15] There is also a right in equity to set off against rent a claim for unliquidated damages arising out of the landlord's failure to repair: *British Anzani (Felixstowe) v. International Marine Management (UK) Limited*[16]; *Melville v. Grapelodge Developments Limited*[17]; *Televantos v. McCulloch*[18]; *Haringey L.B.C. v. Stewart.*[19]

The tenant will not, however, obtain an adjournment of a possession claim or leave to defend an application for summary judgment for the rent merely by making general and unquantified allegations of breaches of repairing obligations: *Asco Developments Limited v. Gordon*[20]; *Agyeman v. Boadi.*[21]

[10] See paras. 10–02, 10–03.
[11] (1879) 27 W.R. 877.
[12] (1980) 257 E.G. 65.
[13] (1823) 2 B.&C. 273.
[14] [1996] 1 All E.R. 303.
[15] See para. 22–03.
[16] [1980] Q.B. 637.
[17] (1979) 39 P.&C.R. 179.
[18] (1990) 23 H.L.R. 412.
[19] (1991) 23 H.L.R. 557.
[20] (1978) 248 E.G. 683.
[21] [1996] E.G.C.S. 14.

If the tenant's unliquidated claim for damages exceeds the amount of rent claimed by the landlord, the tenant should have his costs: *British Anzani (Felixstowe) Ltd v. International Marine Management (UK) Ltd.*[22] In those circumstances it would be "plainly wrong" for any possession order sought on the basis of rent arrears to be made: *Televantos v. McCulloch.*[23] If the claim for unliquidated damages was made bona fide but fails, it will still, in general, be unreasonable for a possession order to be made, providing that the tenant can discharge arrears out of moneys put to one side or paid into court "or, at the very least, . . . put forward proposals for an early discharge of the arrears". The ordinary course might not be followed where the tenant has a long history of late rent payments: *Haringey L.B.C. v. Stewart.*[24]

The tenant's right to set off can be excluded in the tenancy agreement providing clear words are used: *Connaught Restaurants Limited v. Indoor Leisure Limited.*[25] The Unfair Contract Terms Act 1977 does not apply to such an exclusion: *Electricity Supply Nominees Limited v. I. A. F. Group Limited.*[26]

Secure tenants are unable to withhold rent when in receipt of housing benefit: regulation 95 of the Housing Benefit (General) Regulations 1987 (No. 1971).

Quitting

28–05   In *Hussein v. Mehlman*[27] the landlord was in blatant breach of his repairing obligations. The premises had become unfit for human habitation and the landlord was refusing to carry out further repairs. The tenants handed in the keys and left. Mr Stephen Sedley Q.C. as he then was, sitting as an assistant recorder at the Wood Green Trial Centre held that:

(i) A repudiatory breach of a contract of letting is legally possible.

(ii) There was in this case a repudiatory breach by the defendant of the repairing covenants.

(iii) The plaintiffs by vacating the property and returning the keys . . . had accepted the defendant's breach as putting an end to the lease.

---

[22] *Supra.*
[23] *Supra.*
[24] *Supra.*
[25] [1993] 2 E.G.L.R. 108.
[26] [1993] 2 E.G.L.R. 95.
[27] [1992] 32 E.G. 59.

The tenants were accordingly not liable to pay rent after handing back the keys.

It appears, as held in *Hussein v. Mehlman,* that it is possible to repudiate a tenancy agreement or lease in the same way as other contracts, by evincing an intention no longer to be bound by the terms of the agreement and for the tenancy or lease to come to an end by acceptance of that repudiation. A similar conclusion was reached by Mr T Morrison Q.C. sitting as a deputy High Court judge in *W. G. Clark (Properties) Limited v. Dupre Properties Limited.*[28]

The doctrine that leases and tenancy agreements may be repudiated has apparently found root in Canada and Australia in which countries it appears that repudiatory conduct is now attributed to tenants who evince an intention not to pay rent or otherwise comply with their obligations: *Highway Properties v. Kelly*[29]; *Progressive Malting House Property v. Tabali Property.*[30] The doctrine is not without its difficulties because it appears to drive a coach and horses through all forms of statutory security or protection: see *Acceptance of Repudiatory Breaches in Lease* by Mark Pawlowski.[31]

The appointment of managers and receivers

For a full treatment of this topic including the procedures to be followed the reader is referred to *Woodfall: Landlord and Tenant* at Part 2 and Part 7. **28–06**

The High Court has an inherent power to appoint a receiver to take over the management wherever the landlord is in serious default[32]: *Hart v. Emelkirk*[33]; *Daiches v. Bluelake Investments*[34]; *Blawdziewicz v. Diadon Establishment*[35]; *Clayhope Properties v. Evans.*[36] The County Court has similar power by virtue of section 38 of the County Court Act 1984.

Tenants of flats can apply to the County Court for the appointment of a manager under Part II of the Landlord and Tenant Act 1987. The grounds are that the landlord is in breach of a management-type covenant, is likely to continue to be in breach and that it is just and convenient to appoint a manager in all the circumstances: section 24 of the Landlord and Tenant Act 1987.

---

[28] [1992] 1 All E.R. 596.
[29] (1971) 17 D.L.R. (3d) 710.
[30] (1985) 157 C.L.R. 17.
[31] [1995] Conv. 379.
[32] s.37(1) Supreme Court Act 1981.
[33] [1983] 1 W.L.R. 1289.
[34] [1985] 2 E.G.L.R. 67.
[35] [1988] 2 E.G.L.R. 52.
[36] [1986] 1 W.L.R. 1223.

Managers cannot be appointed if the landlord is a specified public body (including local authorities). The manager could be a firm of surveyors or managing agents selected by the tenants, or even the tenant's management vehicle: *Howard v. Midrome*.[37] The court may require the manager to carry out some or all of the landlord's management functions or to act as a receiver: there is power to make a wide range of ancillary orders.

In *Howard v. Midrome* there was a leaking roof which the landlord was bound to repair but showed no intention of repairing. A manager was appointed pending trial, since damage was being caused to individual flats by the water penetration.

Where the appointment of a manager would not be an adequate remedy the court can go further on the tenants' application and make an acquisition order under Part III of the Landlord and Tenant Act 1987: *Gray v. Standard Home and Counties Properties*.[38]

Forfeiture

28–07   If there is a proviso for re-entry in the event of the tenant's failure to repair, the landlord can forfeit the lease. First, he or she has to serve notice complying with section 146 of the Law of Property Act 1925 and section 18 (2) of the Landlord and Tenant Act 1927 and, if applicable, section 1 of the Leasehold Property (Repairs) Act 1938.[39]

For full consideration of forfeiture see *Woodfall: Landlord and Tenant*.

[37] [1991] 1 E.G.L.R. 58.
[38] [1994] 1 E.G.L.R. 119.
[39] See Chapter 26.

PART NINE

MISCELLANEOUS

CHAPTER TWENTY NINE

The Limitation Acts

The basic six-year tort period

The Limitation Act 1980 provides as follows: **29–01**

> **1.—(1) This part of this Act gives the ordinary time limits for bringing actions of the various classes mentioned in the following provisions of this Part.**
>
> **(2) The ordinary time limits given in this Part of this Act are subject to extension or exclusion in accordance with the provisions of Part II of this Act.**

> **2. An action founded on tort shall not be brought after the expiration of six years from the date on which the cause of action accrued.**

Section 2 of the Limitation Act 1980 applies to actions brought by landlords and tenants in nuisance, trespass and negligence (where no personal injury is suffered).

In the case of many torts—negligence and nuisance, for example—it is necessary to prove damage to complete the cause of action. In the case of such torts, the cause of action is completed when damage is suffered and it is at that time that the cause of action accrues for the purposes of the limitation acts.

This can be unfair in cases of latent damage, *i.e.* cases in which the innocent party could not reasonably be expected to realise that he or she has suffered damage until after the expiry of the limitation period: *Cartledge v. E. Jopling & Sons Ltd*[1] (personal injury), *Pirelli*

---

[1] [1963] A.C. 758.

General Cable Works v. Oscar Faber & Partners[2] (property damage).

The limitation acts were amended to ameliorate this source of unfairness.

In cases of personal injury caused by negligence, nuisance or breach of duty,[3] the limitation period became three years, either from the accrual of the cause of action or from the victim's knowledge.[4]

In negligence cases which do not involve personal injury, the limitation period has become, by section 14A Limitation Act 1980, six years from the date of the accrual of the cause of action, or, if later, three years from the victim's date of knowledge, as defined by section 14A Limitation Act 1980. There is however a longstop date of 15 years from the negligent act, even if there has by 15 years been no damage and no knowledge.

The limitation acts have not been amended to provide for any extension of the limitation period by reference to the victim's date of knowledge in other types of tort case, *i.e.* cases in which personal injury has been caused intentionally as opposed to negligently, by for example nuisance or in breach of duty: *Stubbings v. Webb*[5] nuisance cases in which there has been property damage but no personal injury claim has been made, and so forth. *Stubbings v. Webb* was the case in which the plaintiff had allegedly been sexually abused as a minor. She brought proceedings against her abusers within three years of her date of knowledge for the purposes of section 11 of the Limitation Act 1980 but later than six years after attaining her majority. The House of Lords struck out her action on the ground that it was statute barred, section 2 of the Limitation Act applying a flat six-year period to cases in which personal injury had been inflicted deliberately as opposed to negligently. In *Stubbings, J.L. & J.P. v. United Kingdom*[6] the European Commission of European Rights unanimously declared that in those circumstances the effect of section 2 of the Limitation Act infringed the applicants' rights under Article 8 (respect for private and family life) and Article 6 (access to court for determination of civil rights) taken with Article 14 (non-discrimination). The European Court of Human Rights held that there was no violation of Article 8 or Articles 6/14 because the principles of legal certainty and the need to protect people from state claims difficult to defend rendered the

---

[2] [1983] 2 A.C. 1.
[3] As defined by s.11 Limitation Act 1980: see below at para. 29–04.
[4] As defined by s.14 Limitation Act 1980: see below at paras. 29–04.
[5] [1993] 1 W.L.R. 782.
[6] [1995] E.H.H.R. C.D. 32.

limitation acts proportionate and legitimate, having regard to the protection of the criminal law.[6a]

The basic six-year contract period

The Limitation Act 1980 provides as follows: 29–02

1.—(1) This part of this Act gives the ordinary time limits for bringing actions of the various classes mentioned in the following provisions of this Part.
(2) The ordinary time limits given in this Part of this Act are subject to extension or exclusion in accordance with the provisions of Part II of this Act.
5. An action founded on simple contract shall not be brought after the expiration of six years from the date on which the cause of action arose.

An action against a landlord for breach of repairing obligations contained in an oral or written contract (but not a Deed: see para. 29–03) is subject to a basic limitation period of six years from breach.

The cause of action arises when the landlord fails to repair that which he has contracted to keep in repair, providing, in the case of land or parts of land which have been demised, he has had notice of the want of repair and failed to repair within a reasonable period of time: *Bishop v. Consolidated London Properties*[7]; *O'Brien v. Robinson*.[8]

Where the action includes a claim for damages on account of personal injuries, the limitation period may be different.[9]

In contract cases, the cause of action arises when the breach of contract takes place even in cases of latent damage, *i.e.* cases in which the innocent party could not reasonably be expected to realise that there has been a breach and damage does not occur until so long after the breach that the claim is statute-barred: *Midland Bank Trust Co. v. Hett, Stubbs & Kemp*[10]; *Forster v. Outred & Co.*[11]; *D. W. Moore & Co. Ltd v. Ferrier*[12]; *Iron Trade Mutual v. J. K. Buckenham Ltd*[13]; *Bell v. Peter Browne & Co.*[14]

[6a] *The Times*, October 24, 1996.
[7] (1933) 102 L.J.K.B. 257.
[8] [1973] A.C. 912.
[9] See para. 29–06.
[10] [1979] Ch. 384.
[11] [1982] 1 W.L.R. 86.
[12] [1988] 1 W.L.R. 267.
[13] [1990] 1 All E.R. 808.
[14] [1990] 3 All E.R. 124.

The limitation acts were amended in 1963 and in 1986 to allow plaintiffs to start proceedings within three years of the date of knowledge in cases in which:

(1) plaintiffs claimed damages for personal injuries caused by negligence, nuisance or breach of duty, whether the duty exists by virtue of contract or statute or has an independent existence[15];

(2) plaintiffs claim damages for negligence (not causing personal injuries).[16]

There are no provisions for the basic six-year limitation period in contract to be extended in cases of latent damage. The extended period in cases of "negligence" causing latent damage in section 14A of the Limitation Act 1980 applies only to tort negligence and does not apply to actions founded upon the breach of a contractual duty of care: *Iron Trade Mutual Insurance Co. v. Buckenham*[17]; *Islander Trucking v. Hogg Robinson & Gardner Mountain (Marine) Limited*[18]; *Societe Commerciale de Reassurance v. ERAS (Insurance)*.[19] By analogy, section 14A probably does not apply to actions for breach of statutory duty.

The basic 12-year period for deeds

29–03   The Limitation Act 1980 provides as follows:

8.—(1) An action upon a specialty shall not be brought after the expiration of twelve years from the date on which the cause of action accrued.

(2) Subsection (1) above shall not affect any action for which a shorter period of limitation is prescribed by any other provision of this Act.

Specialties have been traditionally defined as contracts or other obligations created by or contained in a document under seal: *Leivers v. Barber, Walker & Co.*[20]; *Alliance Bank of Simla v. Carey*[21]; *R v. Williams*.[22]

An action brought in respect of repairing obligations contained in a contract or lease under seal or by deed has the full 12-year

---

[15] s.11 Limitation Act 1980.
[16] s.14A Limitation Act 1980.
[17] *Supra.*
[18] [1990] 1 All E.R. 826.
[19] [1992] 2 All E.R. 82.
[20] [1943] 1 K.B. 385.
[21] (1880) 5 C.P.D. 429.
[22] [1942] A.C. 541.

limitation period prescribed by section 8 of the Limitation Act 1980.

The Law of Property (Miscellaneous Provisions) Act 1989 abolished the requirement of seals for deeds executed by individuals but section 1(2) of the Act added the requirement that the document be: "clear on its face that it is intended to be a deed by the person making it or, as the case may be, the parties to it (whether by describing itself as a deed or expressing itself to be executed or signed as a deed or otherwise)".

It is questionable whether, since the Law Reform (Miscellaneous Provisions) Act 1989 a document will be a specialty merely because it is sealed, since sealing may not be sufficient to make the document clear on its face that it is intended to be a deed: *Re Compania de Electricidad de la Provincia de Buenos Aires Ltd.*[23]

Contracts made under Leasehold Reform Act 1967 are specialties: *Collin v. Westminster (Duke of)*.[24]

Acts of Parliament have always been treated as specialties and actions founded upon them accordingly prima facie have a limitation period of 12 years. Actions for sums of money "recoverable by statute", however, have an overriding limitation period of six years by virtue of the express provisions of section 9 of the Limitation Act 1980: *Central Electricity Generating Board v. Halifax Corporation.*[25]

Section 8 is expressly subject to different limitation periods prescribed by other sections of the Limitation Act 1980. A further example of an express specific limitation period overriding the general limitation period of 12 years for specialties arising in the context of actions for rent. Section 19 of the Limitation Act 1980 provides that: "No action shall be brought, or distress made, to recover arrears of rent, or damages in respect of arrears of rent, after the expiration of six years from the date on which the arrears became due".

Accordingly, the limitation period even for rent due under a lease made by deed is, subject to Part II of the Act, six years: *Romain and Wolfson v. Scuba TV Limited.*[26] Query whether the limitation period would be six or 12 years in the case of a licence under seal.

Personal injuries actions

The basic three-year period. The Limitation Act 1980 provides a **29–04** basic three-year limitation period for most but not all actions in which a claim for damages for personal injuries is made:

---

[23] [1980] Ch. 146.
[24] [1985] Q.B. 581.
[25] [1963] A.C. 785.
[26] [1996] 2 All E.R. 377.

11.—**(1) This section applies to any action for damages for negligence, nuisance or breach of duty (whether the duty exists by virtue of a contract or of provision made by or under statute or independently of any contract or any such provision) where the damages claimed by the plaintiff for the negligence, nuisance or breach of duty consist of or include damages in respect of personal injuries to the plaintiff or any other person.**

(2) None of the time limits given in the preceding provisions of this Act shall apply to an action to which this section applies.

(3) An action to which this section applies shall not be brought after the expiration of the period applicable in accordance with subsection (4) or (5) below.

(4) Except where subsection (5) below applies, the period applicable is three years from—(a) the date on which the cause of action accrued; or (b) the date of knowledge (if later) of the person injured.

(5) [only applies where the injured person dies].

Section 11 of the Limitation Act 1980 does not apply when the defendant inflicted the personal injury deliberately as opposed to negligently. In that case the plaintiff has the six-year limitation period under section 2 of the Limitation Act but without the possibility of extensions under sections 14 or 33 of the Act: *Stubbings v. Webb.*[27]

Where section 11 of the Limitation Act 1980 applies the limitation period is three years from:

(1) The date the cause of action accrued even if the plaintiff could not reasonably have known at that time that he or she possessed a cause of action: *Cartledge v. E. Jopling & Sons Ltd*[28] (pneumoconiosis); *Higgins v. Arfon Borough Council*[29] (negligent construction of dwelling house);

(2) If later, three years from the "date of knowledge" as defined by section 14 Limitation Act 1980: *Nash v. Eli Lilly & Co.*[30-33] (knowledge of side effects of drug); *Wilkinson v. Ancliff (BLT) Limited*[34] (knowledge of asthma caused by work environment).

---

[27] *Supra.* See paras 29–07.
[28] *Supra.*
[29] [1975] 1 W.L.R. 524.
[30-33] [1993] 1 W.L.R. 782.
[34] [1986] 1 W.L.R. 1352.

Furthermore, the court has an overriding discretion to extend the basic three-year limitation period under the provisions contained in section 33 of the Limitation Act 1980.[35]

Definition of personal injuries. "Personal injuries" are defined by **29–05** section 38 of the Limitation Act 1980 as "[including] any disease and any impairment of a person's physical or mental condition".[36]

The date of knowledge. The date of knowledge for the purposes of **29–06** sections 11 and 12 of the Limitation Act 1980 is defined by section 14 Limitation Act 1980:

14.—In sections 11 and 12 of this Act references to a person's date of knowledge are references to the date on which he first had knowledge of the following facts—
(a) that the injury in question was significant; and
(b) that the injury was attributable in whole or in part to the act or omission which is alleged to constitute negligence, nuisance or breach of duty; and
(c) the identity of the defendant; and
(d) if it is alleged that the act or omission was that of a person other than the defendant, the identity of that person and the additional facts supporting the bringing of an action against the defendant;
and knowledge that any acts or omissions did or did not, as a matter of law, involve negligence, nuisance or breach of duty is irrelevant.
(2) For the purposes of this section an injury is significant if the person whose date of knowledge is in question would reasonably have considered it sufficiently serious to justify his instituting proceedings for damages against a defendant who did not dispute liability and was able to satisfy a judgment.
(3) For the purposes of this section a person's knowledge includes knowledge which he might reasonably have been expected to acquire –
(a) from facts observable or ascertainable by him; or
(b) from facts ascertainable by him with the help of medical or other appropriate expert advice which it is reasonable for him to seek;
but a person shall not be fixed under this subsection with knowledge of a fact ascertainable only with the help of expert advice so long as he has taken all reasonable steps

[35] See paras. 29–05.
[36] s.3 Law Reform (Personal Injuries) Act 1948 and R.S.C. Ord. 1, r. 4 are in the same terms.

to obtain (and, where appropriate, to act on) that advice.

The overriding discretion to extend time under section 33 of the Limitation Act 1980

29–07   Section 33 of the Limitation Act 1980 provides as follows:

33.—(1) If it appears to the court that it would be equitable to allow an action to proceed having regard to the degree to which—(a) the provisions of section 11 or 12 of this Act prejudice the plaintiff or any person whom he represents; and (b) any decision of the court under this subsection would prejudice the defendant or any person whom he represents;

the court may direct that those provisions shall not apply to the action, or shall not apply to any specified cause of action to which the action relates.

(2) ....

(3) In acting under this section the court shall have regard to all the circumstances of the case and in particular to—

(a) the length of, and the reasons for, the delay on the part of the plaintiff;

(b) the extent to which, having regard to the delay, the evidence adduced or likely to be adduced by the plaintiff or the defendant is or is likely to be less cogent than if the action had been brought within the time allowed by section 11 or (as the case may be) by section 12;

(c) the conduct of the defendant after the cause of action arose, including the extent (if any) to which he responded to requests reasonably made by the plaintiff for information or inspection for the purpose of ascertaining facts which were or might be relevant to the plaintiff's cause of action against the defendant;

(d) the duration of any disability of the plaintiff arising after the date of the accrual of the cause of action;

(e) the extent to which the plaintiff acted promptly and reasonably once he knew whether or not the act or omission of the defendant, to which the injury was attributable, might be capable at that time of giving rise to an action for damages;

(f) the steps, if any, taken by the plaintiff to obtain medical, legal or other expert advice and the nature of any such advice he may have received.

In *Camden L.B.C. v. Hawkins*[37] the District Judge at Central London County Court refused the tenant leave to amend her defence and counterclaim in possession proceedings for rent arrears to claim damages for ill health caused by nuisance: a cockroach and ant infestation. The Application to amend was made in 1994. The infestation had begun in 1987 but was, apparently, continuing. The District Judge dismissed the application on the ground that the tenant had known of the effect on her health in 1987 and her claim was statute-barred after 1990. There is no indication in the report as to how the District Judge could have struck out the amendment in so far as it related to the period of three years immediately preceding the amendment application or why, at least in relation to the period from 1988 to 1991 the tenant did not drop the claim for personal injury and claim only for discomfort and inconvenience. The District Judge went on to refuse to exercise his discretion to extend time under section 33 Limitation Act 1980 on the facts of the case.

Mixed causes of action

Section 11 of the Limitation Act 1980 applies the basic three-year limitation period to all actions which include a relevant claim for personal injuries. This is potentially unfair to plaintiff tenants who wish in the same action to claim damages for personal injury and also for discomfort and inconvenience both arising out of breaches by the landlord of his or her repairing obligations. If the plaintiff were to bring separate proceedings for the two causes of action there would be a waste of costs and it would be difficult to resist an application for consolidation.   **29–08**

There are two possible solutions to the predicament of such a plaintiff:

(1) An application under section 33 of the Limitation Act 1980 for an extension of time up to six years in so far as the action claims damages for a breach of contract not causing personal injury.

(2) A submission that section 11 does not apply to breaches of contract causing personal injury.

Extension of limitation period for the claim for discomfort and inconvenience

Section 33 of the Limitation Act 1980 provides that: **29–09**

33.—(1) If it appears to the court that it would be equitable to allow an action to proceed having regard to the

---

[37] (1994) August 9, (*Legal Action*, December 1994, p. 17).

degree to which—(a) the provisions of section 11 or 12 of this Act prejudice the plaintiff or any person whom he represents; and (b) any decision of the court under this subsection would prejudice the defendant or any person whom he represents;

the court may direct that those provisions shall not apply to the action, *or shall not apply to any specified cause of action* to which the action relates.

The section accordingly makes it possible in an action for damages for disrepair for the court to direct that the basic three-year limitation period under section 11 shall continue to apply in so far as the breaches of contract caused personal injury, but that the basic six-year period shall apply in so far as the breaches caused diminution in value or discomfort and inconvenience and so forth.

In *Walkin v. South Manchester Health Authority*[38] the Court of Appeal dismissed a mother's claim for damages on account of a failed sterilisation resulting in the birth of a child. The Court of Appeal held that a mother who became pregnant after a negligent sterilisation suffered a "personal injury" because the unwanted conception was an "impairment of [her] physical . . . condition". The mother in such an action was entitled to claim for her own physical injury (the pain and suffering of pregnancy and delivery) and also for the economic cost of raising the child. Both claims arose, however, out of the unwanted pregnancy and both claims were therefore for damages for personal injury. Both claims were accordingly subject to the time-limits contained in section 11 of the Limitation Act 1980. Auld L.J., however, remarked as follows:

"Finally, there is Mr Wingate-Saul's suggestion that to regard a claim for damages for unwanted pregnancy as a single action regardless of the different heads of damages claimed could unfairly deprive a plaintiff of damages for other than personal injury in the event of the judge refusing to disapply the personal injuries time limit under s.33 of the 1980 Act. As s.11(1) expressly applies to an action for damages where the damages claimed "consist of or include damages in respect of personal injuries", that possibility must have been contemplated by the draftsman. However, in such a case such as this the damages claimed are in respect of personal injury; *and where they are not, the judge has a duty to exercise his discretion under s.33 (1) and (3) equitably, having regard to all the circumstances of the case. Those circumstances would no doubt include the likely prejudice to a plaintiff in being deprived of*

[38] [1995] 4 All E.R. 132.

damages which, if not in respect of personal injuries, form a significant part of his claim."

It is accordingly submitted that the court generally should permit in the same action a 6 year limitation period for discomfort caused by disrepair to co-exist with a 3 year period for personal injuries.

Rejection of three-year personal injury period in cases of breach of contract

Section 11 of the Limitation Act 1980 was recently considered by the House of Lords in *Stubbings v. Webb*[39] in which it was held that: **29–10**

"I cannot agree that the words "breach of duty" have the effect of including within the scope of the section all actions in which damages for personal injuries are claimed . . . Even without reference to Hansard I should not myself have construed "breach of duty" as including a deliberate assault. *The phrase lying in juxtaposition with "negligence" and "nuisance" carries with it the implication of a breach of duty of care not to cause personal injury, rather than the obligation not to infringe any legal right of another person."*

When the Tucker Committee, in its *Report of the Committee on the Limitation of Actions,*[40] recommended a three-year limitation period for personal injuries claims, it had in mind accident cases: "It is I think obvious when reading the report that the committee was confining its recommendations in respect of personal injury to accident cases." *Stubbings v. Webb.*[41]

The Tucker Committee expressly excluded "actions for trespass to the person, false imprisonment, malicious prosecution, or defamation of character" from its recommendations.[42] The effect on actions for personal injury caused by a straight breach of contract was left unclear.

It is widely assumed, but it is not beyond argument that section 11 Limitation Act 1980 applies a three-year limitation period to actions which include claims for personal injuries resulting from a landlord's breach of his or her contractual repairing obligations. A breach of a contractual stipulation contained within a contract is not obviously the same as a "breach of duty . . . [which] exists by virtue of a contract".[43]

[39] *Supra.*
[40] Cm. 7740.
[41] [1993] 2 W.L.R. 120 (*per* Lord Griffiths).
[42] Para. 23 of the report.
[43] s.11 Limitation Act 1980.

The expression "any action for damages for . . . breach of [a] duty . . . [which] exists by virtue of a contract" is apt to cover actions brought by an employee when his or her employer has breached one of the various duties to take reasonable care for the safety of his or her employees which the common law/statute recognise as existing by virtue of that particular type of contract: *Wilsons & Clyde Coal Co. Ltd v. English*[44]; *Paris v. Stepney B.C.*[45]; *Cavanagh v. Ulster Weaving Co. Ltd.*[46] This duty to take reasonable care exists as both an implied contractual term and as a duty in tort: *Davie v. New Merton Board Mills Limited*[47]; *Lister v. Romford Ice and Cold Storage Co. Ltd*[48]; *Mathews v. Kuwait Bechtel Corporation*[49]; *Chesworth v. Farrar*[50]; *Spring v. Guardian Assurance plc.*[51] There are other types of contract which the common law recognises as giving rise to duties to take care, either as an implied contractual term or as a duty in tort: for example, contracts with professionals such as solicitors (*Bell v. Peter Browne & Co.*[52]; insurance brokers (*Iron Trades Mutual Insurance Co. Ltd v. Buckenham Ltd*[53]); architects (*Kensington and Chelsea and Westminster Area Health Authority v. Wettern Composites Ltd*[54] and surveyors (*Smith v. Eric S. Bush*[55]). Such duties can be said to exist "by virtue of" that contract.

When a landlord fails to repair in accordance with a contractual repairing obligation he or she is clearly in breach of contract: he or she is not so clearly in "breach of [a] duty . . . [which] exists by virtue of a contract", although that is the way the courts will probably look at it.

The words of section 11 of the Limitation Act 1980 are however apt to apply a three-year limitation period to all actions including a claim for damages for personal injury which are brought by the tenant or some other person under section 4 of the Defective Premises Act 1972. The reason is that the combination of section 4 and the express and implied terms of a tenancy does create a duty of care. That duty truly can be said to exist "by virtue of a contract or of provision made by or under a statute".

---

[44] [1938] A.C. 57.
[45] [1951] A.C. 325.
[46] [1960] A.C. 145.
[47] [1959] A.C. 604.
[48] [1957] A.C. 555 at p. 587.
[49] [1959] 2 Q.B. 57.
[50] [1967] 1 Q.B. 407.
[51] [1994] 3 All E.R. 129.
[52] *Supra.*
[53] *Supra.*
[54] [1985] 1 All E.R. 346.
[55] [1990] 1 A.C. 831.

Successive and continuing breaches

A series of breaches of a contract or even of a single covenant in   **29–11**
a contract gives rise to a series of separate causes of action: see, for
example, the case of the tenant who fails to pay rent on more than
one occasion: *Archbold v. Scully.*[56] Some breaches may be within
and some breaches may be without the relevant limitation
period.

Alternatively, there may be one continuing breach of covenant or
contract, of which the failure to repair is the classic example: *Spoor
v. Green.*[57] In this case the plaintiff will succeed to the extent and
only to the extent that the failure occurred within the relevant
limitation period.

Section 1 of the Defective Premises Act 1972

There are special limitation provisions in respect of actions   **29–12**
under section 1 of the Defective Premises Act 1972, *i.e.* actions
against landlords who have built the premises negligently. The
cause of action is deemed to accrue at the time the premises are
completed; but if after that time a person who has done work for or
in connection with the provision of the dwelling carries out further
work to rectify the work he or she has already done, any cause of
action in respect of such further work is deemed to accrue at the
time the further work is finished.[58] Since liability under the
Defective Premises Act 1972 is strict the limitation period will be
the normal six-year limitation period under section 2 of the
Limitation Act 1980 and provisions for extension in the cases of
latent damage caused by negligence contained in section 14A of
the Limitation Act 1980 will not apply. If the action includes a
claim for personal injuries, section 11 of the Limitation Act 1980
should apply.

Pleading the Limitation Acts

In general, the limitation acts operate so as to bar the remedy   **29–13**
and not the right. They do not extinguish rights, but impose
procedural time-limits. If the defendant does not plead the limitation acts, the court will not raise the point (unless the defendant is
under a disability) and the plaintiff's rights remain unaffected.[59]

---

[56] (1861) 9 H.L.C. 360.
[57] (1874) L.R. 9 Ex. 99.
[58] s.1(5) Defective Premises Act 1972.
[59] *Re E.G.* [1914] 1 Ch. 927; R.S.C. Ord. 18, r. 8.

The court might not allow an amendment to plead the limitation acts if it is made very late in the day: *Ketteman v. Hansel Properties Limited*[60]; *Easton v. Ford Motor Co. Ltd.*[61]

Agreement or estoppel and the limitation acts

29–14   The parties can by agreement extend or postpone the limitation period: *Lade v. Trill*[62]; *Pearson v. Dublin Corp*[63]; *Lubovsky v. Snelling.*[64]

It is also possible for the defendant to become estopped from relying upon the limitation acts: *Wright v. John Bagnell & Sons Ltd*[65]; *Rendall v. Hill's Dry Dock and Engineering Co. Ltd*[66]; *Commonwealth v. Verwayen.*[67] The fact that the parties have entered into negotiations to settle their dispute will not be sufficient by itself: *Wright v. John Bagnell & Sons Ltd*[68]; *Lubovsky v. Snelling.*[69] It can be difficult to establish that all the necessary ingredients of a recognised estoppel are present: *Alma Shipping Corpn v. Union of India*[70]; *P. S. Chellaram & Co. Ltd v. China Ocean Shipping Co.*[71]

The parties to a contract can agree that the limitation periods should be abridged. Such clauses are exclusion clauses with the result that they will be strictly construed. They will plainly fall within the provisions of the Unfair Contract Terms Act 1977 and may therefore be struck down by the Courts. The Unfair Contract Terms Act 1977 does not, however, apply to any contract "in so far as it relates to the creation or transfer of an interest in land"[72]: *Electricity Supply Nominees Ltd v. IAF Group Ltd.*[73] Since "the repairing covenant is also an integral part of the contract for the creation of the interest in land" (*Electricity Supply Nominees Ltd v. IAF Group Ltd*) a provision abridging the effect of the limitation acts relating to such a covenant would appear to be excluded from the scope of the Act (in the cases of tenancies and leases although not licences). It is possible that the Unfair Terms in Consumer Contract Regulations 1994,[74] which came into effect on July 1,

[60] [1987] 2 W.L.R. 312.
[61] [1993] 4 All ER 257.
[62] (1842) L.J.Ch. 102.
[63] [1907] A.C. 351.
[64] [1944] K.B. 44.
[65] [1900] 2 Q.B. 240.
[66] [1900] 2 Q.B. 245.
[67] (1990) 64 A.L.J.R. 540.
[68] *Supra.*
[69] *Supra.*
[70] [1971] 2 Lloyd's Rep. 495 at p. 502.
[71] [1991] 1 Lloyd's Rep. 493.
[72] Para. 1 Sched. I Unfair Contract Terms Act 1977.
[73] [1993] 1 W.L.R. 1059.
[74] S.I. 1994 No. 3159.

1995, implementing Council Directive 91/13 of April 5, 1993, may cover contracts which create or transfer interests in land. Mr Jon Holbrook writes that it does[75]; *Chitty on Contracts*[76] doubts that it does, and is probably correct.

Where the terms of an agreement to refer disputed claims to arbitration provide for an abridged limitation period the High Court has power under section 27 of the Arbitration Act 1950 to extend time, unless the provision extinguishes claims not presented with the relevant period: *The Stephanos*.[77]

Set-offs and counterclaims

A counterclaim or set-off is deemed to have been made, for the **29–15** purposes of the limitation acts, on the date the plaintiff issued proceedings. Thus counterclaims for damages for simple breach of contract will cover a period of six years going back from the date the plaintiff issued proceedings rather than from the date of service of the defence and counterclaim. Section 35 of the Limitation Act 1980 provides as follows:

35.—(1) For the purposes of this Act, any new claim made in the course of any action shall be deemed to be a separate action and to have been commenced—

(a) In the case of a new claim made in or by way of third party proceedings, on the date on which those proceedings were commenced; and

(b) in the case of any other new claim, on the date of the original action.

(2) In this section, a new claim means any claim by way of set-off or counterclaim, and any claim involving either—

(a) the addition or substitution of a new cause of action; or

(b) the addition or substitution of a new party and "third party proceedings" means any proceedings brought in the course of any action by any party to the action against a person not previously a party to the action, other than proceedings brought by joining any such person as defendant to any claim already made in the original action by the party bringing the proceedings.

(3) Except as provided by section 33 of this Act or by rules of court, neither the High Court nor any county court shall allow a new claim within subsection (1)(b) above, other than an original set-off or counterclaim, to be made

[75] *Legal Action*, August 1995, at p. 24.
[76] 27th ed., 1994, at para. 14–090.
[77] [1989] 1 Lloyd's Rep. 506.

in the course of any action after the expiry of any time limit under this Act which would affect a new action to enforce that claim.

For the purposes of this subsection, a claim is an original set-off or an original counterclaim if it is a claim made by way of set-off or by way of counterclaim by a party who has not previously made any claim in the action.

Section 35(4) and (5) of the Limitation Act 1980 and rules of court set out the conditions on which new claims by way of counterclaim and set-off will be allowed.

A tenant's claim against his or her landlord for damages on account of the landlord's failure to repair gives rise to the defence of equitable set-off to any claim brought by the landlord for arrears of rent: *British Anzani (Felixstowe) v. International Marine Management (UK)*[78]; *Melville v. Grapelodge Developments*[79]; *Asco Developments v. Gordon*[80]; *Televantos v. McCulloch.*[81]

It is questionable whether section 35 of the Limitation Act 1980 applies to equitable set-offs such as this. The reason lies in section 36 of the Limitation Act 1980, which provides as follows:

36.—(1) The following time limits under this Act, that is to say—
(a) the time limit under section 2 for actions founded on tort;
(b) the time limit under section 5 for actions founded on simple contract; . . .
(d) the time limit under section 8 for actions on a specialty;
(e) the time limit under section 9 for actions to recover a sum recoverable by virtue of any enactment . . .
shall not apply to any claim for specific performance of a contract or for an injunction or for other equitable relief, except in so far as any such time limit may be applied by the court by analogy in like manner as the corresponding time limit under any enactment repealed by the Limitation Act 1980 was applied before July 1, 1940.
(2) Nothing in this Act shall affect any equitable jurisdiction to refuse relief on the ground of acquiescence or otherwise.

---

[78] [1980] Q.B. 137.
[79] (1979) 39 P.&C.R. 179.
[80] (1978) 248 E.G. 683.
[81] [1991] 1 E.G.L.R. 123.

When equitable relief is sought, the normal time limits under the Limitation Act 1980 do not apply, although the court has a discretion to apply them "by analogy": *Brooksbank v. Smith*[82]; *Knox v. Gye*.[83]

It is arguable that equitable set-offs are not caught by limitation periods contained in section 35 Limitation Act 1980. That was the view of Lord Denning M.R. in *Henrisksens Rederi A/S v. THZ Rolimpex*.[84] He said:

"By section 28 [now section 36] a counterclaim, which arises out of a separate transaction, is on the same footing as a set off. If it is not time-barred at the time when the plaintiff issues his writ, the defendant can raise it in opposition to the plaintiff's claim without being affected by any intervening running of time.

All this is when the set off or counterclaim arises out of a separate transaction. When it does not arise out of a separate transaction, but out of the same transaction, then it is not within section 28 at all. It can be raised, as I will soon show, as a matter of defence, either legal or equitable, so as to reduce or extinguish the claim and, being matter of defence, it is not subject to a time bar."

Cairns and Roskell L.JJ. expressed strong disagreement with Lord Denning's views which were, nonetheless, followed (*obiter*) by Hobhouse J. in *Kleinwort Benson Ltd v. Sandwell B.C.*[85]

If the limitation acts do not apply to equitable set-offs, then the limitation acts can not limit a tenant's claim for damages if raised by way of set-off.

Persons under a disability

The Limitation Act 1980 provides as follows: **29–16**

28.—(1) Subject to the following provisions of this section, if on the date when any right of action accrued for which a period of limitation is prescribed by this Act, the person to whom it accrued was under a disability, the action may be brought at any time before the expiration of 6 years from the date when he ceased to be under a disability or died (whichever first occurred) notwithstanding that the period of limitation has expired.

[82] (1836) 2 Y.&C. Ex. 58.
[83] (1872) L.R. 5 H.L. 656.
[84] [1974] Q.B. 233, 1 W.L.R. 185.
[85] (1993) 91 L.G.R. 323.

A person is under a disability for the purposes of the Limitation Act 1980 whilst he is an infant (i.e. under 18 years) or of unsound mind.[86] The Act contains provisos to which regard should be had in unusual cases.

Where a child of the tenant suffers personal injury or property damage and brings an action against the landlord under, for example, section 4 of the Defective Premises Act 1972, the limitation period does not expire until six years after the child attains his or her majority. It seems that where there is a continuing injury, *e.g.* asthma or upper respiratory tract infections caused by the landlord's breach of contract, the child who sues during his or her minority can claim for the entire period, even if it exceeds six years. If the child commences proceedings after he or she attains the age of 18 years, but within six years of that date, the position is not so clear.

---

[86] s.38 of the Limitation Act 1980.

CHAPTER THIRTY

Actions for Loss Suffered by Members of the Tenant's Family

Actions brought by the tenant

The law on privity of contract is summarised by *Chitty on Contracts*[1] **30–01**
as follows:

> "The doctrine of privity means, and means only, that a person
> cannot acquire rights, or be subjected to liabilities, arising
> under a contract to which he is not a party. For example, it
> means that, if A promises B to pay a sum of money to C, then
> C cannot sue A for that sum."

There are a number of exceptions to this basic rule, all of which
are considered in detail in *Chitty on Contracts*. The possibility of an
exception being made in the case of contracts entered into by one
parent for the benefit of his or her family was first raised in *Jackson
v. Horizon Holidays Limited*.[2] Mr Jackson booked a holiday with the
defendant for himself, his wife and their three children. It cost
£1,200, but was a disaster. The hotel accommodation was sub-
standard, the food was horrible and there were few amenities in the
hotel. Lord Denning M.R. said:

> "We have had an interesting discussion as to the legal position
> when one person makes a contract for the benefit of a party. In
> this case it was a husband making a contract for the benefit of
> himself, his wife and his children. Other cases readily come to

---

[1] 27th ed., 1994, at 18–014.
[2] [1975] 1 W.L.R. 1468.

mind. A host makes a contract with a restaurant for a dinner for himself and his friends . . . . It would be a fiction to say that the contract was made by all the family, or all the guests . . . and that he was only an agent for them . . . . It would equally be a mistake to say that that in any of these instances there was a trust . . . .

What is the position when such a contract is broken? At present the law says that the only one who can sue is the one who made the contract. None of the rest of the party can sue, even though the contract was made for their benefit. But when that one does sue, what damages can he recover? Is he limited to his own loss? Or can he recover for the others? . . . . I think he can . . . . The case comes within the principle stated by Lush L.J. in *Lloyd's v. Harper*[3]:

'I consider it to be an established rule of law that where a contract is made with A for the benefit of B, A can sue on the contract for the benefit of B, and can recover all that B could have recovered if the contract had been made with B himself.'

. . . . I think that the figure of £1,100 was about right. It would have been excessive if it had been awarded only for the damage suffered by Mr Jackson himself. But when extended to his wife and children, I do not think it is excessive."

In *Woodar Investment Development Limited v. Wimpey Construction Co. Limited*[4] the House of Lords refuted Lord Denning's reasoning, pointing out that the passage of Lush L.J. in *Lloyd's v. Harper* applied only to cases in which there was a trust (an established exception to the privity rule) and did not establish the broad principle on which Lord Denning M.R. had relied. On the other hand, all members of the House of Lords expressed dissatisfaction with the state of the law on privity. Lord Wilberforce said, additionally:

"I am not prepared to dissent from the actual decision in that case. It may be supported either as a broad decision on the measure of damages (*per* James L.J.) or possibly as an example of a type of contract—examples of which are persons contracting for family holidays, ordering meals in restaurants for a party, hiring a taxi for a group—calling for special treatment. As I suggested in *New Zealand Shipping Co. Limited v. A M Satterthwaite & Co. Limited*[5] there are many situations of daily

---

[3] (1880) 16 Ch.D 290, 321.
[4] [1980] 1 W.L.R. 277.
[5] [1975] A.C. 154, 167.

life which do not fit neatly into conceptual analysis, but which require some flexibility in the law of contract."

"Special treatment" is common in disrepair actions. In *Radford v. de Froberville*[6] damages for failure to perform a contract to rebuild a wall were not reduced because the landlord had entered into the contract partly for the benefit of his tenants. In *Calabar Properties Limited v. Stitcher*[7] the County Court judge awarded general damages of £3,000 "for the disappointment, discomfort, loss of enjoyment and bouts of ill-health which he [the tenant's husband] suffered during the five years that he was occupying what was supposed to be a high-class flat". There was no challenge based upon privity and the court of appeal saw nothing remarkable in the award. In *Credit Suisse v. Beegas Nominees Limited*[8] Lindsay J. made a substantial award of general damages to a limited company which had had to occupy commercial premises which the landlord had failed to repair in these terms:

> "I am unconvinced that one evaluate inconvenience to a tenant in occupation by reference simply to the diminution in prospective letting value to some hypothetical other tenant. General damages are notoriously at large, but doing the best I can to have regard to the inconvenience suffered by staff and customers in these expensive and prestige premises over the period I have described I fix general damages at £40,000."

Damages for discomfort and inconvenience suffered by family members are frequently awarded to plaintiffs in the County Court and it is difficult to imagine this practice ceasing except in response to a clear contrary decision by the Court of Appeal, which it is also difficult to imagine occurring.

Actions brought by the family member

At least when the landlord knows or ought to know that   **30–02** members of the tenant's family are in occupation, the landlord owes such persons the duty of care to prevent personal injury or damage to property contained in section 4 of the Defective Premises Act 1972.[9] If that duty is breached, the family member is entitled to sue the landlord in his or her own right.

Family members may also acquire the right to sue directly in nuisance[10] or under the Occupier's Liability Act 1957.[11]

---

[6] [1977] 1 W.L.R. 1262.
[7] [1984] 1 W.L.R. 287.
[8] [1994] 1 E.G.L.R. 76.
[9] See paras. 5–05 and 11–13 to 11–19.
[10] See Chapter 12.
[11] See Chapter 14.

Such actions are commonly for personal injuries. The combination of such a claim which has the tenant's non-personal injuries claim raises potential difficulties under the limitation acts.[12]

In *C (A Minor) v. Hackney L.B.C.*[13] the Court of Appeal held that:

(1) A consent order whereby the mother received £15,000 general damages for disrepair did not give rise to a *res judicata* which prevented an action on behalf of her infant daughter for personal injury under section 4 of the Defective Premises Act 1972 arising out of the same disrepair.

(2) A solicitor who brings separate actions on behalf of the tenant and other family members without good reason may be made subject to a wasted costs order.

(3) Where it is intended that the settlement of a tenant's claim should also compromise the claims of other family members under a disability, such persons should be made parties if they are not already parties and the approval of the court to the settlement obtained under C.C.R. Ord. 10, rr. 10 and 11. Otherwise not only is the person under disability not protected, the defendant cannot rely on the judgement or settlement as defence to future claims.

---

[12] See para. 29–06.
[13] [1996] 1 All E.R. 973.

CHAPTER THIRTY ONE

The New Small Claims Limit

Introduction

The importance of the new small claims limit hardly needs to be **31–01** stated. Where the new limit applies, tenants who wish or need to take proceedings for compensation or an order of specific perform-ance are unlikely to obtain legal aid to bring the action or be able to obtain professional assistance with the claim.

The effect is likely to be severe in the case of periodic tenants of dwelling houses, in both private and public sector. Since it is in practice impossible for the vast majority of such tenants to bring proceedings in person, the new arbitration limit and the absence of legal aid for claims which now fall victim to it, means that thousands will either never receive compensation or get repairs carried out, or will only be able to do so if they remain tenants enduring the conditions for a considerable period of time. The new arbitration limit inflicts financial loss, personal misery and illness upon the least well-off in our society and their children. It is deeply regretted by all those who have seen how damp and mould can ruin beyond repair belongings which the poorer tenants simply cannot replace, and otherwise inflict privation, discomfort and ill health on such tenants and their children.

The text of the new rule

C.C.R. Ord. 19, r. 3 now reads as follows (the version below **31–02** indicates the changes which have taken place):

3.—(1) Any proceedings *except those mentioned in para-graph 1(A),* **in which the sum claimed or amount involved**

does not exceed £1,000 £3,000 (leaving out of account the sum claimed or amount involved in any counterclaim) shall stand referred for arbitration by the district judge upon the receipt by the court of a defence to the claim

(1A) *Paragraph (1) shall not apply to proceedings which include—*

(a) *a claim for possession of land;*

(b) *a claim for damages for personal injuries which exceeds £1,000.*

(2) Where any proceedings are referred for arbitration by the district judge under paragraph (1), he may, after considering the defence and whether on the application of any party or of his own motion, order trial in court if he is satisfied—

(a) that a difficult question of law or a question of fact of ~~exceptional~~ complexity is involved; or

(b) that fraud is alleged against a party; or

(c) that the parties are agreed that the dispute should be tried in court; or

(d) that it would be unreasonable for the claim to proceed to arbitration having regard to its subject matter, the size of any counterclaim, the circumstances of the parties or the interests of any other person likely to be affected by the award.

....

(4) For the purposes of paragraph (1), "a defence to the claim" includes a document admitting liability for the claim but disputing or not admitting the amount claimed.

Exceptions to the general rule

31–03   Actions in which the "sum claimed" or "amount involved" does not exceed £3,000 will, if defended, as a general rule stand referred to arbitration. There are two exceptions: (1) when the proceedings include a claim for the possession of land; (2) when the proceedings include a claim for damages for personal injuries exceeding £1,000.

Proceedings including a claim for the possession of land. When and whilst the landlord sues for possession no counterclaim, however small, will be referred to arbitration.

The tenant who takes the risk of withholding rent because his or her landlord has failed to repair the premises and who relies upon the right of set-off stands, accordingly, to benefit in the sense that neither claim nor counterclaim will be referred to arbitration. The normal costs rule will apply and legal aid will be available in principle.

Secure tenants in receipt of housing benefit are simply not able to withhold rent.[1] Withholding rent is in any event always risky, even if the tenant acts on the basis of expert advice.

Proceedings including a claim for personal injuries exceeding £1,000. C.C.R. Ord. 19, r. 3 provides that the automatic reference to arbitration shall not apply to proceedings which include "a claim for damages for personal injuries which exceeds £1,000". Where tenants or members of the tenant's family have suffered injury as a result of the landlord's breaches of his or her obligations, the old limit is retained. The requirement is that the personal injuries element of the claim (rather than the global value of the claim including the personal injuries element) exceeds £1,000.

Providing one or more of the plaintiffs[2] have suffered personal injuries giving rise to a claim individually or collectively exceeding £1,000 there will not be a reference to arbitration.

It is not difficult to claim this level of compensation where there has been personal injury for several years. In *McCaffery v. Lambeth L.B.C.*[3] young children were awarded between £400 and £600 per annum because of illness from chest problems to aggravated bronchitis/asthma over a two to six year period. In *Bygraves v. Southwark L.B.C.*[4] a child whose asthma was severely aggravated (there were hospital admissions on average once a year over four years) was awarded damages for pain and suffering of around £1142.86 [£1,428] per annum.

"Personal injuries" are defined by section 38 of the Limitation Act 1980 as "[including] any disease and any impairment of a person's physical or mental condition". Section 3 of the Law Reform (Personal Injuries) Act 1948 and R.S.C. Ord. 1, r. 4 are in the same terms. In *Page v. Smith*[5] Lord Lloyd said "If a working definition of 'personal injury' is needed, it can be found in section 38(1) of the Limitation Act 1980".

How to calculate the sum claimed or the amount involved

The sum claimed. C.C.R. Ord. 19, r. 3 directs attention to "the **31–04** sum claimed" in "any proceedings".

A plaintiff may in one action claim against a defendant in respect of more than one cause of action, providing the parties sue and are

---

[1] Reg. 95 of the Housing Benefit (General) Regulations 1987 (No. 1971).
[2] See para. 31–04.
[3] (1994) *Kemp* F2–045/3.
[4] (1990) *Kemp* F2–035/2.
[5] [1992] 2 All E.R. 760.

sued in the same capacity.[6] "The sum claimed" in proceedings will be the combined value of all sums claimed in respect of all causes of action.

"Two or more persons may be joined together in one action as Plaintiffs" providing all claims (whether joint, several or alternative) "arise out of the same transaction or series of transactions" and raise "some common question of law or fact".[7] All County Court proceedings are brought by action.[8] "The sum claimed" in the proceedings is the combined value of all sums claimed by all plaintiffs joined in the action.

The court has the power to sever causes of action and plaintiffs to prevent the trial being delayed or embarrassed or for reasons of convenience[9] (although mis-joinder will never result in the action itself being "defeated"[10]).

The courts will undoubtedly order separate trials if it appears that plaintiffs have been joined into one action for the sake of increasing the sum claimed for the purposes of C.C.R. Ord. 19, r. 3, and might even penalise the solicitors in costs. There are cases, however, in which there is a legitimate reason for joinder. Where the facts of individual cases are substantially linked, *e.g.* where all the plaintiffs are members of the same family who have been living together, where there is a large estate on which all tenants have been subject to noise and dust caused by building works, a block of flats or street in which all tenants have experienced similar drainage, rising/penetrating damp problems, joinder can be appropriate, particularly if individual cases raise only slightly different issues as to quantum.

Including a claim for the cost of repairs. The plaintiff is entitled to claim the cost of the works of repair as damages.[11]

Claiming the cost of the works (plus VAT and the costs of professional supervision) instead of or in addition to claiming specific performance, will in many cases mean, in principle, that the total sum claimed/involved exceeds £3,000.

It means that proceedings have to be issued before the landlord repairs. It also means that experts have to be able to estimate the likely cost of the works plus supervision (and VAT).

Disrepair claims where the sum claimed or amount involved does not exceed £3,000 stand to be referred to arbitration even though there is a claim for specific performance. The logic is that

[6] C.C.R. Ord. 5, r. 1.
[7] C.C.R. Ord. 5, r. 2.
[8] C.C.R. Ord. 3, r. 1.
[9] C.C.R. Ord. 5, r. 3.
[10] C.C.R. Ord. 5, r. 4.
[11] See paras. 22–02 to 22–04.

small money claims and small claims for specific performance are equally suited to arbitration. The logic of including the likely cost of the works in the action is that the action is shown to be for relatively substantial compensation and for relatively substantial works.

The amount involved. C.C.R. Ord. 19, r. 3 refers to "the sum claimed or the amount involved". Even where the plaintiff does not claim the estimated cost of the works as damages, that cost would appear to be part of the "amount involved" in the litigation. If the tenant succeeds, the landlord will have to lay out that amount of money in order to comply with an order of specific performance, or with a subsequent order under R.S.C. Ord. 45, r. 8.[12]

In *Joyce v. Liverpool City Council, Wynne v. Liverpool City Council*[13] the value of the action for the purposes of the then small claims limit of £1,000 was treated by the district judge and the circuit judge in the County Court and by the Court of Appeal as including the cost of the repairs (which had been pleaded and particularised) as well as the likely amount of compensation. The point, however, does not appear to have been put in issue by the local authority.

Interest

Statutory (as opposed to contractual) interest is not to be taken into account in assessing the value of the claim.[14]   **31–05**

Rescission of the reference to arbitration

Proceedings are referred to arbitration by the district judge upon receipt of a defence. But, after consideration of the defence, on application or on his or her own motion, the district judge may rescind the reference. The plaintiff may wish to consider including objections to a reference to arbitration in the particulars of claim, where the sum claimed is clearly under the new limit. This is an area where a broad discretion is vested in the district judge: Sir Thomas Bingham M.R. said in *Joyce v. Liverpool City Council, Wynne v. Liverpool City Council*[15]:   **31–06**

"While in the ordinary way low value claims will be determined under the small claims arbitration procedure the final decision must rest with the district judge who is charged with the task of doing substantial justice in the particular case. It is

---

[12] See para. 22–05.
[13] [1995] 3 All E.R. 110.
[14] s.69(8) County Courts Act 1984.
[15] *Supra.*

for him to decide, making a judgment in accordance with the rules, whether—

> it would be unreasonable for the claim to proceed to arbitration having regard to its subject matter . . . the circumstances of the parties or the interests of any other person likely to be affected by the award.[16]

He, as the final decision-maker, is likely to be the best judge whether that test is met in any given case or whether it is not. Great respect should be paid to his decision, not only because of his experience of dealing with individual cases but also because of the knowledge he will have of the local situation.

It is of course true that an accident at work is, in fact and in law, very different from a landlord's breach of a repairing covenant. But that is in itself of little or no significance. In either field, difficult questions of fact and law may arise in borderline cases. But in either, the solution is likely to be fairly obvious in the ordinary run of cases. It may be that expert evidence will be more important in s 11 claims than in many claims against employers, but armed with an expert's report (which will have been obtained, usually with legal assistance, before proceedings are issued) the burden on the tenant of preparing and presenting his case is proportionately reduced. It must also be borne in mind that the common defects likely to fall within the financial scope of the small claims arbitration procedure—immovable or ill-fitting windows, minor leaks in the roof, over-flowing drains, defective boilers—are not things which the average tenant (or the tenant's spouse) will find it hard to understand or describe."

Difficult questions of law/complex questions of fact

31–07   Sir Thomas Bingham M.R.'s list of "straightforward" defects contains no reference to damp beyond "minor leaks to the roof". In many cases there is a dispute as to whether damp is or was caused by a failure to repair or by the inherently defective construction of the premises when that is not also a breach of covenant. Such a dispute always raises a complex issue of fact.

The Court of Appeal in *Afzal v. Ford Motor Co. Ltd.*[17] had before it cases in which expert evidence was agreed (and which, in some cases, liability was admitted). In *Joyce v. Liverpool City Council, Wynne v. Liverpool City Council*[18] Sir Thomas Bingham M.R. had cases in contemplation where there was no dispute, or only a

---

[16] C.C.R. Ord. 19, r. 3(2)(d).
[17] [1994] 4 All E.R. 720.
[18] *Supra.*

dispute for which the plaintiff required factual and not expert evidence in order to establish liability. Where there is a need for true expert, *i.e.* opinion evidence (as to what is/is not covered by a particular repairing obligation, as to causation of defects and so forth) one has almost by definition a complex question of fact.

Many tenancy agreements contain specific, possibly unique express terms as to repair and, in some cases, improvement. Interpretation or such terms in the factual context often raise a difficult question of law. Test cases will almost certainly not be referred to arbitration: *Afzal v. Ford Motor Co. Ltd.*[19]

Whether any particular case does raise a complex factual issue or a difficult question of law will depend to a considerable extent on what parts of the plaintiff's case the defendant admits and why he or she disputes allegations which are not admitted. Where a reference to arbitration is possible, the tenant's advisor should, therefore, at an early stage ascertain from the landlord what aspects of liability or the expert evidence are in dispute and why.

It is futile to attempt to define "difficult" and "complex". The new C.C.R. Ord. 19, r. 3 removes the requirement that the question of fact be of "exceptional" complexity. The standard of complexity has, accordingly, clearly been reduced; but to what degree, it is more difficult to say. The test appears to be objective. The words "difficult" and "complex" do not appear to be intended to include all issues of law or fact which are not capable of being described as "simple" or "straightforward". On the other hand, it would probably be wrong to compare the relevant legal or factual issues with issues arising in other disrepair cases, as opposed to other cases commonly referred to arbitration. In *R. v. Legal Aid Board, ex p. R. M. Broudie,*[20] for example, the court considered the meaning "exceptional circumstances of the case" in paragraph 3(b) of Schedule I of the Legal Aid in Criminal and Care Proceedings (Costs) Regulations 1989[21] and held that in determining whether circumstances are "exceptional" comparison should be made with the generality of criminal cases and should not be restricted to comparisons with other similar cases.

C.C.R. Ord. 19, r. 3(2)(d)

There is nothing intrinsically unsuitable for arbitration about **31–08** disrepair claims: *Joyce v. Liverpool City Council, Wynne v. Liverpool City Council.*[22] It is not permissible to reintroduce under this head

---

[19] *Supra.* at p. 734C.
[20] *The Times*, April 11, 1994.
[21] S.I. 1989 No. 343.
[22] *Supra.*

legal or factual issues which are not "difficult" and "complex": *Afzal v. Ford Motor Co. Ltd.*[23-24] "Subject matter" refers to:

"some quality of the subject matter of the claim of sufficient importance to the parties or one of them to justify trial in court: for instance, a claim for damages for trespass which could have far-reaching consequences for the rights of the parties or a claim involving ownership of a family heir-loom . . . "

The fact that a tenant will be legally unrepresented whilst the landlord will be represented is not of itself a ground for rescinding a reference to arbitration as C.C.R. Ord. 19, r. 7(4) expressly provides for such an inequality of arms: *Afzal v. Ford Motor Co. Ltd.*

On the other hand, due weight has to be given to "the circumstances of the parties": "The rule suggests that the circumstances of the parties and whether they are represented are separate considerations for the arbitrator. The circumstances of the parties may, for example, include physical disability, poor sight, pronounced stammer or inability to read." *Afzal v. Ford Motor Co. Ltd.*[25]

Legal aid

31–09 The test in section 15(2) of the Legal Aid Act 1988 is that the applicant "has reasonable grounds for taking, defending or being a party to proceedings". A certificate may however be refused if "in the particular circumstances of the case it appears to the Board – (a) unreasonable . . . ".[26]

Applicants in housing disrepair cases tend to have strong legal merits. Section 15(3), however, permits the Legal Aid Board to refuse a certificate if, inter alia, the proceedings are not likely to be cost effective.

When writing an opinion on merits it is the barrister's duty under paragraph 3.1(ix) of The General Council of the Bar's Legal Aid Guidelines to confirm that the proceedings are likely to be cost effective, having regard in particular to the statutory charge. The barrister has to consider at that stage whether there will be a reference to arbitration and its effect on cost effectiveness.

Actions worth £2/3,000 *may* still be cost effective even via arbitration. *Notes for Guidance* 6–11 requires only that there is likely to be a benefit net of costs of £1,000 plus (less, if the action is of overriding importance e.g. because of the need for repairs).

[23-24] *Supra.* at p. 734.
[25] *Supra.* at p. 735a.
[26] s.15(3). See also the *Notes for Guidance*, paras. 6–06—6–08, 6–11.

The Legal Aid Board's position on the expanded arbitration limit, subject to challenge in the courts, is set out in *Legal Aid Focus*[27] and the *Focus Supplement*. The text is as follows:

"*Legal Aid Focus (15th Issue, April 1996)*

On 8th January 1996 the small claims limit increased to £3,000.00. This affected all cases where proceedings were issued on or after that date, except defended possession cases and personal injury claims over £1,000.00.

Cases that fall within this expanded jurisdiction will automatically be referred to arbitration on the filing of a defence. As arbitration cases do not, by their nature, generally require representation of the parties it would not be justified for legal aid to be granted for them.

In order to assist solicitors in handling such cases the Board's position can be summarised as follows:

WHEN SHOULD GREEN FORM ADVICE BE GIVEN?

Advice and assistance is available to litigants in person, subject to financial eligibility. Solicitors will be able to advise on the merits of the proceedings and assist the litigant in any necessary steps to be taken. Advice may include the likely success of an application to rescind the reference to arbitration. The advice given should enable the litigant to proceed in person and make representations in support of an application to rescind.

Green form extension applications will be considered on the basis of reasonableness having regard to all the issues, including what is at stake, the costs involved, the prospects of successful recovery and the operation of the solicitor's charge.

The solicitors may also, where appropriate, prepare written representations for the application to rescind. It is expected that the majority of such applications will be dealt with on the papers. If, after written representations have been submitted by either party, the district judge requests an oral hearing a limited legal aid certificate may be appropriate. For legal aid to be granted there must be a tangible benefit to the litigant and the costs/benefit position must be considered carefully having particular regard to the operation of the statutory charge.

If a solicitor is advising a potential litigant but the value of the claim is uncertain the investigative work in order to establish quantum should be done under the green form scheme.

---

[27] April 1996, 15th issue.

Whilst the nature of the small claims procedure does not generally justify the grant of full legal aid, in some cases the litigant in person may require additional legal assistance. Examples of this are where the litigation has some form of disability which leads to a lack of understanding or comprehension of the proceedings, such as mental handicap, illiteracy or poor grasp of English. It may be appropriate in those circumstances for a McKenzie friend to be used under the green form to assist the litigant. To justify this there must be a need for legal help rather than help or support which could be provided by a social worker or relative.

The solicitors' charge under the green form scheme falls to be protected and recovered by solicitors. Advice in the proceedings can be piecemeal. Solicitors should ensure that the client is fully aware of the effect of the charge in the event of recovery of damages and/or property and must take all necessary and reasonable steps to protect their charge. This is likely to include notifying the other side and obtaining an unequivocal undertaking from the client that any recovery/preservation must pass via the solicitor and to repay the charge amount. Should the client decline to provide such an undertaking it would be justified for the solicitor to refuse to provide advice and assistance.

WHEN WILL FULL LEGAL AID BE AVAILABLE?

An application for legal aid for a case falling within the expanded small claims jurisdiction is likely to fail the merits test under section 15(3)(a) of the Legal Aid Act 1988.

It is only likely to be justified to grant legal aid where there are exceptional circumstances warranting representation by a solicitors and where such representation will produce sufficient tangible benefit to the client, having regard to the costs likely to be incurred and the operation of the statutory charge.

Cases in which the reference to arbitration is rescinded may be the subject of a legal aid application in the normal way. It is unlikely that legal aid will be granted for representation on an application to rescind, unless the court requests an oral hearing and the case is otherwise meritorious.

If a case remains within the small claims procedure the limited costs allowable in arbitration will mean that any financial advantage by representation would be reduced or negated by the workings of the statutory charge. Examples of cases where the grant of legal aid may be justified will be those that involve violence or harassment, e.g. an assault or trespass/

illegal eviction injunction. In such cases the costs/benefit equation will be considered carefully.

Whilst the costs/benefit test is not the sole or decisive factor in the grant of legal aid exceptional cases should involve a sufficient tangible benefit to the client. It is recognised that cases with a value at the upper end of the expanded jurisdiction might satisfy the costs/benefit test. Factors to consider in the evaluation of costs/benefit will be what is at stake (financially or otherwise), the likely costs, the strength of the case and the prospects of successful recovery."

"Focus Supplement (15th Issue, April 1996)

1.4.1 In most cases of disrepair the initial two hour limit would normally be sufficient for the solicitor to take full instructions, identify the issues and advise the client as to the appropriate remedies. Full instructions would include details of the property, the tenancy, the disrepair, losses caused by the disrepair and any health problems suffered by the family. Advice would be given on possible proceedings, and/or negotiations with the Environmental Health Department, and/or with the landlord to ensure that the repairs are carried out.

1.4.2 If a civil legal aid certificate is unlikely to be granted, because for example, the claim is to be conducted under the small claims procedure, an extension of about 10 units may be necessary to cover a full letter before action and notice of disrepair to the landlord.

1.4.3 Once it becomes clear that a remedy based on disrepair will be sought in the county court, an application for civil legal aid should be submitted normally within the initial limit. However in some circumstances, an extension of about 5 units may be justified if a notice of disrepair and a full letter before action were dealt with under the green form. Because the solicitors is able to provide details of the disrepair, it would not normally be necessary to obtain an expert's report from an environmental health officer or from a surveyor to support the application.

1.4.5 When a solicitors is giving advice and assistance in relation to an Environmental Health Act case, an extension to cover an expert's report may be appropriate. Fees for a report may range from between £150.00 and £300.00. The amount that can be justified will depend upon the particular expert's services, travelling costs and the scarcity of experts. In the magistrates' court, the client will be acting in person, and the solicitor may also have to obtain a medical report, advise on the drafting of the information to the magistrates, obtain a schedule of works and correspond with the landlord. The client will have to be advised as to court procedure and the remedies available. Further extensions of between 2 to 4 hours (20 – 40 units) plus disbursement may be justified to enable the solicitor to undertake all these steps."

The costs position in arbitration proceedings

31–10   If there has been an automatic reference to arbitration (as opposed to a reference under C.C.R. Ord. 19, r. 9) party and party costs are drastically restricted. C.C.R. Ord. 19, r. 4 provides that:

> **(2) No costs shall be allowed as between party and party in respect of any proceedings referred to arbitration under rule 3 except—**
>> **(a) the costs which were stated on the summons or which would have been stated on the summons if the claim had been for a liquidated sum;**
>> **(aa) in proceedings which include a claim for an injunction or for an order for specific performance or similar relief, a sum not exceeding £260 in respect of the cost of legal advice obtained for the purpose of bringing or defending that claim;**
>> **(b) the costs of enforcing the award; and**
>> **(c) such further costs as the district judge may direct where there has been unreasonable conduct on the part of the opposite party in relation to the proceedings or the claim therein.**
> **(3) Nothing in paragraph (2) shall be taken as precluding an award of the following allowances—**
>> **(a) any expenses which have been reasonably incurred by a party or a witness in travelling to and from the hearing or staying away from home;**
>> **(b) a sum not exceeding £50 in respect of a party's witness or a witness's loss of earnings when attending a hearing;**
>> **(c) a sum not exceeding £200 in respect of the fees of an expert.**
> **(4) Where trial in court is ordered, paragraph (2) shall not apply to costs incurred after the date of the order.**

Where trial is ordered

31–11   Where trial is ordered, the effect of C.C.R. Ord. 19, r. 4(4) is that the plaintiff recovers small claims costs up to that date, but normal party and party costs thereafter. Given that in almost all conceivable circumstances trial in court will be ordered on the basis that the claim is and always has been suitable for trial in court, this rule appears to be illogical. Its parsimony is explicable only by reference to the political object of the new small claims procedure.

Inflated claims

If a plaintiff claims in excess of the small claims limit but recovers **31–12** less, his or her costs are likely to be restricted to costs allowed by C.C.R. Ord. 19, r. 3 if the plaintiff knew or should have known that he or she could not reasonably expect to receive more than £3,000. This is so, even though the defendant does not apply to have the case referred to arbitration: *Motley v. Courtaulds plc.*[28] If the plaintiff had reasonable grounds for supposing that an award might exceed £3,000 then the plaintiff should recover costs on the appropriate scale (lower scale or scale 1): *Cunningham v. B. L. Components.*[29] Presumably no costs sanction will be applied if the plaintiff does not overstate the value of his or her claim but issues it on the basis of a reasonably held belief that it ought not to be referred to arbitration because C.C.R. Ord. 19, r. 3(2) applied.

Unreasonable conduct

It may be unreasonable conduct to file a defence which disputes **31–13** liability when in reality only quantum is in dispute: *Newland v. Boardwell.*[30]

In *Afzal v. Ford Motor Co. Ltd*[31] it was said that: "The parties should bear in mind that the overstatement of the amount of damages claimed or the raising of the speculative and unsupportable defence may be regarded as unreasonable conduct . . . "

In *Clarke v. McBrien Civil Engineering*[32] the plaintiff recovered £624.95. The claim had not been referred to arbitration because the plaintiff had claimed over £1,000. The court held that the plaintiff had abused the process of the court by putting forward a claim that was obviously inflated. The plaintiff recovered fixed costs only. Further, the plaintiff had failed to recover more than a sum offered by the defendant in a *Calderbank* letter. The defendant had been entitled to send a *Calderbank* letter rather than make a payment into court (acceptance of which means the plaintiff is entitled to costs). Because the plaintiff failed to beat the *Calderbank* letter he was ordered to pay the defendant's costs from the date of the letter.

---

[28] [1990] 12 L.S.Gaz.R. 39, C.A.
[29] [1987] C.L.Y. 2965.
[30] [1983] 3 All E.R. 179.
[31] *Supra.*
[32] Reading County Court, [1992] C.L.Y. 3419, November 1992, para. 376.

APPENDIX ONE

TABLES OF DAMAGES AWARDS[1]

Awards for Inconvenience and Discomfort

Awards exceeding £2,000 per annum

Court of Appeal

In *Elmcroft Developments Limited v. Tankersley-Sawyer*[1a] **A1–01**
judgment was given in the County Court in June 1983. The Court
of Appeal refused to interfere with an award of £2,600 [£4,758] for
two years of discomfort and inconvenience: [£45.75 per week] to a
single, female plaintiff. There was rising damp throughout a
basement flat up to 1 to 1 1/2 metres high. The flat was in an
expensive and fashionable part of London. If felt and smelt damp.
The bedroom was so damp the electric blanket needed to be on
constantly to keep the bedclothes dry. Entertaining guests was
impossible. The plaintiff probably suffered from throat and chest
infections as a result of the damp. Plaster and decorations were
ruined throughout. The landlord was responsible for the rising
damp to the main walls. The tenant was responsible for the rising
damp to the interior non load-bearing walls and to the floors and
the damages awarded took no account of such damp. The county
court judge held that there had been a two-year period of liability,
but that conditions had worsened significantly in the six months
before trial.

In *Personal Representatives of Chiodi v. de Marney*[2] the
County Court judge in July 1987 awarded general damages for
inconvenience and discomfort at the rate of £1,560 [£2,371] per
annum to a single woman in her early thirties. Between late 1980
and late 1983 the flat, which was not noted to be in a particularly
expensive area, suffered from water penetration, the hot water
supply ceased, there were frequent electrical problems, some

---

[1] (Figures in square brackets represent the value of the award as at March
1996.)
[1a] (1984) 15 H.L.R. 63.
[2] (1988) 21 H.L.R. 6.

windows were very rotten and one was broken. The judge made a
further award of £1,500 [£2,280] for aggravation of the plaintiff's
arthritis and a number of colds and influenza symptoms suffered
by her. The Court of Appeal was critical of the county court
judgment which "does approach the tolerable limits of brevity". It
was, for example:

" . . . impossible to tell over what periods of time any particular head of complaint continued . . . The Court is therefore
placed in the position of being invited to say that an award
based on £30 per week is too high for a woman in a poor state
of health, who spent much time in her home because the
evidence shows that she was unemployed; who could not
escape from the consequences of damp and cold by using
some other part of the premises, because all parts of the flat
were affected and who was forced to live, for this time, in
circumstances which the judge described as 'quite intoler-
able' . . . the award was, in my judgment, high—that is to say,
at the very top of what at this time could in my view be
regarded as a proper award on these facts. But for the reasons
I have given, by itself that is not enough for this Court to
interfere with it."

The award in *Personal Representatives of Chiodi v. de Marney*[3] was
described as at the very top of what an award could be on those
(somewhat obscure) facts. The case is not, however, to be regarded
as setting some upper limit on damages awards. The suggestion
that it did was made in *Brent L.B.C. v. Murphy*[4] but summarily
dismissed: "The facts in that case may have been different from the
facts in the present case".

In **Brent L.B.C. v. Carmel**[5] the full Court of Appeal refused to
grant leave to appeal an award made by the County Court judge in
March 1994 at rates which for the last years of disrepair were
£2,808.84 per annum [£3,005.46]. The tenancy of the local
authority flat began in 1981. There was water penetration throughout right from the start and the central heating system was "wholly
inadequate". In the winter one and sometimes two out of the three
bedrooms were uninhabitable. The plaintiff's teenage boy and girl
had to share her bedroom, while their clothes were stored in the
living room. The County Court judge and four of the five members
of the Court of Appeal who had dealings with the case found that
the local authority's behaviour had been "outrageous" and that in

---

[3] *Ibid.*
[4] (1995) 28 H.L.R. 203, C.A.
[5] (1995) 28 H.L.R. 203, C.A.

terms of property management (rather than disrepair) "This was as bad a case as can be imagined".

In *Ezekiel v. McDade*[6] the court of appeal substituted £4,000 [£4,400] for an award of £6,000, made by the official referee on December 13, 1993. The surveyor who carried out the plaintiff's survey before purchasing negligently failed to detect that the house was defectively built and unmarketable. The plaintiff lost his job and tried to sell the house but was unable (the mortgagor eventually re-possessed). General damages were for the physical discomfort of having to occupy temporary accommodation after re-possession. The plaintiff, his wife and their three children were in a one bedroom bed and breakfast hotel for 10 weeks, and in a two bedroom house for about 10 months which had a gas fire in the living room, no other heating and was cramped.

High Court

In *Sampson v. Wilson*[7] Roger Cooke, sitting as a deputy High Court judge, had to deal with a case in which the premises were in substantial disrepair. The landlord was an absentee and his agents carried out works of repair in such a manner as to deliberately make matters worse and drive out the tenants. Because works were carried out without permission or exceeding any permission there was a trespass (in addition to a breach of contract) thereby permitting an award of exemplary damages to be made. H.H.J. Cooke held as follows (leaving it to the reader to up-date): **A1–02**

"(1) For the relevant period each plaintiff should be taken as having suffered damage equivalent to the whole of his rent; that is, having an uninhabitable home and losing the whole value of it.

(2) But I have also to consider exemplary damages.

As to (1) the number of weeks for Mr Sampson—April 17 to November 26—is 32 weeks; for Mr Kohlbacher they were from April 17 to January 4, which is 37 weeks. Mr Sampson's rent was £25 per week, Mr Kohlbacher's £40. Mr Sampson comes out at £800 and Mr Kohlbacher at £1,480 . . . it is a proper case for exemplary damages . . . I am, of course, limiting myself to the period before the tenants go . . . I award against Mitchell at this point £2,000 in respect of each tenant."

---

[6] [1995] 47 E.G. 150.
[7] (1994) 26 H.L.R. 486.

In *Credit Suisse v. Beegas Nominees Limited*[8] there was water penetration as a result of defective cladding from June 1985, when the plaintiff purchased the residue of the term until trial, in September 1993. The tenant in fact moved out of the premises in November 1988. The premises in question was first class commercial accommodation in SW1. There were large number of leaks, every time it rained, sufficiently serious to cause damage to surrounding decorations and fittings. Prior to moving out in November 1988, staff had to lay towels around affected windows and use baskets and bins to catch drips. From time to time staff had to stop work to mop-up. Water sometimes leaked on to chairs and desks. The premises smelt damp. Lindsay J. held that the landlord was in breach from early 1987 and, bearing in mind that the tenant moved out in late November 1988, made an award of general damages "in respect of nearly two years' inconvenience". He said "I am unconvinced that one evaluate inconvenience to a tenant in occupation by reference simply to the diminution in prospective letting value to some hypothetical other tenant. General damages are notoriously at large, but doing the best I can to have regard to the inconvenience suffered by staff and customers in these expensive and prestige premises over the period I have described I fix general damages at £40,000 [£42,000/£22,000 pa]". It was not significant that the physical discomfort and inconvenience was in fact suffered by employees and customers of the plaintiff company.

County Court

A1–03   In *Walker v. Lambeth L.B.C.*[9] the County Court judge awarded the single, female tenant, who had a young child and for half the period of 18 months in question was pregnant, the sum of £3,750 [£4,200] for 18 months in which one of two lifts was out of operation and the other was subject to frequent breakdowns. The tenant was on the 15th floor of a 21 storey block, was on one occasion trapped in the lift and frequently had to use the stairs.

In *Adams v. Melhuish and Kensey*[10] the county court judge awarded general damages to an apparently single tenant at the rate of £2,080 [£2,225.60] per annum where there had been serious water penetration affecting every room of an old house causing the plaster to become saturated and mouldy throughout.

In *Clarke v. Brent L.B.C.*[10a] the tenant and her 3 young children occupied a flat affected by severe condensation. The

---

[8] [1994] 1 E.G.L.R. 76.
[9] *Legal Action*, September 1992, p. 21.
[10] *Legal Action*, August 1994, p. 17.
[10a] *Legal Action*, August 1994, p. 17.

heating was defective and there was some penetrating damp. The county court judge awarded £18,630 for a nine year period.

In *Foster v. Donaghey*[11] the district judge awarded the single, male tenant damages of £2,000 [£2,140] for eight months in a two bedroom house with extensive rising and penetrating damp, windows which did not keep out the elements, a gas fire which emitted fumes, a toilet which did not flush and only one operable tap (cold). The damages included compensation for two minor incidents of harassment.

In *Essapen v. Jouaneau* (1995)[12] the county court judge awarded £10,240 [£10,649.60] for 33 months (including £9,240 for diminution in value) in which there was water penetration around the windows, which were inoperable, and through the roof, the electrical installation was defective and there was only intermittent heating.

In *Ali v. Birmingham City Countil*[13] the county court judge awarded £15,750 for rising damp through floors and penetrating damp through walls in a traditional victorian terraced house occupied by a family between before March 1987 and April 1992. The family was in temporary accommodation from April 1992 until January 1993 but the works were not fully completed until November 1994.

In *Banton v. Lambeth L.B.C.*[14] the county court judge awarded the single, male tenant £12,000 [£12,48] for damp penetration from a leaking central heating pipe in the flat above which spread and got worse over a seven-year period to the point where the walls in the hall, bathroom and lounge became wet and the whole flat smelt musty. Additionally, for two winters the central heating and hot water were inoperable.

In *Hardy v. Maund* (1995) 21 August[15] the district judge awarded a single tenant £2,475 (including £975 diminution in value) for six months of very severe rising and penetrating damp in all parts of a modest bedsit.

In *Symons v. Warren*[15a] the district judge awarded an assured shorthold tenant paying £175 per week damages at the rate of £2,470 [£2,568.50] per year for a period of five months in which the light and extractor fan in the bathroom/toilet did not work. The single, male tenant had to use candles in the bathroom and odours would not clear.

[11] (1994) C.L.W. April 22.
[12] *Legal Action*, June 1995, p. 22.
[13] *Legal Action*, June 1995, p. 22.
[14] *Legal Action*, December 1995, p. 22.
[15] *Legal Action*, December 1995, p. 22.
[15a] *Legal Action*, December 1995, p. 22.

In **Bell v. Mazehead Limited** (1995) 18 May[16] the recorder awarded £15,250 [£15,860] for five years of water penetration through the roof and other dampness (£10,250 of the award was for diminution in value).

In **Rayson v. Sanctuary Housing Association Limited** (1996) 16 January[17] the county court judge awarded £4,750 to what appears to have been a single, female tenant for two years of severe, unsightly and worrying structural cracking.

Awards between £1,000 and £2,000 per annum

Court of Appeal

A1–04   In **Calabar Properties Limited v. Stitcher**[18] the county court judge on December 14, 1982 awarded £3,000 [£5,760/£1,152 p.a.] general damages "for the disappointment, discomfort, loss of enjoyment and bouts of ill-health which [the tenant's husband] suffered during the five years that he was occupying what was supposed to be a high class flat". The tenant acquired the residue of the term of a long lease of a flat for £40,000 in October 1975. She and her husband redecorated immediately. By January 1976 they were complaining of water penetration. External woodwork began to rot, mastic sealing around the windows perished and there was substantial water penetration. The tenant's husband suffered two attacks of pleurisy and one of bronchitis. In January 1981 the tenant and her husband left the flat to live permanently on the Isle of Man. The judge held that "They were forced to leave" by the landlord's failure to comply with its covenant to repair the structure and exterior of the building.

In **Lubren v. Lambeth L.B.C.**[19] the county court judge on June 29, 1987 awarded £4,000 [£6,080] for five years. The plaintiff was a woman whose two adult sons lived with her. The flat became cold and damp as the result of unspecified disrepair, deteriorating from a reasonable condition at the outset to being "appalling". In the last two years the hot water heating system worked intermittently and caused significant additional inconvenience. The Court of Appeal commented that the average yearly sum of £800 [£1,216] was too high for the earliest part of the period and too low for the latest part of the period. The County Court judge also awarded £500 [£760] (about a third of the rent of the premises) for a period of 14 months when the plaintiff was

---

[16] *Legal Action*, March 1996, p. 14.
[17] *Legal Action*, March 1996, p. 15.
[18] [1984] 1 W.L.R. 287, C.A.
[19] (1988) 20 H.L.R. 165.

in alternative accommodation waiting for the works to be completed, when the defendant had undertaken that the works would only take three months. Those premises had been recently repaired and "there was nothing from first to last wrong with them".

In *Davies v. Peterson*[20] the County Court judge on February 19, 1988 awarded the single, female plaintiff £250 [£367.50] for about 12 months of damp which severely affected one bedroom and the living room. The Court of Appeal increased the award to £1,000 [£1,470]. Kerr L.J. said:

"In the case of *Saunders v. Edwards*,[21] I suggested that it was important that in cases involving disappointment and loss of amenity, which was the subject matter of an award of £500 general damages in that case, substantial, albeit moderate damages should be awarded and that a higher figure would have been justified . . . . In the present case we are dealing with a claim for general damages in a context which is more important than mere disappointment and loss of amenity. We are dealing with physical discomfort and possible damage to health. It is therefore not surprising, and welcome, to find that realistically substantial damages have been awarded in a number of cases . . . . I agree entirely that £250 is nowadays no more than a nominal figure. It is just the sort of sum which I considered in *Saunders v. Edwards* should not be awarded, because it is little more than nominal or cosmetic."

In *Sturolson & Co. v. Mauroux*[22] the county court judge on June 4, 1987 awarded £5,895 [£8,960.40] to an elderly male plaintiff for about 11 years of disrepair. There had been water penetration through external walls of the flat and around the windows, insufficient hot water for washing and for the radiators, poorly lit corridors, an electrical system which was often unusable, blocked drains and defective bath and sink. The County Court judge found that the premises had become "appalling" by the 1970s and continued to be appalling until late 1982/1983. That leaves an average of £536 [£814.72 per annum]. The average is, however, misleading as: (a) the judge treated the claim for damages as having been satisfied in part by the registration of fair rents which are required by statute to take into account the "state of repair" of the dwelling house; (b) it appears that the County Court judge awarded damages by reference to yearly rates which increased as the disrepair worsened: it seems as though the worst period lasted about four and a half years from 1978 to 1983. The Court of Appeal

---

[20] (1988) 21 H.L.R. 63.
[21] [1987] 1 W.L.R. 1116 at pp. 1128 and 1129.
[22] (1989) 20 H.L.R. 332, C.A.

dismissed the landlord's appeal: there had been no cross-appeal by the tenant.

In **Watts v. Morrow**[23] the official referee on November 6, 1990 awarded a professional couple £4,000 [£5,080] each for distress and discomfort caused by having a occupy (during the weekends) their expensive weekend cottage for a period of about eight months whilst substantial repairs were carried out to it. Repairs which their surveyor negligently failed to advise them before their purchase would be required, included upgrading and replacement of some of the windows, installation of lead flashings, specialist woodworm treatment to first floor timbers with renewal of some boarding, some repointing of the chimneys and main walls involving the erection of scoffolding, substantial renewal of the roof. The plaintiffs stayed at the house for most but not all weekends. The Court of Appeal noted that the plaintiffs did not have to stay at the house at all but did so to supervise more extensive works which they were taking the opportunity to carry out. The Court of Appeal held that damages should not be awarded merely for distress and disappointment, but only for physical discomfort and distress directly related thereto and that in cases where purchasers had to endure repairs as a result of negligence awards should be restrained. The Court of Appeal awarded general damages of £750 [£952.50] to each plaintiff. The judgment of Ralph Gibson L.J. contains a useful sketch of general damages awards made in similar cases prior to 1991.

High Court

A1–05   In **Loria v. Hammer**[24] Mr John Lindsay Q.C. on July 31, 1989 awarded the single, female plaintiff £900 [£1,224] for five months of rainwater penetration through the roof which caused severe damp to the plaster of the flat. The plaintiff was a paediatrician, "often away for weeks at a time". The judge observed "I have no doubt that Dr Loria has a good claim under this head. My only difficulty in this nebulous area is in fixing a sum."

County Court

In **Tuoma v. Raad** (1994) 26 May[25] the County Court judge awarded the tenant general damages at the rate of £1,820 [£1,947.40] per annum for water dripping into his bathroom from the flat above causing some plaster to fall and leaving him without a fixed light fitting in the bathroom.

---

[23] [1991] 1 W.L.R. 1421.
[24] [1989] 2 E.G.L.R. 249.
[25] *Legal Action*, August 1994, p. 17.

In *Staves & Staves v. Leeds City Council*[26] it is recorded that the county court judge on November 24, 1989 awarded £5,000 [£6,800] for four years in which condensation and some penetrating damp through the ceiling had caused damp and mould to the gable walls in the bedrooms so that the plaster deteriorated. The plaintiffs were a married couple with three young children.

In *Hussein v. Mehlman*[27] Mr Stephen Sedley Q.C. sitting as an assistant recorder on March 5, 1992 awarded one of the three tenants, a young single female, the sum of £600 [£672] for the landlord's failure to put three gas heaters into working order over the 1989/90 winter. The tenants did buy calor gas fires which mitigated the discomfort to an extent. He also awarded the three tenants jointly £1,250 [£1,400] for eight months in which one bedroom had had a collapsed ceiling letting in damp and cold draughts to the rest of the house, there was a bulging sitting room ceiling for about 13 months (caused by the incursion of rainwater). The judge observed:

> There is no "tariff" as there is in most personal injuries cases, for awards of this kind, but a line of recent cases has given some indication of the proper range. In particular I have had regard to *Lubren v. Lambert L.B.C.*[28] . . . In general, the passage of time produces a "taper" effect in damages . . . ."

In *Joyce v. Southwark L.B.C.*[29] the district judge awarded tenants at a block of flats damages of £600 per annum on account of very poor collection of communal rubbish by landlords (the rubbish was infrequently removed leading, *inter alia*, to smells and flies in the summer (occasionally scavenging animals and once a fire)) so that the tenants refrained from using their back gardens or opening their rear windows.

Awards under £1,000 per annum

Court of Appeal

In *Taylor v. Knowsley Borough Council*[30] the Court of   **A1–06**
Appeal refused to interfere with the award of the county court judge made on an unspecified date probably in mid-1984. The award was £32 [£55.68] for being without hot water for five months and being without a central light in the living room for three months. The plaintiff was a young single man who had bathed at relative's houses and received an award of special

[26] (1990) 23 H.L.R. 107.
[27] [1992] 32 E.G. 59.
[28] (1987) 20 H.L.R. 165.
[29] [1996] C.L. 378.
[30] (1985) 17 H.L.R. 376.

damages for that. It was decided that he simply had not suffered any significant inconvenience: "This was not a case of a woman with a young family—it was a case of a young man in his 20s who had relatives in the neighbourhood, and once he had made arrangements with them . . . it is difficult to see on the evidence that the general damage to him was very great". There was also an award of £59 [£102.66] for eight months' dripping from a pipe in the bathroom ceiling which again was considered not to have caused any significant inconvenience to this particular plaintiff.

In **Minchburn v. Peck**[31] the county court judge on July 10, 1987 awarded the plaintiff £800 [£1,216] for two years of water penetration as a result of defective roof slates and three to four years of cracks to the party walls which spoilt the decorations. The plaintiff appears to have been a single man. The report gives no indication of the severity or extent of the water penetration and one would therefore assume that it was intermittent and slight: the roof did, however, require 100 to 140 new slates. The Court of Appeal refused to interfere with the award except to reduce it to take into account a failure to mitigate on the part of the plaintiff.

In **Sella House Limited v. Mears**[32] the county court judge on June 15, 1988 awarded £1,250 [£1,837.50] to a single, male plaintiff occupying a fairly high-class flat for the condition of the hall and stairs in the common parts, which became "fairly shabby", with the carpet scuffed and marked in places and in need of a "thorough cleaning". Although the rest of the common parts were "basically clean" some of the window ledges out of the cleaning lady's reach were "filthy". The period in question was seven years and the Court of Appeal declines to interfere with the award.

In *Joyce v. Liverpool City Council, Wynne v. Liverpool City Council*[33] the county court district judge and judge had decided that Mr Wynne could not reasonably expect to receive more than £718 [£746.72] for his general damages. There was, on his pleaded case, disrepair for a two year period involving two badly spalled bricks, a blocked-side gully and missing grid, warped casement windows in one room, minor decay to external casement timbers, a broken power socket and insecure switch, some missing and loose vinyl floor tiles in the kitchen and bathroom, deteriorated sink base, constant blocking of sink waste outlet, missing ceramic tiles behind sink, seizing of bedroom window casements and defective hinges. The Court of Appeal observed that not all these items fell within the landlord's repairing covenants, that the defects

---

[31] (1987) 20 H.L.R. 392; [1988] 1 E.G.L.R. 53.
[32] (1988) 21 H.L.R. 147.
[33] [1995] 3 All E.R. 110.

were of the DIY variety and that the plaintiff who seems to have been a single man was not put to any significant discomfort.

County Court

In *Makan v. British Gas plc*[34] the county court judge awarded   **A1–07**
the home owners £2,000 [£2,140] the defendant's negligence caused a hot water cylinder to flood down into their living room causing the ceiling to collapse. The plaintiffs lost the use of the living room for about nine months presumably because they did not have funds to immediately repair it.

In *Hallett v. Camden L.B.C.* (1994) 4 May[35] the recorder awarded the tenant damages at the rate of £300 [£321] per annum for draughty windows which were "low in the scale of possible defects".

In *Lewin v. Brent L.B.C.*[36] the county court judge awarded the tenant about £600 [£624] per annum for an ineffective rubbish collection service, grass in common areas not kept clean and service areas in disrepair. He awarded £800 [£832] per annum for two years in which the sewers had overflowed from time to time.

In *Newham L.B.C. v. Hewitt*[37] the county court judge awarded the single, male tenant in his fifties £850 [£884] per annum over a period in which the bedroom and hallway radiators and one of the three living room radiators failed to work so that, during the winter months, the tenant had to wear a coat in the living room and go to bed in his clothes. In addition the judge awarded £600 [£624] because the cold made the tenant's bad foot feel "dead".

Cases of noise nuisance

In *Sampson v. Hodson-Pressinger*[38] the Court of Appeal   **A1–08**
refused to interfere with the trial judge's award of £2,000 for noise nuisance consisting of footsteps and conversations which could be heard from above in the plaintiff's sitting room. The period was from August 1978 to August 1980 and was awarded in respect of "diminution in value of the plaintiff's flat". The award is not, however, reliable because: (a) the County Court judge indicated that the award he would have made had he been free to do so would have been higher (the County Court limit at that time was £2,000);

---

[34] (1994) C.L.W. 374.
[35] *Legal Action*, August 1994, p. 17.
[36] (1995) C.L.W. 3/95.
[37] *Legal Action*, June 1995, p. 23.
[38] [1981] 3 All E.R. 710.

(b) the Court of Appeal treated that award as including an (unspecified) sum for carrying out remedial works.

In *Power v. Hammersmith L.B.C.*[39] the County Court judge awarded the single, male tenant general damages at the rate of £1,000 [£1,100] for poor sound insulation resulting in him being able to hear normal domestic noise from the flat above.

In *Toff v. McDowell*[40] determined in July 1993 the plaintiff leaseholder downstairs could plainly hear music, footsteps and even activities such as snoring in the flat above by sub-tenants of the upstairs leaseholder. The court awarded the plaintiff damages against the upstairs leaseholder at the rate of £2,200 per annum between July 1990 and January 1991, at which time his sub-tenants had behaved unreasonably, and £1,100 per annum thereafter. The freeholder was insolvent. Evans-Lombe J. held that:

> "I have really no evidence upon which I can base any measurement of damage save that I know that the plaintiff, when he took his assignment of the flat, paid the sum of rather more than £60,000 for the unexpired portion of the lease. It is submitted that a flat purchased with such a purchase price would be likely to command an annual rental or approximately £3,000 a year. It seems to me that, as I have been told in many other similar cases, the court must simply do the best it can and to some extent that must result in plucking a figure out of the air. I find that the diminution in the flat's enjoyment during the six-month period of the occupation by the three tenants between July 1990 and January 1991 diminished the enjoyment of the plaintiff of his flat at the rate of £2,000 per annum but that otherwise the diminution of his enjoyment can be valued at approximately £1,000.00 [per annum]."

Personal Injury

A1–09   *Pneumonia. McCoy & Co. v. Clark.*[41] Mr Clark, a single man in his mid to late 40s rented a flat which suffered from water penetration and condensation dampness. He contracted Left Lower Lobe Pneumonia, spent nine days in hospital in considerable pain and five to six weeks afterwards feeling ill. There was then complete recovery. The Court of Appeal doubled the County Court judge's award of £100 to £200 [£384]. Damages were reduced by 50 per cent owing to the tenant's failure to look after himself properly (there was no appeal on that point). The Court of Appeal disapproved of the County Court judge's reduction of

---

[39] *Legal Action*, March 1993, p. 14.
[40] (1993) 25 H.L.R. 650.
[41] (1982) 13 H.L.R. 89.

damages because the tenant had had a comfortable time in hospital

Depression. In **Yilmaz v. Hackney L.B.C.** (1994) 29 November[42] the parents and their two children suffered anxiety and depression caused in material part (but less than 20 per cent) by the disrepair. In addition to general damages for discomfort and inconvenience the County Court judge approved a settlement where by the children received £1,000 [£1,070] and the adults £500 [£535] each for personal injury.

Asthma. In **Bygraves v. Southwark L.B.C.**[43] the County Court judge on September 20, 1990 awarded a child born into a damp and mouldy house, five years old at the time of the award, £4,000 [£5,080] for ill health, pain and suffering upon proof that the housing conditions materially exacerbated the asthma which the child would anyway have suffered. The child's asthma was severe, requiring constant treatment and involving four attacks requiring admission to hospital for up to seven days. The judge further awarded £5,000 [£6,350] for future pain and suffering caused by the aggravated asthma, disruption to schooling and possible psychological consequences up to the age of 18.

In **McCaffery v. Lambeth L.B.C.**[44] the County Court judge awarded damages for personal injury to three young girls. The first suffered upper respiratory tract infections and asthma over a period of four and a half years including nine full blown attacks but no hospital treatment, but mainly suffering from wheezing and shortness of breath. She received damages at the rate of £600 [£642] per annum. The second suffered a large number of colds over a five and a half year period and developed asthma, requiring treatment from her G.P. on a number of occasions. She received compensation at the rate of £450 [£483.64] per annum. The third suffered intermittently from chest problems and wheeziness sometimes requiring antibiotics. She received damages at the rate of £400 [£428] per annum. The relationship between the landlord's breaches of covenant and damage to health, according to the report, was simply that after being rehoused the children's illnesses "improved".

In **Camden L.B.C. v. Witten and Witten**[45] the county court awarded the adult male tenant £17,500 at an assessment of damages hearing at which there was uncontested medical evidence

---

[42] *Legal Action*, March 1995, p. 15.
[43] See *Kemp & Kemp* at F2–035/2.
[44] See *Kemp & Kemp* at F2–045/3.
[45] *Legal Action*, September 1993, p. 15.

that the tenant had contracted asthma at least in part as a result of the disrepair. The report gives no further information.

Awards arising out of infestations

A1–10   *Cockroaches.* **Brent L.B.C. v. Roberts.**[46] Joint tenants with five children in a three bedroom flat experienced a cockroach infestation for four years of varying severity. All rooms save the tenants' bedroom came to be infested. Spraying by tenants and council had brought temporary relief, but the infestation was heavy shortly before the trial. General damages were awarded for a four-year period of £5,200 [£6,032]: £1,300 [£1,508] per annum. Special damages were awarded for loss of food, damaged photographs, damaged wallpaper and insecticide.

In **Hodder v. Tower Hamlets L.B.C.**[47] the district judge awarded general damages at the rate of £1,500 [£1,620] over a seven year period for a severe cockroach infestation.

In **Lambeth L.B.C. v. Wright**[48] the county court judge awarded the tenant £1,440 [£1,584] per annum for a heavy cockroach infestation.

Clark v. Wandsworth L.B.C.[49] The judge awarded general damages of £3,500 [£3,745] per annum for a period of one year. The tenant was a single parent with two children aged 10 and three years. The flat was heavily infested. The Court of Appeal refused leave to appeal.

In **Habinteg Housing Association v. James**[50] the Court of Appeal noted without comment that had the county court judge found the landlord liable he would have awarded the tenant £10,000 [£10,700] general and special damages for a cockroach infestation of a little over six years which contaminated food, damages furnishings and disrupted her and her family's life.

McGuigan v. Southwark L.B.C.[51] The Recorder awarded general damages of £3,000 [£3,120] for 1986/7 for a severe ant infestation with some cockroaches; £1,000 [£1,040] for 1987/8 for a light cockroach infestation; £2,500 [£2,600] for 1988/9 and 1989/90 for a heavy infestation; £3,500 [£3,640] for 1990/91 for an extremely serious infestation. By 1990/91 no food could be kept in the house and the tenant began to stay elsewhere. She became

---

[46] (1991) October 8–9, Willesden County Court, H.H.J. Lowe (*Legal Action*, April 1991, p. 21).

[47] (1993) September 3 (*Legal Action*, August 1994, p. 17).

[48] (1993) December 10 (*Legal Action*, August 1994, p. 18).

[49] (1994) April 21, Wandsworth County Court, H.H.J. Sumner (*Legal Action*, June 1994, p. 15).

[50] (1994) 27 H.L.R. 299.

[51] (1995) September 15, Central London County Court, Recorder Rose (*Legal Action*, March 1996, p. 14).

profoundly depressed and suicidal and had to receive psychiatric counselling. She was advised to leave her belongings behind in case she took the infestation with her and was unable to replace them: she received a further award of £500 per annum for the next four years when she was without replacement furniture.

Mice and Rats. In **Dadd v. Christian Action (Enfield) Housing Association**[52] the tenant with two young children rented a flat from the defendant in a house which was infested with rats. The rats never entered the flat but could be heard at night squeaking and gnawing. After treatment rate carcasses attracted flies and the rats returned a few weeks later. There was some dampness in the kitchen and problems with the hot water and heating. The district judge awarded general damages at the rate of £2,090 [£2,236.30] per annum.

Ants. **McGuigan v. Southwark L.B.C.**[53] The Recorder awarded general damages of £3,000 [£3,210] for 1986/7 for a severe ant infestation with some cockroaches.

In **Ryan v. Islington L.B.C.** (1996) February 21, H.H.J. Marr-Johnson at Clerkenwell County Court awarded general damages at the rate of £2,500 per annum for over four years of infestation by Pharoah ants. It was difficult to keep the ants away from food, the premises required constant cleaning, as did clothes and furnishings, the mother became depressed, the children got bite marks (whether Pharoah ants actually do bite seems to be matter of expert controversy) and the family were unable to invite friends round. Although ants are smaller than cockroaches, they are not nocturnal but are capable of creating a nuisance 24 hours a day.

Beetles. In **Syrett v. Carr & Neave**[54] the official referee awarded general damages of £9,360 [£11,887.20] to a home-owner who suffered an infestation of death watch beetles for slightly less than two years. The award as damages for surveyor's negligence was criticised, however, by the Court of Appeal in *Watts v. Morrow.*[55]

Discomfort caused by works of repair. In *Watts v. Morrow*[56] the official referee on November 6, 1990 awarded a professional couple £4,000 [£5,080] each for distress and discomfort caused by having a occupy (during the weekends) their expensive weekend cottage for a period of about eight months whilst substantial repairs were

---

[52] (1994) September 28 (*Legal Action*, December 1994, p. 18).
[53] *Supra.*
[54] [1990] 2 E.G.L.R. 161.
[55] *Supra.*
[56] [1991] 1 W.L.R. 1421.

carried out to it. Repairs which their surveyor negligently failed to advise them before their purchase would be required, included upgrading and replacement of some of the windows, installation of lead flashings, specialist woodworm treatment to first floor timbers with renewal of some boarding, some repointing of the chimneys and main walls involving the erection of scoffolding, substantial renewal of the roof. The plaintiffs stayed at the house for most but not all weekends. The Court of Appeal noted that the plaintiffs did not have to stay at the house at all but did so to supervise more extensive works which they were taking the opportunity to carry out. The Court of Appeal held that damages should not be awarded merely for distress and disappointment, but only for physical discomfort and distress directly related thereto and that in cases where purchasers had to endure repairs as a result of negligence awards should be restrained. The Court of Appeal awarded general damages of £750 [£952.50] to each plaintiff. The judgment of Ralph Gibson L.J. contains a useful sketch of general damages awards made in similar cases prior to 1991.

Televentos v. McCulloch.[57] The bulk of the award of £1,700 related to a period of 10 months during which the landlord was carrying out repairs with the tenant in occupation. The work should have taken 10 weeks or so. The tenant was partly to blame for the delay because she was not co-operative. It is difficult to understand from the report what works were carried out, what the inconvenience was, and how much of the award was attributable to periods before the works of repair.

In **Sampson v. Wilson**[58] H.H.J. Roger Cooke, sitting as a deputy High Court judge, had to deal with a case in which the premises were in substantial disrepair. The landlord was an absentee and his agents carried out works of repair in such a manner as to deliberately make matters worse and drive out the tenants. Because works were carried out without permission or exceeding any permission there was a trespass (in addition to a breach of contract) thereby permitting an award of exemplary damages to be made. H.H.J. Cooke held as follows (leaving it to the reader to up-date):

> "(1) For the relevant period each plaintiff should be taken as having suffered damage equivalent to the whole of his rent; that is, having an uninhabitable home and losing the whole value of it.
>
> (2) But I have also to consider exemplary damages.

[57] [1991] 19 E.G. 18.
[58] (1994) 26 H.L.R. 486.

As to (1) the number of weeks for Mr Sampson—April 17 to November 26—is 32 weeks; for Mr Kohlbacher they were from April 17 to January 4, which is 37 weeks. Mr Sampson's rent was £25 per week, Mr Kohlbacher's £40. Mr Sampson comes out at £800 and Mr Kohlbacher at £1,480 . . . it is a proper case for exemplary damages . . . I am, of course, limiting myself to the period before the tenants go . . . I award against Mitchell at this point £2,000 in respect of each tenant."

In *Hannant and Curran v. Harrison*[59] the owners of a bungalow were awarded £1,000 for loss of their bedroom for 6 months caused by incompetent improvement works. They had to sleep in the lounge.

Miscellaneous awards. In *Smith v. Nixon*[60] a property developer stripped the roof from the house next door to the plaintiff's exposing it to the elements. For a period of over three years, draughts, damp and vermin spread into the plaintiff's house. General damages for nuisance of £8,000 [£832] were awarded.

Fines and damages for breaches of orders of specific performance and undertakings

In *Bloombury v. Lambeth L.B.C.*[61] the county court judge   **A1–11** fined the defendant £500 and ordered it to pay costs on an indemnity basis after it failed to comply with an interlocutory injunction. The judge observed that had he not been persuaded that a "new wind" was blowing through the housing department and had not counsel been persuasive and the witnesses of good calibre the fine "might have been 10 times higher".

---

[59] [1995] 2 C.L. 157, Hull County Court.
[60] (1995) C.L.W. 34/96.
[61] (1995) April 21 (*Legal Action*, June 1995, p. 23).

APPENDIX TWO

INFLATION TABLES

INFLATION TABLE

SHOWING THE VALUE OF £ AT VARIOUS DATES

In the left-hand column of this table is the year and in the right-hand column the multiplier which should be applied to the £ in January of that year to show its value in terms of the £ in September 1996.

A2–01

Year	Multiplier	Year	Multiplier
1948	18.55	1973	6.79
1949	17.79	1974	6.07
1950	17.19	1975	5.06
1951	16.62	1976	4.10
1952	15.17	1977	3.52
1953	14.69	1978	3.20
1954	14.48	1979	2.93
1955	14.08	1980	2.47
1956	13.45	1981	2.19
1957	13.28	1982	1.95
1958	12.54	1983	1.86
1959	12.31	1984	1.77
1960	12.31	1985	1.69
1961	12.16	1986	1.60
1962	11.65	1987	1.54
1963	11.34	1988	1.49
1964	11.13	1989	1.39
1965	10.63	1990	1.29
1966	10.18	1991	1.18
1967	9.82	1992	1.13
1968	9.57	1993	1.12
1969	9.02	1994	1.09
1970	8.59	1995	1.05
1971	7.92	1996	1.02
1972	7.32		

This table has been calculated from the Official Retail Prices Index, the value of the £ being taken from the figures published in January of each year, ending with January 1996.

RETAIL PRICES INDEX

	JAN.	FEB.	MAR.	APR.	MAY	JUN.	JUL.	AUG.	SEP.	OCT.	NOV.	DEC.
1996	150.20	150.90	151.50	—	—	—	—	—	—	—	—	—
1995	146.00	146.90	147.50	149.00	149.60	149.80	149.10	149.90	150.60	149.80	149.80	150.70
1994	141.30	142.10	142.50	144.20	144.70	144.70	144.00	144.70	145.00	145.20	145.30	146.00
1993	137.90	138.80	139.30	140.60	141.10	141.00	140.70	141.30	141.90	141.80	141.60	141.90
1992	135.60	136.30	136.70	138.80	139.30	139.30	138.80	138.90	139.40	139.90	139.70	139.20
1991	130.20	130.90	131.40	133.10	133.50	134.10	133.80	134.10	134.60	135.10	135.60	135.70
1990	119.50	120.20	121.40	125.10	126.20	126.70	126.80	128.10	129.30	130.30	130.00	120.90
1989	111.00	111.80	112.30	114.30	115.00	115.40	115.50	115.80	116.60	117.50	118.50	118.80
1988	103.30	103.70	104.10	105.80	106.20	106.60	106.70	107.90	108.40	109.50	110.00	110.30
1987	100.00	100.40	100.60	101.80	101.90	101.90	101.80	102.10	102.40	102.90	103.40	103.30
1986	96.25	96.60	96.73	97.67	97.85	97.79	97.52	97.82	98.30	98.45	99.29	99.62
1985	91.20	91.94	92.80	94.78	95.21	95.41	95.23	95.49	95.44	95.59	95.92	96.05
1984	86.84	87.20	87.48	88.64	88.97	89.20	89.10	89.94	90.11	90.67	90.95	90.87
1983	82.61	82.97	83.12	84.28	84.64	84.84	85.30	85.68	86.06	86.36	86.67	86.89
1982	78.73	78.76	79.44	81.04	81.62	81.85	81.88	81.90	81.85	82.26	82.66	82.51
1981	70.29	70.93	71.99	74.07	74.55	74.98	75.31	75.87	76.30	76.98	77.79	78.28
1980	62.18	63.07	63.93	66.11	66.72	67.35	67.91	68.06	68.49	68.92	69.48	69.86
1979	52.52	52.95	53.38	54.30	54.73	55.67	58.07	58.53	59.11	59.72	60.25	60.68
1978	48.04	48.31	48.62	49.33	49.61	49.99	50.22	50.54	50.75	50.98	51.33	51.76
1977	43.70	44.13	44.56	45.70	46.06	46.54	46.59	46.82	47.07	47.28	47.50	47.76
1976	37.49	37.97	38.17	38.91	39.34	39.54	39.62	40.18	40.71	41.44	42.03	42.59
1975	30.39	30.90	31.51	32.72	34.09	34.75	35.11	35.31	35.61	36.12	36.55	37.01
1974	25.35	25.78	26.01	26.89	27.28	27.55	27.81	27.83	28.14	28.69	29.20	29.63

	JAN.	FEB.	MAR.	APR.	MAY	JUN.	JUL.	AUG.	SEP.	OCT.	NOV.	DEC.
1973	22.64	22.78	22.92	23.35	23.52	23.64	23.75	23.82	24.03	24.50	24.69	24.87
1972	21.01	21.12	21.19	21.38	21.49	21.63	21.70	21.87	21.99	22.30	22.37	22.49
1971	19.43	19.53	19.69	20.11	20.25	20.39	20.51	20.52	20.55	20.67	20.79	20.89
1970	17.91	18.00	18.11	18.38	18.44	18.49	18.62	18.61	18.70	18.90	19.03	19.16
1969	17.06	17.15	17.22	17.41	17.38	17.46	17.46	17.42	17.47	17.60	17.64	17.76
1968	16.07	16.15	16.20	16.49	16.51	16.57	16.59	16.61	16.63	16.71	16.74	16.97
1967	15.66	15.67	15.67	15.79	15.78	15.85	15.75	15.71	15.70	15.82	15.91	16.02
1966	15.11	15.12	15.15	15.33	15.44	15.48	15.41	15.50	15.48	15.52	15.61	15.63
1965	14.47	14.47	14.52	14.80	14.85	14.89	14.89	14.92	14.93	14.95	15.01	15.08
1964	13.84	13.85	13.90	14.02	14.14	14.19	14.19	14.25	14.25	14.26	14.38	14.43
1963	13.57	13.69	13.71	13.74	13.73	13.73	13.65	13.61	13.65	13.71	13.74	13.77
1962	13.22	13.23	13.28	13.47	13.51	13.60	13.55	13.43	13.41	13.40	13.45	13.52
1961	12.63	12.63	12.68	12.74	12.78	12.89	12.89	13.01	12.99	13.01	13.15	13.17
1960	12.36	12.36	12.34	12.41	12.41	12.47	12.50	12.42	12.43	12.53	12.59	12.62
1959	12.42	12.41	12.41	12.32	12.27	12.29	12.26	12.29	12.23	12.28	12.37	12.40
1958	12.16	12.10	12.19	12.33	12.28	12.40	12.20	12.18	12.19	12.31	12.35	12.40
1957	11.74	11.73	11.71	11.75	11.77	11.89	11.99	11.97	11.93	12.05	12.11	12.17
1956	11.25	11.25	11.39	11.55	11.53	11.52	11.47	11.51	11.48	11.55	11.60	11.63
1955	10.70	10.70	10.70	10.76	10.74	10.97	11.00	10.93	11.00	11.11	11.29	11.29
1954	10.28	10.26	10.35	10.39	10.36	10.42	10.60	10.53	10.51	10.56	10.61	10.66
1953	10.14	10.17	10.24	10.33	10.30	10.35	10.35	10.29	10.27	10.27	10.30	10.26
1952	9.71	9.72	9.77	9.93	9.93	10.09	10.08	10.02	10.00	10.09	10.08	10.15
1951	8.60	8.68	8.74	8.88	9.10	9.13	9.27	9.31	9.38	9.44	9.48	9.54
1950	8.28	8.30	8.32	8.35	8.37	8.33	8.33	8.30	8.35	8.44	8.47	8.52

	JAN.	FEB.	MAR.	APR.	MAY	JUN.	JUL.	AUG.	SEP.	OCT.	NOV.	DEC.
1949	7.99	8.01	7.98	7.96	8.11	8.14	8.15	8.16	8.19	8.23	8.23	8.25
1948	7.64	7.78	7.80	7.91	7.90	8.04	7.92	7.92	7.93	7.95	7.97	7.98
1947	—	—	—	—	—	7.33	7.38	7.34	7.37	7.43	7.58	7.60

GROSS RETURN ON INDEX-LINKED GOVERNMENT SECURITIES

Date		Gross Return (%)	After Deduction of Tax at 25%	After Deduction of Tax at 40%
1995	Jan.	3.89	2.92	2.33
	Feb.	3.89	2.92	2.33
	Mar.	3.87	2.90	2.32
	Apr.	3.79	2.84	2.27
1994	Jan.	2.93	2.20	1.76
	Feb.	3.26	2.45	1.96
	Mar.	3.41	2.56	2.05
	Apr.	3.50	2.63	2.10
	May	3.90	2.93	2.34
	June	3.95	2.96	2.37
	July	3.98	2.99	2.39
	Aug.	3.76	2.82	2.26
	Sept.	3.86	2.90	2.32
	Oct.	3.89	2.92	2.33
	Nov.	3.86	2.90	2.32
	Dec.	3.88	2.91	2.33
1993	Jan.	3.71	2.78	2.23
	Feb.	3.47	2.60	2.08
	Mar.	3.41	2.56	2.05
	Apr.	3.57	2.68	2.14
	May	3.56	2.67	2.14
	June	3.52	2.64	2.11
	July	3.38	2.54	2.03
	Aug.	3.24	2.43	1.94
	Sept.	3.18	2.39	1.91
	Oct.	3.14	2.36	1.88
	Nov.	3.08	2.31	1.85
	Dec.	2.86	2.15	1.72
1992	Jan.	4.29	3.22	2.57
	Feb.	4.29	3.22	2.57
	Mar.	4.57	3.43	2.74
	Apr.	4.49	3.37	2.69
	May	4.31	3.23	2.59
	June	4.35	3.26	2.61
	July	4.58	3.44	2.75
	Aug.	4.72	3.54	2.83
	Sept.	4.11	3.08	2.47

DATE		GROSS RETURN (%)	AFTER DEDUCTION OF TAX AT 25%	AFTER DEDUCTION OF TAX AT 40%
	Oct.	3.67	2.75	2.20
1992	Nov.	3.88	2.91	2.33
	Dec.	3.83	2.87	2.30
1991	Jan.	4.14	3.11	2.48
	Feb.	4.16	3.12	2.50
	Mar.	4.14	3.11	2.48
	Apr.	4.14	3.11	2.48
	May	4.22	3.17	2.53
	June	4.36	3.27	2.62
	July	4.39	3.29	2.63
	Aug.	4.31	3.23	2.59
	Sept.	4.22	3.17	2.53
	Oct.	4.23	3.17	2.54
	Nov.	4.30	3.23	2.58
	Dec.	4.45	3.34	2.67
1990	June	4.21	3.16	2.53
	July	4.30	3.23	2.58
	Aug.	4.32	3.24	2.59
	Sept.	4.35	3.26	2.61
	Oct.	4.34	3.26	2.60
	Nov.	4.17	3.13	2.50
	Dec.	4.18	3.14	2.51

REAL AND NOMINAL INTEREST RATES AND PRICE INFLATION 1970–90

YEAR	PRICE INFLATION (%)	NOMINAL INTEREST RATE (%)	REAL INTEREST RATE (%)
1970	6.52	9.21	2.69
1971	9.18	8.85	−0.33
1972	7.48	8.90	1.42
1973	9.13	10.71	1.58
1974	15.94	14.77	−1.17
1975	24.05	14.39	−9.66
1976	16.62	14.43	−2.19
1977	15.91	12.73	−3.18
1978	8.20	12.47	4.27
1979	13.45	12.99	−0.46
1980	18.03	13.78	−4.25
1981	11.88	14.74	2.86
1982	8.70	12.88	4.18
1983	4.44	10.80	6.36
1984	5.01	10.69	5.68
1985	6.04	10.62	4.58
1986	3.40	9.87	6.47
1987	4.16	9.47	5.31
1988	4.92	9.36	4.44
1989	7.79	9.58	1.79
1990	9.44	11.08	1.64

AVERAGES FOR REAL AND NOMINAL INTEREST RATE TABLE

Year	Price Inflation (%)	Nominal Interest Rate (%)	Real Interest Rate (%)
1970–90	10.01	11.54	1.52
1970–79	12.65	11.95	−0.70
1980–90	7.62	11.17	3.55

Notes
1. Price Inflation is calculated as the rate of change of the Consumer Price Index.
2. The Nominal Interest Rate is based on the rate on 20 year British Government Securities.
3. Data taken from *Economic Trends Annual Supplement*, 1991.
4. These tables are taken from Appendix A of Law Commission Consultation Paper No. 125: "Structured Settlements and Interim and Provisional Damages."

APPENDIX THREE

SPECIMEN DOCUMENTS: TENANT'S ACTION FOR DISREPAIR

IN THE BUSY COUNTY COURT   CASE NO:
BETWEEN:

THE TENANT
CHILD ONE (suing
by her mother and next friend the tenant)

Plaintiffs

and

THE LANDLORD

Defendant

PARTICULARS OF CLAIM

1. By an agreement made in writing on January 1, 1995 the First **A3–01** Plaintiff became the tenant of the Defendant at the premises known as No 1, The Street, The Town, The Postcode ("the premises"). She has at all material times dwelt at the premises with her children: the Second Plaintiff, Child One (born on January 1, 1990), Child Two (Born on January 1, 1992) and Child Three (born on January 1, 1994).

2. It is an express term of the tenancy that the Defendant will:

2.1 Keep in repair the structure and exterior of the premises, including its fixtures;

2.2 Keep in repair internal walls including their plaster, skirting boards, doors and door frames, floors and ceilings of the premises;

2.3 Keep in repair gas, electric and water installations which serve the premises and which are further defined in the tenancy agreement.

3. The terms implied by section 11 of the Landlord and Tenant Act 1985 apply to the tenancy.

4. The duties imposed by section 4 of the Defective Premises Act 1972 apply to the tenancy and have at all material times been owed both to the First and to the Second Plaintiff.

5. The Defendant has been in breach of the aforesaid express and implied terms and duties since the tenancy began.

PARTICULARS

A3–02   (1) There are and have been since the tenancy began three broken roof tiles on the rear elevation with the result that there has been rainwater penetration into the First and Second Plaintiffs' bedroom since January 1, 1995.

(2) The plaster on the ceilings and walls of the First and Second Plaintiff's bedroom has been saturated and crumbling since about February 1995.

(3) The damp course has broken down to the front external wall of the living-room on the ground floor, which has been damp and stained since the commencement of the tenancy.

6. The Defendant has had notice of its aforesaid breaches.

PARTICULARS

A3–03   (1) By inspecting the premises on January 2, 1995 in the company of the First Plaintiff who drew his attention to the aforesaid defects.

(2) By inspection of the Defendant's surveyor on August 1, 1995.

(3) By letters written by the First Plaintiff on February 1, 1995 and September 1, 1995.

(4) By oral complaint of the First Plaintiff by telephone and in person at the Defendant's offices on occasions too numerous to particularise.

7. As a result of the Defendant's aforesaid breaches the First Plaintiff has suffered loss, damage, discomfort, inconvenience and distress and the Second Plaintiff has suffered personal injury and distress.

PARTICULARS OF SPECIAL DAMAGES

A3–04   (1) The rental value of the premises has been reduced by 50 per cent throughout the period of the tenancy.

(2) The First Plaintiff's belongings set out in the schedule annexed hereto have been ruined beyond economic repair by damp.

PARTICULARS OF GENERAL DAMAGE

A3–05   (1) The premises have been damp, cold and unpleasant to live in;

(2) The Second Plaintiff's asthma has been materially exacerbated by the condition of the premises, as shown by the report of The G.P. dated January 1, 1996 annexed hereto.

8. The Plaintiffs claim interest pursuant to section 69 of the County Courts Act 1984 on damages awarded at such rate and for such periods as to the court appears just.

AND THE PLAINTIFFS CLAIM

(1) An order requiring the Defendant to carry out the works set out in the Schedule of Work annexed hereto.
(2) Damages exceeding £5,000.00.
(3) Interest pursuant to section 69 of the County Courts Act 1984.

Dated the   day of   1996

....
The Solicitors

Ref:

To the District Judge and
To The Defendant

(Backsheet omitted)

IN THE BUSY COUNTY COURT   CASE NO:
BETWEEN:

THE TENANT
CHILD ONE (suing
by her mother and next friend the tenant)

Plaintiffs

and

THE LANDLORD

Defendant

DEFENCE

A3–06   1. The Defendant admits paragraphs 1, 2, 3 and 4 of the Particulars of Claim.

2. The Defendant admits that the premises currently are in the condition described at paragraph 5 of the Particulars of Claim, but makes no admissions as to when the defects first arose and denies any breach of the terms and duties pleaded.

3. The Defendant denies paragraph 6(1), (3) and (4) of the Particulars of Claim. The Defendant's case is as follows:

3.1   On or about July 15, 1995 the First Plaintiff complained to the Defendant orally by telephone about water penetration into her bedroom.

3.2   The Defendant admits and avers that he sent his surveyor to inspect the premises on August 1, 1995.

3.3   The Defendant further admits and avers that his surveyor reported to him on August 2, 1995 that the premises were in the condition alleged by the Plaintiffs at paragraph 5 of the Particulars of Claim.

3.4   The Defendant made appointments with the First Plaintiff for his builders to repair the premises on September 1, 1995, October 10, 1995 and December 15, 1995 but on each occasion without prior warning the First Plaintiff has refused access to the builders on the ground that she required to be rehoused by the Defendant whilst the works of repair are carried out.

4. The Defendant denies that any breach by him caused the damage set out at paragraph 7 of the Particulars of Claim and makes no admissions as to the occurrence of the damage pleaded.

5. Save in so far as the same have been expressly admitted or not admitted the Defendant denies each and every allegation contained in the Particulars of Claim as if set out separately herein and traversed seriatim.

Dated the   day of   1996

....
The Other Solicitors

Ref:

To the District Judge and
To The Plaintiffs

(Backsheet omitted)

APPENDIX FOUR:

SPECIMEN DOCUMENTS: PROCEEDINGS UNDER SECTION 82 ENVIRONMENTAL PROTECTION ACT 1990 INFORMATION

IN THE TOWN MAGISTRATES' COURT

Dated January 1, 1996

Defendant: The Landlord

Address: The Landlord's Address

Alleged Offence: That on this 1 January 1996 a statutory nuisance as defined by section 79(1)(a) of the Environmental Protection Act 1990 exists at [The Tenant's Premises] and continues to exist and that the nuisance (particulars of which are given in the annexed report) is the responsibility of the [Landlord] and in so far as it results from structural defects is the responsibility of [The Landlord] as the owner.

The complaint of: [The tenant] who being a person aggrieved for the purposes of section 82 of the said Act complains that the Defendant is responsible for the said nuisance, has given the required notice to bring these proceedings and asks that the accused be summoned to answer this complaint.

Address: The Tenant's Solicitors

Take before me this 1 January 1996

....

Justice of the Peace/Clerk to the Justice

INDEX

Quitting, 28–05

Reasonableness,
access, 21–02
alternative accommodation, 22–11
ancillary property, 8–08
damage, 6–01
damages, 19–04, 19–21, 20–01
defective premises, 11–15
impecunious plaintiffs, 19–20
implied terms, 8–08, 10–01,
    11–15
mitigation, 19–21, 21–02, 21–03
notice, 5–05, 10–01
repairs, 21–03
special damages, 22–04, 22–11
Rebuilding,
construction of agreement, 3–03
damage, 6–04
drafting, 7–05
underpinning, 6–04
Receivers, 28–06
Recoupment, 22–03, 22–04, 28–01
Rectification, 3–01
Reinstatement, 22–04
Relevance,
damage, 6–01
locality, 6–01
Remedial works,
betterment, 22–02, 22–07
clean up, 22–02, 22–07
costs, 22–02, 22–07
decoration, 22–07
special damages, 22–02, 22–07
Remoteness, 19–05 to 19–06,
    19–10, 19–13, 19–17
distress, 23–05
general damages, 23–02, 23–05
injury to feelings, 23–05
special damages, 22–14
Renewals,
construction defects, 6–09
design, 6–09
drafting, 7–03
improvements, 6–08
patching, 6–11
repair, 6–11, 6–12
Rent,
damages, 20–01 to 20–09, 21–08
exemplary, 21–08
diminution in value, 20–09
discomfort, 20–08
estoppel, 11–10
failure to pay, 21–08

Rent—*cont.*
implied terms, 11–01, 11–04,
    11–11
limits, 11–04
mitigation, 21–08
recoupment, 22–03, 28–01
self-help, 28–01
set-off, 2–09, 28–04
small claims, 31–03
specific performance, 21–08
tenant,
    remaining in occupation, 20–02
        to 20–03
    work carried out by, 22–03
time limits,
Repairs,
access, 8–07
blockage of conduits, 4–06
condensation, 4–03
definition, 4–02
decoration, 4–08
deterioration, 4–03, 4–05, 4–08
failure to carry out, 21–03
fitness for human habitation, 4–01,
    4–03
future damage, 4–07
implied terms, 8–02, 8–03, 8–05,
    8–09, 8–11
Landlord and Tenant Act 1985
    s. 11, 4–01
Law Commission: *Landlord and
    Tenant: Responsibility for State
    and Condition of Property,* 4–01
obligation to, 4–01 to 4–09
    put into repair, 4–09
qualifying, 27–12
renewals, 6–08 to 6–09
residential property, 4–01
standard, 4–09
water ingress, 4–04
Replacement, 7–05
Repudiation, 28–05
Residential property,
business efficacy, 8–09
defective premises, 11–14
furnished, 8–04
implied terms, 8–04, 8–09, 11–08,
    11–14
licences, 8–05
notice, 10–02
personal injuries, 10–02
repair, 4–01
right of entry, 10–02
small claims, 31–01
specific performance, 27–01,
    27–02